SLOW-TECH

SLOW-TECH

Manifesto for an Overwound World

Andrew Price

Atlantic Books

London

First published in hardback in Great Britain in 2009 by Atlantic Books,
an imprint of Grove Atlantic Ltd.

1 2 3 4 5 6 7 8 9

A CIP catalogue record for this book is available from the British Library.

ISBN 978 1 84354 726 6

Printed in Great Britain by MPG Books Ltd, Bodmin

Atlantic Books
An imprint of Grove Atlantic Ltd
Ormond House
26–27 Boswell Street
London
WC1N 3JZ

www.atlantic-books.co.uk

CONTENTS

Acknowledgements

While I was researching and writing the various drafts of *Slow-Tech*, many gave generously of their time, providing information or sources of information, discussing ideas, reviewing chapters or parts of chapters, or simply providing encouragement. In particular, I would like to thank and acknowledge the following, although, of course, any errors in fact or logic remain my own:

Sara Abdulla, Paul Abel, Jane Abel, Judy Armstrong, Marlin Atkinson, Sylvia Bernard, Adam Blackley, Simon Blackley, Alan Bodfish, Seán Boyle, Nicholas Brealey, Peter Bryan, Brian Clegg, Mike Coates, Jack Cohen, Orin Courtenay, Hugh Doherty, Mike Donlan, John Elder, Melinda Elder, John Ellis, Dessale Fishalzion, Will Gaze, Howard Gibbon, Les Goodall, Alain Jeudy de Grissac, Al Harris, Martin Hartley, David Hartshorn, Julie Hawkins, David Jones, Artemis Kassis, Betty Kay, Matt Keeling, Fareed Krupp, Keith Leppard, Anna Lloyd, Stanley Mann, Desi Maxim, Jacquie McGlade, Mark McKergo, Jeff NcNeely, Graham Medley, 'E.J.' Milner Gulland, Andrew Moulson, Duncan Macdonald, Peter Neumark, Peter Nicholls, Sebastian Nokes, Robert Old, Michael Pearson, Marcus Pembrey, Carsten Potsch, Jules Pretty, David Price, Joseph Price, Muireann Price, Sarah Price, Callum Roberts, Julie Robotham, Charles Sheppard, Peter Smith, Gary Steele, Avril Stewart, Ian Stewart, Philip Strickland, Peter Tallack, Simon Taylor, Mike Tildesley, Virginie Tilot, Nelly Trevelyan, Philip Trevelyan, Alicia Venkatachalam, Marcela Vlad, Tom Walker, Geert Wassink, Mike Willoughby, Tony Wilson, Trisha Wilson, John Zarb.

Special thanks go to the many individuals at Atlantic Books involved in the production of *Slow-Tech*; in particular Toby Mundy for taking on the project, for his help and unwavering enthusiasm throughout; my editor, Emma Grove, for unstinting support and the unenviable task of preventing me from swerving too far off course; and Caroline Knight, Sarah Norman, Sachna Hanspal and Annie Lee.

It would be an omission not to express gratitude to my late parents, Jane ('J.') and Peter ('Jake'), and to David and Anna. I am grateful to them for the many opportunities and shared experiences which influenced the writing of this book. Finally, I thank my own family, Sylvia, Muireann and Joseph, for their support and for having to suffer above-normal levels of obsession while I was researching and writing *Slow-Tech*.

PROLOGUE

Therefore love moderately: long love doth so;
Too swift arrives as tardy as too slow.
— William Shakespeare, *Romeo and Juliet*

Our family never totally bought into efficiency.

At 108 kilos, my father was built for the long haul, and chose his vehicles in his own image (although he himself refused to go metric). Windswept and chilled, my brother and I – both children of the 1950s – would arrive for school in a 1930 racing Bentley. For reasons we never fully understood, my father named the car Phyllis.

To describe this piece of machinery as massive would be an understatement, for at two and half tons it had more in common with a truck than a normal car. With a chassis resembling two steel girders separated by huge crossbars, our Bentley dwarfed almost everything else on the road. Yet so powerful was the beast that a standing start in top gear was effortless – and a party piece my father relished, to the very end. The Great Bentley's 'oomph' lay, of course, in its gargantuan, no-frills, slow-revving engine, all six and a half litres of it. Some claimed that the six cylinders, or pots, were reminiscent of the bore of a mains sewage pipe, but without the sludge.

Yet our car was no slouch. In its heyday, 'GF8511', better known as Bentley Team Car No. 3, achieved top speeds in excess of 120 mph at Brooklands race track in England – and, more famously, at the Le Mans 24-hour race (and still does, decades later). As testament to the capability of these slow-tech British racing-green giants, Ettore Bugatti, builder of the invincible Bugatti racing cars of that era, once exclaimed: 'The Bentley is the fastest lorry I have ever seen!'

Of course, vintage Bentleys could never compete with today's Formula

1

One racing cars. On the other hand, the latter's engines are, effectively, disposable: they only have to last two race weekends. And as one Formula One website puts it: 'Unsurprisingly, engine-related failures remain one of the most common causes of retirement in races.' Bentley engines were entirely different: after a race weekend, they were stripped down for checking and precautionary maintenance, then the same parts were carefully reassembled – no need for complete replacement. In fact, Billy Rockell, who built virtually every Bentley racing engine and was one of the firm's most trusted mechanics, claimed to have had few, if any engine failures. As further testament to the durability of these extraordinary machines, many original Bentley engine parts (racing and non-racing) remain in place, and in order, seventy years down the line. One three-litre car, in fact, is still racing on all the original parts fitted at Cricklewood over eighty years ago.

Solid and 'unrefined', maybe, yet such apparent lack of sophistication belies an approach to engineering that some say was ahead of its day: absolutely nothing was left to chance, so anything that might go wrong was backed up. The car's designer, W.O. Bentley, and those who built these cars firmly believed in the wisdom of 'over-design', and wide margins of safety. If, for example, both of our Bentley's electric fuel pumps happened to conk out, the driver could pump up and pressurize the forty-five-gallon petrol tank, manually, and force-feed the carburettors that way. More amazing still, if the starter motor failed, all was not lost: a knob on the dashboard would trigger off a shower of sparks from the 'trembler' coil into the cylinders. And, hey presto, as if by magic, the powerhouse under the bonnet would roar into action. If even that failed, there was always the starting handle. The ignition system was doubled up, too, as were the rear brakes. You could lose the braking on any two wheels and the car would still stop in a straight line.

To ensure our Bentley kept going during long-haul races, there were some very cunning devices, all installed for insurance and back-up. If, for example, heavy use of the brakes wore them down, the driver could easily adjust them, while still in the saddle, by using a handily placed adjuster which you turned as you drove along; there was no need for a pit stop. Similarly, if oil consumption rose as the revs were cranked up over prolonged periods, turning a tap under the dashboard would instantly drop an extra gallon into the engine's enormous (six-gallon) sump.

On top of that, the slow-revving Bentley engines were comparatively efficient at converting fuel to power; at 2,500 rpm, the Speed Six would generate 230 brake horsepower – it was a very big 'bang for your bucks', even by Formula One standards today. A modern Formula One engine, in contrast, will rev eight times as fast for just under four times the power gain; and it will have a far worse fuel consumption than the Speed Six, which is bad enough (ten to fourteen miles per gallon) – though, admittedly, a far greater power to weight ratio, and speed.

Longevity was another signature of old Bentleys, and an outcome of their massive construction and complete absence of corner-cutting – and, of course, of some tender loving care, though less than one might suppose. Nearly eighty years on, and now with a new owner, ours just keeps on going: a piece of living motor-racing history.

Bentleys still in use are, unquestionably, ace gas-guzzlers; their colour may be green, but not so their emissions or their 'ecological footprint' (although a well-tuned vintage Bentley is still capable of passing the modern emissions test). Yet if factors such as prolonged existence – reducing the need to scrap or recycle – and absence of electronic chips (which carry environmental costs) are taken into account, claims that these vintage relics are little more than inefficient, polluting monsters may be slightly wide of the mark.

Being able to keep on going, even against the odds, was my father's approach to life, too – aided, it must be said, by a physique as unmistakable and imposing as his beloved Bentley. The surprising thing was that he was remarkably speedy, at least when it came to long-distance swimming races and water polo back in his youth. But it would be a mistake to suppose that his performance had anything whatsoever to do with a high-tech, let alone sensible diet. Were he alive today – in an era of slow-release carbs, balanced proteins and fats, high-nutrient drinks and the like – he would have none of it. Quite the opposite. Shortly before a swimming event, my father merely stoked calories, whatever their form. Treacle pudding and custard was, we recall, his favourite racing formula. Yet at water sports he excelled, and his regimen seemed to pay dividends; at least, it never held him back.

Years later at the seaside, his competitive days long over, my father would ferry my sister and me through the waves, one perched on each shoulder. As a final testament to his unassailability, consider the following incident. Once, en route to work in Manchester after doing the school round, the Bentley suffered a puncture. Without ado, he pulled off the road, jacked up the car and began to change the wheel. Like a bolt from the blue another car, totally out of control, came hurtling round the corner. Worse still, it slid off the road and squashed my father; we do not recall if it was between the two cars or against the embankment. Either way, in hospital later that day, he admitted to losing all the air from his lungs, to which the doctor replied that he was lucky that was not all he had lost. Astonishingly, besides bruising, he escaped virtually unscathed.

When it came to boats – our family's second great passion – my father found little to be gained from anything bordering on the flimsy or insubstantial. Summer holidays were spent sailing around Anglesey and Ireland, not in a yacht of the day, but in our family's massive pilot cutter, built in the early days of the twentieth century. Graced by a gilded semi-clad mermaid, her bow sliced impressively through the water while struggling to keep up with the times. Yet *Mermaid*, and other traditional sailing craft like her, carried an impressive pedigree and record, particularly when it came to safety.

Like the example of the old Bentleys, the following tales about sailing sum up, for me, everything beneficial that *Slow-Tech* claims about over-provision – you could call it the wisdom of 'overkill'. Nothing could be more different from corner-cutting for 'efficiency', the unstoppable but dangerous crusade modernity chose to embark upon a century or more back.

In their heyday, English pilot cutters ventured on modest sorties, from the UK's sheltered waters to the open Atlantic or North Sea. Their purpose: to escort incoming shipping through the hazardous shallow waters to the safety of port, winter or summer. Rivalry was intense, as British sailor and writer Tom Cunliffe points out; so there were some 'very fast pilot cutters driven hard by some really desperate characters'. Not surprisingly, then, pilot cutters were seaworthy and reliable, returning to port at a quick tempo if it was blowing hard. Centenarians, maybe, but for the likes of my father, being at sea with something solid beneath your feet was what counted most. In his eyes, only this sort of packhorse was capable of providing the no-nonsense cruising experience he sought and achieved.

But it is not just their stout construction, or kindly sea-motion, that makes pilot cutters so safe and appealing. More subtle forces, paradoxically, also come to bear. Because of their old-fashioned features – straight stem, long keel and old-fashioned gaff-rigged sail plan – these boats can actually steer themselves, unassisted. Without anyone standing at the helm, or an auto-pilot, they just keep sailing. These boats manage to hold their course, simply with the helm lashed. Put another way, pilot cutters are virtually immune against being knocked off course; but, should that happen, they automatically get back on track. With a falling barometer, rising seas and a seasick crew, what could be a more worthwhile boat trait? For one, it gives the helmsman, whose eyes are normally glued to the compass for hours on end, a welcome break.

Modern yachts, at best only tolerated by my father, are indisputably faster and more responsive, which of course is what helps them win races. But their lighter construction and flighty behaviour carries a down-side; for high-tech yachts, unlike their sturdier elders, will not so easily stay on course unless, of course, steered manually or by an auto-pilot.

But perhaps nothing illustrates more forcefully the remarkable capacity of a vessel – especially traditional sailing craft – to chill out when confronting stormy seas than a slow-tech, safety measure called 'heaving to', which it amounts to sailing-but-stalled. Once in that state, with the helm lashed, a boat can be more or less left to its own devices. It involves having the sails on opposite sides, instead of on the same side, and the boat lying about fifty degrees from the wind. In one story, while a storm raged in North America's eastern waters, yachtsman Tom Cunliffe and crew simply went below deck in their Bristol Channel pilot cutter, *Hirta*. It was comfortably 'hove to' and they decided to play Scrabble. Snugged down, it enabled them to bide time until the weather abated.

Heaving to also has a calming effect *on the sea*, not just on the crew. By drifting slowly, obliquely to the wind, the keel of a boat in that condition actually creates its own smooth slick of water, on which the vessel safely perches and bobs. Yet just metres beyond, the seas boil in anger. According to yachtsman Larry Pardy, heaving to may be the ultimate survival strategy for impending hurricane-force winds.

Quite plainly, when it came to cars and boats, strength, safety and sustainability were what our family believed mattered most. No less substantial was the Aga, an old-fashioned, oil-fired heat-storage cooker. Centre-stage in the kitchen and packed with sixteen cubic feet of natural insulation (vermiculite), it occupied more space even than my father. The Aga sustained us and breathed warmth and life into our home, day in, day out. The only trouble was it ran constantly, except during rare heatwaves. Invented and patented in 1922 by Dr Gustaf Dalén, a Swedish Nobel prize-winning physicist, this cooker is by conventional reckoning inefficient – nothing less than a cast-iron dinosaur that devours £10 notes one after the other. But this is only half the tale, a lopsided and incomplete portrayal of an Aga's true performance.

Fast forward two decades to the 1970s, and out in the cut-and-thrust workplace I realized that my family's fondness for sustainability, its admiration for the strength and quality of a bygone era, was both nostalgic and eccentric. After all, slickness of operations through corner-cutting and other efficiency drives already had much of the Western world in its thrall. To our contemporaries, efficiency had come to symbolize per-formance, effectiveness and even satisfaction. At least part of me, too, had come to accept that retaining the inessential was inefficient and verging on history: being 'lean and mean' really was the name of the game.

Yet I could not completely dispel some nagging doubts. My professional background as an ecologist and environmental scientist made me realize that nature is complex and full of constraints and compromises. With insufficient in reserve, too little 'spare capacity' to bounce back after a catastrophic event, such as a serious disease or major oil spill, populations of species dwindle, or crash: in extreme cases, extinction is the price tag. Perhaps my father's sentiments about insurance and back-up in cars, boats and Agas – the very opposite of squeezing things to the limit – did, after all, contain nuggets of truth. Quite possibly, they might even provide some valuable lessons for modernity. Like the early nineteenth-century English Luddites, who destroyed textile machines – but only because they felt they threatened their livelihood – my father was not totally anti-technology. In his eyes, though, there was no guarantee that cutting-edge stuff was inevitably superior to the old, or the best way forward, either.

In 1981, virtually becalmed for fifty-five days in the Indian Ocean, I began to have even more serious doubts about the wisdom of modernity's obsession with efficiency, and reluctance to keep sufficient, if anything, in reserve. We were on a slow boat to China: 'Sindbad voyagers' on a replica of a ninth-century Arab sailing ship. On this international expedition I was resident marine biologist. In the damp and salty conditions, one by one *Sohar*'s few electronic gadgets failed; corrosion by hydrogen sulphide from deep in the ship's bowels probably made things worse.

Those gizmos had not lasted long. Just days before our departure from Muscat in November 1980, the chandlers in England had sent out a replacement depth-sounder, plus some other electronics. They were hardly in keeping with the mission: sailing a stitched, medieval look-alike vessel along the ancient Spice Route. The aids were partly to verify the ancient navigational methods being tested, and also to add a little security and comfort to our lives. But during the frenetic preparations for departure, one of the crew had thrown the ship's electronics – still wrapped – on to the fire along with other rubbish. Their charred remains were needed in England for insurance purposes. By the time the voyage ended in China, eight months later, few of the replacement units were functioning.

The insight, when it came, struck suddenly, perhaps an aftershock from the lightning that bolted through my arm while I was collecting rainwater on deck. A second power, currently eclipsed by conventional views of efficiency, was needed to counterbalance and temper its supremacy: robustness, something in reserve – the upshot of deliberately retaining or adding 'unproductive' baggage. That's robustness simply put. Yet from it comes something more powerful and profound than toughness and the ability of things to keep going when the going gets tough.

INTRODUCTION

An alternative to the big squeeze

Disappearing under our feet

The power of the 'inessential' is a simple message, but it resonates far
and wide. For keeping sufficient in reserve adds power to the present
and insures against the impending. Yet modernity has been remarkably
slow to grasp such a fundamental 'law of nature'. Perhaps the huge toll
from the 2004 Sumatran tsunami – more than 283,000 deaths – is really
what awoke us from a complacent slumber; and, less than one year later,
the devastating effects from hurricanes Katrina, Rita and Stan in the
USA and Central America. These events began to shake the world, quite
literally, like never before.

In the case of the damage to New Orleans by Hurricane Katrina in
2005, the artificial floodwalls or levees were supposed to have protected
the city against a 100-year storm – one so severe it might only strike
once in a century. When the Army Corps of Engineers constructed the
levees, decades earlier, individuals in charge must have believed – or
silently prayed – that sufficient insurance had been made in the town's
coastal defence. Anything more, in their eyes, would be unnecessary and
an inefficient use of costly resources.

The problem is, though, that much of New Orleans and coastal
Louisiana are below sea level. On top of that, the city was sinking under
its own weight, and worse still, certain activities were accelerating the
process. Consider, for example, the extraction of natural resources. By
withdrawing groundwater and oil from sediment beneath it, New Orleans
was, quite literally, pulling the ground out from under its own feet.

Given the precarious setting of the city, blind faith in levees that lacked sufficient over-provision – an engineering solution that provided only partial insurance – proved to be a dangerous precedent. As TV viewers the world over witnessed, the effects of Katrina were devastating; and predictably so. On top of over 1,800 (direct and indirect) deaths, and loss of homes, came the ruining of livelihoods. If that was not enough, there was the silencing, albeit temporarily, of one of the world's greatest musical hubs, as musicians joined the throng of fleeing residents.

The stark reality is that Katrina dealt the worst civil engineering disaster in American history, largely because high-tech buffers to protect New Orleans were insufficiently substantial and fell wide of the mark, nature's own free defences having already been undermined.

The Dutch, incontestably the world's elite when it comes to engineered coastal defences, so-called 'hard construction' techniques, are more cautious: they design flood barriers with serious overkill, to withstand a 10,000 year mother-of-surges. As in New Orleans, though, most inhabitants of the Netherlands live below sea level, and Dutch society is also one where lives and livelihoods hang, delicately poised, on dependable coastal protection. But if steel-and-concrete fixes are necessary, the only ones worth having, in their eyes, are ones that really work. Reliable artificial defence, of course, does not come cheap, especially as it means deliberately instilling 'spare capacity' that would be superfluous and unnecessary most of the time.

Wider fallout

The uncomforting tale of Katrina exposes something more profound and far-reaching than the power of the 'inessential', the need for adequate engineering and technological fixes – whether to save our skin, or in situations which are not so life-threatening. What we're talking of here is why the world is experiencing so many different environmental and other disasters large and small, in the first place, and whether going high-tech is always 'the one best way' so often acclaimed.

Added to the problem of coastal vulnerability, in fact linked to it in the case of increasing hurricane strength, are the scary effects of climate change and sea-level rise. More alarming still, tropical storms seem to be on the increase and they are becoming more ferocious. Engineered structures previously relied upon to do the job properly can themselves, all of a sudden, become fragile, especially if coastal development has already damaged the coral reefs, wetlands – 'worthless swamps' – and other natural habitats which should have provided natural defences. In the case of the USA, according to its Geological Survey, New Orleans and the wider state of Louisiana has lost 1,900 square miles of wetland over the past seven decades to pave the way for roads, marinas, condominiums and business facilities. In a way this is understandable. After all, they have got to go somewhere and, surely, some sacrifices of nature are inevitable. Besides, many planners and engineers probably felt that ridding the region of disagreeable wetlands was actually doing local society a favour; that is, of course, in addition to providing sites for development.

Yet in their zest for economic expansion, without bothering to look over their shoulder, the people who called the shots had overlooked something fundamental: wetlands absorb and store floodwater, and act like a giant sponge. The irony was that these areas turned out to be anything but inessential. They should, and could, have helped provide New Orleans with physical defence against Hurricane Katrina. But over-zealous developments had seriously cut into this invaluable protection and insurance service. Quite plainly, nature's buffers are not so dispensable after all. Hurricane Gustav provided another stark reminder in 2008.

Environmental researcher Alicia Venkatachalam, based at Warwick University, recently conducted a survey in southern Sri Lanka in the aftermath of the 2004 tsunami. This revealed that 94 per cent of the 297 fishermen interviewed believed that mangrove vegetation decreased the number of human fatalities caused by the tsunami waves. (Actually, 498 fishermen were interviewed, but 201 respondents scored mangroves as 'not present' and did not provide an opinion about their possible role in coastal protection.) A similar picture emerged when it came to protection by mangroves against housing damage.

Of course, no shock-absorber, natural or made-made, could possibly have given full protection against such an unprecedented, deadly assault; casualties, sadly, were an inevitable outcome. Some mathematical models even cast doubt on mangroves being any help at all against the tsunami (although, it has to be said, inundation distance was their measure of impact, something that may be very different from fatalities). On the other hand, one study after another, around the world, has opened our eyes to the protective and other benefits of natural habitats.

So much so that the USA and other developed nations are beginning, albeit gradually, to see the wisdom of going with nature rather than battling against it. First and foremost, by avoiding, where possible, whole-scale clearing of so-called 'worthless swamps' in the first place. And if intervention is necessary to bolster up coastal defences – when, for example, natural systems have been dramatically mined and undermined – 'soft construction' can work wonders. One example is the simple low-tech expedient of using planted vegetation to trap blown sand. For this encourages the growth of dunes, the first line of defence, not unlike pawns in a game of chess: little clout individually, yet, in a line, an arsenal to be reckoned with. When it comes to protecting development structures against the environment (or, paradoxically, vice versa), slowing the flow that way entails little more than use of natural materials and natural processes. Admittedly, the 'soft fix' is not an immediate solution. Compared with 'hard construction' techniques, though, these slow-tech ways are cheaper to construct and maintain and, what's more, they may be self-sustaining.

An even more radical and enlightened alternative to coastal protection, and simpler still, goes one step further. It entails, quite literally, going with the flow. What we are talking of here is that long-known army tactic called, euphemistically, managed retreat: in the present context, it is little more than deliberately allowing an area that was previously high-and-dry to become flooded by the sea and washed by sediment – the raw building material, of course, for terra firma.

Sooner or later this creates new inter-tidal land, salt marsh or coastal vegetation. Were he alive today, it is an approach that my father – purveyor par excellence of slow-tech – would have sanctioned with heart and soul.

As the news reminds us, we are experiencing catastrophes like the ones mentioned on a grand scale, with devastating impacts on ourselves and our world. Nature's ability to withstand such shocks has been weakened. In no small way, it is the outcome of habitual and repetitive 'mining' of the earth's natural resources. Much of it boils down to a product-hungry world, economic growth and unfettered development, whatever the wider costs. To make this all possible, corporate bosses insist that returns must always be bigger, year on year.

What is so surprising, given what is at stake, is that unrestrained economic growth has been allowed to go on for so long. On top of that, of course, there is the relentless squeeze from humanity's burgeoning population, particularly in poorer parts of the world. No one can deny that sheer numbers exert a big pressure on the environment, too. What's more, the global population is still increasing. One way or another, both our lives *and* our economic necks are now on the line, like never before.

The harsh reality is that damage to environmental resources, and their inability to spring back, can be enough to push a civilization over the tipping point; or, in less extreme situations, to make life exceedingly uncomfortable. In order to retain the earth's natural ability to withstand such onslaughts, we need to *keep* some spare capacity – the so-called inessential. The deliberate act of retaining 'unproductive baggage' can, ironically, mean that crisis management through high-tech restoration projects can actually become unnecessary in the first place, or at least far less costly. Either way, it helps avoid catastrophic failures. Consider, as a bleak reminder, what happened to New Orleans. And, if we have been unwise enough to trade too much of the 'inessential', for short-term pursuits and products, then re-instilling it invariably gives a pay-off.

Robustness in a nutshell

Robustness is that visible or invisible whiz that allows a system to absorb shocks and surprises, without failing catastrophically, then continue (sometimes through re-structuring) more or less 'business as usual'. Whether we are talking of the wetlands around New Orleans, or protective coral reefs, many of the individual ecosystems that the earth consists of are naturally robust. When not weakened by profit-driven intervention, or relentless population pressures, they are resilient against all sorts of attack: they self-repair, they have spare parts, and they can endure for millennia; often, in fact, much longer, if only given the chance.

In this respect, the human body behaves no differently. During a lifetime, our bodies are exposed to an onslaught of assaults – from unwelcome bacteria and viruses to concussion and broken bones – and sometimes insults, too. Yet, more often than not, we live to greet another dawn. A Bentley (or more modern machine) enduring a tough race after being hammered around the track, or a yacht surviving a gruelling sea passage, echoes precisely the same principles. Robustness, one way or another, is what helps ecosystems, humans or objects to keep going, even when the going gets tough.

Persistence, especially through solidity, is the most down-to-earth type of robustness. That a concrete wharf is robust hardly takes rocket science to know: through extreme 'over-engineering', its massive construction instils robustness against virtually everything – save being rammed by a tanker. Most of the time, though, the wharf does not really need to be that strong; there is deliberate 'overkill' or redundancy, just in case. It is a case of over-engineering on a grander scale than even our 6½ litre Bentley. To a lesser degree, this is what enables a coral reef to withstand day-to-day knocks and scrapes. Being struck and mounted by a cruise ship is, of course, quite another matter. That is robustness at its crudest, a notion that chimes with our intuition. Overdosing on materials is not all that counts, though. 'Design' plays its part, too, as in the case of the shell of a nut, whose curves and form imbue it with the toughness and durability that enhance chances of survival.

Paradoxically, though, robustness is normally something far more subtle and enigmatic, yet, at the same time, more powerful.

Robustness through spare parts is another approach to back-up. Having more than one part of the system perform the same or similar tasks is a very different, more refined, approach to redundancy than brute strength alone. This type of spare capacity has another advantage: it can also create flexibility – against problems now, and others that might arise in the future. We are glad to have two kidneys, not just one – especially if one has to be removed, either because of an untreatable condition (especially if it might affect other organs) or for transplant into someone else: normally one kidney is enough, and the other inessential, but it can be risky to bank on it, especially in a hot climate.

According to biologist Andreas Wagner at the Santa Fe Institute and University of New Mexico, back-up through spare parts is the main 'pillar of system reliability' in engineering. It is partly because building systems with spare parts is straightforward, at least conceptually, although technically this may not always be quite so easy. Just as in the human body, aircraft demonstrate, reassuringly, that duplication of critical parts is one sure way of instilling robustness. Take the Boeing 777 or Airbus. Extreme weather – high winds, torrential rainstorms and lightning strikes – or engineering failures, anywhere from nose to tail, are disturbances that can potentially create disaster in countless ways. The only trouble is that added extras don't always come cheap – if not in dollars, then in weight or space. To the aircrew and passengers up at 10,000 metres, though, nothing could be better value for money.

We cherish the 'inessential', not surprisingly, when it comes to saving our own skin, for example when we fly in aircraft. It is a different matter, though, in the case of the environment. Here we seem quite happy to treat robustness of ecosystems as 'surplus to requirements', and trade it to fuel economic progress and development – whatever the costs, and whatever the outcome. And we should be under no illusions: the collateral damage is immense. That's the irony, given that, even in our high-tech era, natural ecosystems remain our bread-and-butter, both for food and finance.

The concepts, and several examples above, come from man-made or 'engineered' systems. This book is mainly about natural systems, but it takes many words from the jargon used to describe engineering. These also provide helpful analogies as to why robustness around us matters, and is less dispensable than we care to believe. In the case of redundancy, the earlier tale about our old Bentley's double electric fuel pumps (plus a mechanical back-up system) is one such instance. Few would pretend, of course, especially in today's climate, that a vintage car can come anywhere near a blueprint, *leitmotif* or last word in design and engineering; the Bentley's fondness for fuel, for example, has already been mentioned. Besides, these relics of a bygone era now change hands for such colossal sums that they are, except for the seriously well off, simply unaffordable.

The real point here, though, is that the degree of duplication of parts might seem excessive: indeed, for most of the time carrying two additional, identical pumps *was* inessential. But, on more than one occasion at Le Mans 24-hour races, you can bet there was a pay-off. Precisely the same principles apply when it comes to having sufficient spare provision in ecosystems, and in fact in almost every system, and what these mean, for the environment and society alike.

Robustness through self-adjustment is another type of 'robustness through flexibility'. This works even more cunningly than back-up by means of identical parts. Here, interaction of numerous and *different* system parts ensures smooth working while compensating for effects of disturbance. For reasons that will become clear, this is sometimes called 'distributed robustness'. Unlike straightforward redundancy, where two or more system parts perform the same function, distributed robustness is not simply other parts standing in for the failed part.

This type of robustness is spread across the system. For organisms, including us humans, Andreas Wagner believes, distributed robustness (through complex genetic architectures) may be more important than simply overdosing on spare parts. The same goes for the Boeing 727, despite the need to duplicate or triplicate really critical bits. Similar principles apply to the environment and ecosystems, with their myriad different species – whose roles will vary to a greater or lesser extent. For example, some massive reef builders, as in the case of certain *Porites* corals, act like a breakwater and provide physical defence. Yet other corals, ones that on the face of it are less stout, deliver services that may be no less dispensable. For they provide a more subtle, rearguard action if, for example, environmental conditions change out of the blue. As an aside, it may be added that the significance of particular species (like all sorts of other system parts) often transpires only once they have disappeared; hence, there really is wisdom in the precautionary principle.

Tendency to self-regulation, self-repair or self-replication are examples par excellence of distributed robustness. For many systems, this adjust-as-you-go behaviour provides an astonishing degree of plasticity; that invisible and magical whiz, working away in the background and taken for granted. Purring along smoothly is what nature does much of the time, assuming, of course, that modernity has not carved it up too much in the process of development; so too do certain mechanical systems – as in the case of old-fashioned governors on steam engines or, closer to home, the automatic switching on and off of household central heating.

In fact, negative feedback – the jargon used to describe this sort of behaviour – helps create smooth running and robustness in all biological systems. For an organism's ability to maintain constant states in the face of change, physiologist Walter Cannon coined the term 'homeostasis' back in 1932. Just as an electrical thermostat regulates the switching on and off of radiators, so too, via a sensor in the brain, our body keeps close to an optimal temperature of thirty-seven degrees; for example by sweating or shivering. Negative feedback operates in all sorts of complex systems, at higher and higher scales right up to ecosystems and even the planet; for example, forests (indirectly) lead to cloud formation. Both provide essential checks and balances that assist in climate regulation and moderation, and instil robustness, at least up to a point.

This is the essence of James Lovelock's Gaia hypothesis; a daring pronouncement that the earth is a self-regulating system. Once the 'tipping point' is reached, though, the system can easily fail to compensate. Worse still, once flipped into an altered state, positive feedback – precisely the opposite of negative feedback – can then easily kick in and take over. Positive feedback leads to an increase in (rather than dampening of) an effect; often this creates greater fragility and, in the case of climate, it can make it warm up very rapidly. That, it turns out, is what seems to be happening, right now.

The **myth of immutability** or, in engineering jargon, the 'robust-yet-fragile' paradox, is one of the most tantalizing features of living and non-living systems. To all who knew him, my father was the epitome of robustness. His ability to walk away, virtually unscathed (though to say smiling would be an exaggeration), after being crushed by a car bears testament to this. By most reckonings, it was a miracle he came out alive. Yet, at the age of only sixty-six years, he succumbed to a rare auto-immune disease: an illness amounting to the body's tissues attacking its own immune system. In his case, it was polyarteritis nodosa, in which the body's blood vessels become damaged and, one by one, different organs start to pack up. The condition can be stabilized, but the cause is unknown and there is still no proper cure. Perhaps smoking at least sixty cigarettes a day from the age of seventeen (or younger) eventually took its toll.

Despite best efforts to instil robustness, complete guarantees are never possible. It is little short of a quest for the unattainable. The fact is that fool-proof disease control eludes us, as the fate of my father reminds us. Similarly, an ecosystem or species might survive the harshest of winters but collapse unexpectedly when a new virus appears. Take the influenza pandemic of 1918–19. That virus killed more people than died in World War I: 20 million or possibly even 40 million people. According to some, it was the most devastating epidemic in world history. Known as 'La Grippe' or 'Spanish Flu', the virus wiped out more people than any other single disease outbreak, surpassing even the Black Death of the Middle

Ages. Sequencing the virus's RNA, collected from the lung tissue of a dead soldier, pointed to a novel H1N1 influenza A virus of exceptional virulence. The weird thing is that, over their lifetime, most victims must have fended off a host of other bugs and immune system assaults. One wonders what might have happened if the H5N1 avian flu virus had really taken hold in 2007. The really scary thing is that scientists believe the 1918 virus infected humans by mutating from bird flu.

Or consider coral reefs: like the human immune system, some things they can tolerate, others they cannot. The calcareous outer skeleton of many corals can withstand the relentless pounding of waves, even from a violent storm. Exposure to sediment plumes from nearby coastal construction operations, on the other hand, can be completely crippling – to the coral animal's inner workings and, sooner or later, to the reef's overall condition and health. On the face of it, you might regard sand grains as a mild and innocuous disturbance. Yet it is one from which a coral reef may not easily recover.

The 'robust yet fragile' paradox is an inescapable reality. To lose what robustness and insurance a system does possess can, therefore, be extremely hazardous. As TV and news reports remind us, almost daily, this is happening more and more to natural systems, often through the 'unnatural' actions of ill-conceived development projects, all, ironically, in the name of progress.

Robustness, as the above illustrations demonstrate, plainly portrays an extraordinary richness of meaning. As testament, mathematician Erica Jen and colleagues have posted eighteen or so different ways of characterizing robustness on the website of the Santa Fe Institute.

It should also be said that robustness theory is not yet mature. Unlike at least superficial measures of efficiency, there is no simple equation for robustness. Its meaning is even broader and more enigmatic and ethereal than efficiency. But this richness of meaning – including, curiously and paradoxically, **innovation** and **change** (the very opposite of how we normally expect robustness to act) – is actually far more its strength than a limitation, for it helps us get to the very heart of performance. Robustness, it turns out, is also the best tool we have for understanding and retaining what counts, for most of the time.

It is not that we should simply turn the clocks back, or ditch silicon for iron and rope. By striking a better balance between immediacy and the long view, though, nature and the things we create would be less highly strung.

What is so surprising is that robustness can spring to the fore from such low-tech, unsophisticated fixes: planting vegetation to help create sand dunes for coastal protection, and so on. Furthermore, repairs of any sort would often be unnecessary, had we not tampered with natural systems, inadvertently and in ignorance, in the first place. It turns out that many high-tech interventions, for example from some agribusinesses, do not actually turn out to be miracle solutions at all, and worse still, some, quite plainly, are doing more harm than good.

Sacrificing the 'indispensable': why robustness so easily gets eclipsed

Modernity's casual indifference to robustness – verging on disdainful neglect – has accompanied a growing love affair with immediacy and 'efficiency'. As just one reminder, consider the fate of 'worthless swamps', often sacrificed to make way for unfettered development and economic growth. Robustness so often plays second fiddle and gets ditched.

In many ways, opting for 'development at all costs' was inevitable. Throughout the twentieth century, for example, over-provision – making things stronger than seems really necessary – was to become the epitome of *in*efficiency; our racing Bentley, hugely over-engineered and great for the long haul, was a prime example in the motor car industry. Pruning down – whether for outright speed, or for leanness and efficiency more generally – was thought to be the best way forward. In the eyes of many, this was the fastest if not the only gateway to performance, efficiency and even satisfaction. But with it can come something less agreeable.

It is the same whether we're talking businesses, motor racing, national economic growth or globalization. Immediacy is what counts, never mind any inconvenient knock-on effects. But the price modernity pays for the short view – efficiency at all costs – has been colossal. Quite plainly, the environment has been one sacrificial pawn in the game. The real irony, though, is that economic interests can suffer, too. Often this arises from unanticipated and disagreeable knock-on effects, created by a weakened environment, as in the case of New Orleans and hurricane Katrina. (Of course squeezing commercial enterprises too far can have more direct, adverse effects on performance.)

We may now be in the second millennium, yet, judging from the environmental consequences of our actions, it is hardly an era of enlightenment; or one that future generations are going to look back on and thank us for.

As a result of our obsession with immediacy, and an increasingly product-hungry public, our focus simply does not penetrate far into the future. The long view, more reverently 'sustainability', may be admired and practised by environmental groups such as Greenpeace, and by health worshippers. Even the global sporting giant Adidas-Salomon declares itself 'dedicated to socially responsible, safe and environmentally sustainable practices in the company'. Or take Toyota, Alcoa – the world's largest producer of aluminium – and British Petroleum. These corporate lions, including Adidas, happened to be among firms specially earmarked in 2005 for superior sustainability.

The truth, though, is that in many private and public sector eyes sustainability means greater concern for the environment than the job in hand, too many staff, or too much stock. Worse still, they exclaim, it is a stranglehold on efficiency, a corporate straitjacket; and in our competitive world slickness, trimming things down, is all that really counts. Little wonder, then, that the coastal wetlands that 'invisibly' protected New Orleans were barely spared a thought, as development, and other dictates of free enterprise, propelled the city through the twentieth century and into the next.

It is hardly surprising, then, that efficiency – focusing on what *seems to* count, *now*, and disregarding or cutting what does not – has become the holy grail of performance measures: the rallying cry of a quasi-moral crusade. One major and often overlooked problem, though, is deciding and agreeing what is 'important'; efficiency is invariably subjective and ambiguous. The questions 'Efficiency for whom?', 'Efficiency at what cost?' and 'Efficiency over what time?' are seldom asked. In fact, narrow or ill-defined measures of efficiency now influence virtually every sphere of modern life, so powerful is the grip of the efficiency trap. But, if modernity is brutally honest, it is also an efficiency delusion.

Efficiency acclaims the merits of production with minimal effort. It embodies the quest for getting more from less, or even something for nothing; engineers see it as the ratio of output to input. In the business world it relates to the cost of achieving a certain aim – and it is here that the concept has had a love affair with people like no other. Corporate giants and small companies alike strive for ever higher annual profits by becoming lean and mean; hang the indirect fallout, on the environment or wherever else knock-on effects might strike. Even though it can be a risky business, quite literally, anything except 'more and faster' amounts, in their eyes, to poor practice, and second best . . . or worse.

Outside the corporate world, the fast track – the dangerous lane – can also provide rewards; better still, immediate gratification. Take heavy smoking, drinking or fast driving. You can hardly dismiss these quick fixes as merely youthful indulgences, or minority activities. In fact, childhood dares, extreme sports and other 'cerebral climaxes' seem to be precisely what humans crave. Might the quick fix, whether for speed efficiency in the corporate world, or simply for leisure, have some inherent logic after all?

Seen in this light, it is almost as if we are actually hard-wired for the quick fix, an immediate solution; something that is at least partly genetic. Consider, as one of many illustrations, that universal survival extinct – the fight-or-flight response. This is triggered by the adrenalin rush and, as mentioned, our fondness for daredevil pursuits; these might suggest at least some 'in-built' impermanence or transience about human behaviour. The truth is that in desperate (and sometimes not so desperate) situations, cannibalism is a grim reality. As a nerve-jangling reminder, consider what sometimes happened to sailors adrift for weeks in a small boat, once the food had run out: eat for survival now, and hang the consequences, is what made sense in their eyes.

What, ultimately, is at stake

The here-and-now mindset, being on the go, at lightning speed 24/7, seems to be modernity's approach to going about daily affairs. It is, after all, what many now believe it takes for 'efficiency' and 'success'. The approach is one that could not be more different from the more enlightened ways reminiscent of bygone days – yet, curiously, still alive and well in sòme places; that is, building for the long haul, through robustness, in an attempt to avoid catastrophic failure and for assured performance. As many examples demonstrate, this is not simply scaremongering or pie-in-the-sky theory, unlinked to reality. For disaster can easily strike anywhere down the line, including the environment, and, as mentioned, the pursuit of efficiency can backfire in more direct ways.

Simply put, many recurring issues and choices confronting modernity boil down to a conflict of interests: '*efficiency* of industry and development'; globalization, mass commercialization and capitalism, immediate gratification – lubricated, invariably, by high technology versus '*robustness* of ecosystems'; nurturing natural resources, localization, not-for-massive-profits, self-sufficiency, delayed gratification and adoption of less invasive technology.

Ever since the Luddites tried to defend their textile jobs by destroying factory looms in the early 1800s, the '*efficiency* of industry'/'*robustness* of ecosystems' camps have disagreed over these two opposing and fiercely contested sets of interests and alternatives. After 200 years advocates of '*efficiency*' (at-all-costs), by and large, still crack the whip. They proclaim that the environment is a luxury which, inevitably, must bow to the dictates of industry and development. Yet chasms in this simplistic and flawed ethos and dream world are beginning to open up, before our very eyes; the tide may be gradually beginning to turn. For example, the recent Paris Declaration is starting to bring about more effective and appropriate aid. Likewise, the Equator Principles insist on international business operating in a more socially and environmentally sound manner.

Because 'industry/ecosystem' issues are so fundamental to us all, they are a major part of this book's thrust. It would, naturally, be naïve and wide of the mark to suppose that nothing else drives the world, both forwards and backwards; but that is not what *Slow-Tech* is trying to claim. Besides the impositions and repercussions from ever-greater '*efficiency* of industry and development', there are now also huge (environmental and social) pressures simply from the sheer numbers of people going about their daily business, often in traditional and relatively modest ways. That is one case in point and an issue already mentioned. Yet the collateral from their activities, even if they are not 'industrial' or necessarily 'efficient', can also be substantial.

On the other hand, there seems little doubt that environmental fallout from modernity's quest for ever-greater '*efficiency* of industry and development' now equals, and in many places exceeds, that created by less pushy or commercial actions of society; that is from people not under the spell of efficiency at all costs. Writer and environmentalist George Monbiot, for one, believes economic activity to be the immediate and overwhelming threat. Either way, the '*robustness* of ecosystems' – an excellent buffer and antidote, up to a point, against the quivers and shocks imposed on nature – ends up on the line.

Why robustness matters, though, goes beyond safeguarding the integrity of environmental systems, and the many goods and services that flow from its natural captial – but which, all too easily, can slow from a flood to a trickle. Undeniably, the environment remains the cornerstone and powerhouse for the life, prosperity and well-being of our civilization, even if many corporate leaders and politicians have become blind to such a simple fact. What we're talking of here, though, is an influence of robustness that is no less pervasive and universal: the wisdom of retaining sufficent slack (and other froms of robustness) in *all* systems, as an alternative to driving most of it away in virtually everything we do, touch or create. This feckless behaviour – efficiency fanatics' solution to pretty much everything – has plunged society deep into an 'efficiency trap' entirely of its own making, though far from everyone's liking.

The modern world now marches to the beat of the corporate drum. With all spare capacity removed in today's managerial style, though, 'efficient' systems often fail to deliver. On close inspection, it becomes clear that robustness is lacking in many spheres of life, often the result of squeezing everything too far.

It's the same whether we are talking about environmental health, business health, the performance of military systems or even our own health. Instead of focusing solely on the here-and-now, driven by shortsightedness, the condition of virtually everything – ourselves included – would be far better off with greater robustness. This, too, is a major argument, especially later in the book. As many examples demonstrate, 'real efficiency' (robustness retained or instilled) is vastly more superior than 'superficial efficiency' (too much robustness squeezed out).

It is also clear that a constant high level of performance, excellence over time, is almost impossible to achieve. This holds for the environment, the corporate landscape and everything else, too. Robustness is, nevertheless, the best tool we have for understanding and maintaining what counts most, for most of the time: a step towards real efficiency. It means, paradoxically, keeping some of the 'inessential' instead of driving it all out, as many efficiency fanatics strive to do. Robustness science is still in its infancy; it is exciting and developing, and we still have much to learn. It is already clear, though, that robustness is something extending far beyond the long view, insurance and sustainability.

Slow-Tech paints a fresh and radically different picture of performance and how to assess it. It is one that will prevent us becoming stuck in an efficiency trap – and creating an environmental mess – enthralled by high-tech solutions, whatever the costs. Part of the solution true performance seekers should be waking up to is more enlightened thinking; not always getting rid of excessive baggage, which often proves to be far from 'superfluous'. That is what is needed as an antidote to the here-and-now mentality driven by shortsightedness.

To this end the book argues that we need a better integration of the concept of robustness into that of efficiency if we are to prevent the modern world from plunging further into an efficiency trap. Trading robustness for superficial saving for short-term efficiency is highly risky. Efficiency through robustness is so integral to agriculture, the environment, fisheries, cities and civilizations that we cannot afford to do nothing. It is a fact that modernity was by no means the first to discover.

CHAPTER 1 CIVILIZATION IN CRISIS

Over-consume and become a loser

The Inca way and less robust ways

Stretching 4,000 kilometres along the west coast of South America there was once an empire which, in its heyday, was the largest on earth. By any reckoning it was vast, enveloping sizeable chunks of present-day Ecuador, Peru, Chile, Bolivia and Argentina. This 'Land of Four Quarters' came together at the capital, Cuzco.

For its people, survival in the rugged terrain high in the Andes, in the inhospitable Atakama Desert and deep inside the steamy Brazilian rainforest was no trivial thing. Nor was the building and maintaining of 20,000 kilometres of roads, often across difficult terrain. The empire in question is, of course, that of the Incas. They may have lived back in the 1400s and 1500s, but the wealth, sophistication, knowledge and advanced ways of their legendary civilization knew no limits. It continues, what's more, to fascinate anthropologists, mathematicians, engineers and doctors right up to the present time.

But no less significant than these accomplishments, grand and ingenious as they were, was something more fundamental, down to earth: sustainable environmental management. Using agro-forestry practices still relevant today, it emerged quite recently, the Incas tapped into the multiple flow of ecosystem benefits without demolishing them. On the sides of the mountains, they terraced the land and boosted crop production. As enlightened farmers, the Incas realized that the answer lay in the soil. To this end, they developed irrigation, drainage systems and canals to extend and increase agricultural output.

It was old-fashioned technology through and through; at least, that is how modernity would view it. On many counts, though, it was far more advanced and successful than a lot of modern, yet short-sighted and ill-conceived solutions to land management.

Of course, we should not pretend that our ancestors always got things right; it is now clear, from archaeological and other research, that they did not. Either way, though, we seem not to have cottoned on to one glaringly obvious but disquieting fact, as modernity blasts off the launch pad into the new millennium: that insufficient attention to the maintenance of our surroundings is no less crazy than contemplating a car journey from one coast of the USA to the other without bothering to check the engine oil or water on the way.

The truth is that many developers today are over-zealous and care not a jot for the robustness of the soil, nor for the people and livelihoods reliant on it; that is, of course, assuming that some natural habitat is still there among all the concrete.

With enough resources put in, even a country as arid as Saudi Arabia can grow wheat – in fact it did so for several decades, up until early this century. Some might view such growth as a fiery statement to the world that nothing is beyond the realm of high-tech and petro-dollars; not even when it comes to defying nature against all odds by attempting to 'green' the desert, using temperate crops. The trouble was that this particular enterprise was thirsty in more ways than one: together with other non-sustainable schemes, it drew so heavily on the aquifer below that it lowered the water table and agriculture across the entire Arabian Peninsula suffered as a result.

This high-tech spectacle in the heartland of Arabia – more a debacle, and a tragedy, many would argue – was a step backwards from the Inca ways all those years earlier. For instead of impoverishing the land, an indelible signature of the Arabian experience, the Incas actually nourished it. Ensuring that resources remained renewable year on year was a practice that plainly paid off. In contrast to many civilizations (both past and present), it was an impressive environmental legacy, and one that long outlived the Incas themselves.

Natural cogs in modernity's machinery: ecosystems fuel development

Just as nurturing the environment helped enrich Inca society, so today our civilization depends on secure natural capital, and the uninterrupted productivity that flows from it: goods like timber, crops and fish, as well as free services through the physical protection of towns and population centres, or water purification and removal of wastes, for example by wetlands. Directly or indirectly, ecosystems are responsible for all this, and far more.

At one level, an ecosystem is simply nature; little more than a physical habitat, like a desert or wetland, plus all the creatures that happen to live there. But when the non-living and living come together, or 'synergize' – which is what happens in a healthy ecosystem – something incredibly vibrant and powerful comes about. For what you see, superficially, is considerably *less* than the totality of what you get. In fact, if you really want to think big (by stretching things only slightly), consider 'the ecosystem' as the synchronized operation of the earth, the environment, as well as the human race and other species in it.

Seen in that light, it is not difficult to see why maintaining the robustness of ecosystems is worth some sacrifices elsewhere, even if that means some commercial ones. As many examples demonstrate, this is our best bet for a productive present and a secure future; a far wiser alternative to development for quick returns, whatever the costs. Yet modernity continues to be unfased by squeezing the '*robustness* of ecosystems' from under its feet.

The reasons for the erosion of our surroundings are many and complex. One over-arching one is that we march to the beat of the corporate drum; in other words, the '*efficiency* of industry and development' carries huge clout. To this we could add something related: our fondness for unrestrained behaviour. Even when it comes to national or international assets, modernity can get away with blue murder, blemish-free, despite flagrant acts of rape and plunder. As a chilling reminder, consider what is now happening to the world's atmosphere. Rising energy consumption and greenhouse gas emissions are, unquestionably, adding to any natural climate trends and cooking the planet further.

Then there is the 'out of sight, out of mind' syndrome; again, though, this often follows from modernity's pursuit of '*efficiency* of industry and development', or other manifestations of a here-and-now society. Dump toxics like PCBs (a synthetic compound used, for example, as a coolant in transformers) in the sea, or even discharge synthetic oestrogen from contraceptives into sewage systems, and you might well get away with it. Companies and people have for decades, partly because the contaminant cocktail is not entirely of *their* own making. Undeniably, nature does a good clean-up job by flushing, dilution and redistribution – at least up to a point. Sooner or later, sometimes not for several generations, disagreeable side-effects start to emerge, for marine if not for human life.

But there are also less obvious factors at play, ones that nevertheless can erode the '*robustness* of ecosystems', little by little, until nature's ability to spring back and do its job all but disappears. Salt marshes, mangroves and other wetlands, as many examples demonstrate, have considerable 'off-site' value; you could call it 'out-of-sight' or invisible value, too. For example, young fish and shrimp often grow up, feed and are safe from predators in mangroves. In fisheries jargon, the ecosystem is an important 'nursery' area. When older, though, many fish migrate, sometimes to fishing areas far away, where they are exploited. Nevertheless, mangroves are extremely useful, even when not in close proximity to a fishery, as it may depend indirectly on them. Because their nursery role can go unnoticed, however, mangroves easily become the sacrifice of harmful activities, ones linked, for example, to '*efficiency* of industry and development'.

A similar sort of indirect ecosystem service is the protection, already described, against hurricanes, tsunamis and floods, even in distant areas. Simply put, it is insurance through robustness that intact and healthy natural systems provide. Although seldom acknowledged (except through lip-service), let alone accounted for, these sorts of 'off-site' benefits can be as great as 'on-site' ones linked more obviously to wetlands: timber, paper, seafood, animal fodder and the like. Unless you are firmly on guard, though, developers will try to bamboozle you into believing, as they themselves conveniently do, something very different: that wetlands are nothing but a thorn on the rose of progress and prosperity; quite literally a pain and, in their eyes, justifiably maligned and best eclipsed by development. Undeniably, wetlands can be mosquito-ridden, but they also generate numerous benefits.

There is the same sort of cavalier attitude when it comes to other species, too, in particular ones for which money may not change hands. Among these are useful plants, normally free and there for the picking by local people. The Sinai in Egypt is one of many regions whose communities have long utilized plants for their medicinal properties. It turns out that the ancient Egyptians suffered from ailments such as constipation much the same as we do, and used natural remedies such as castor oil, figs and bran – familiar to us today. Likewise, celery and saffron were effective against rheumatoid conditions. These and many other valuable natural products come from so-called 'non-marketed' species (although Egyptologists are now finding evidence of former distant trade). By and large, they were freely available; many products still are, when people can find them.

Because such products may not have a cut-and-dried value, or even any monetary value at all – unlike teak, potatoes and other marketed goods – modernity's bean counters seem blind to the fact that non-marketed species hold any value at all, let alone that they can be worth saving or are life-saving.

Of course pharmaceutical (and biotechnology) companies are beginning to cotton on to the value of the pharmacologically active compounds that many plants contain; and some of these are exploited, directly or indirectly, for commercial gain. Echinacea to help boost the immune system, and St John's Wort for depression, are just two examples. But even commercial interest, ironically, provides no guarantees for the conservation of some medicinal plants, either; in fact sometimes it does the very opposite. The problem is especially acute when loss of habitat, and hence decline in 'robustness of ecosystems', accompanies unsustainable harvesting of the medicinal plants themselves.

It is hardly surprising then, that in no time at all nature's green veneer can become replaced and eclipsed by glitzy hotels, shopping malls and marinas. That is why, in a market-force driven (and over-populated) world, ecosystem robustness (and sometimes ecosystems themselves) easily becomes the sacrificial lamb.

Of course, decline or loss of the odd species here or there may not be totally crippling, or even noticeable at first. The problem comes from the collective collateral, the loss of too many species, whether we're talking medicinal plants, wetlands or other natural vegetation. It is also something that can easily happen, from too much commercial development, or simply from 'urban creep'.

Yet the simple expedient of interspersing developments – even inner cities – with parks and other green areas can work wonders. Besides the obvious benefit for wildlife conservation, open space can simply help rejuvenate the weary city-dweller. There are huge pay-offs for relatively little expenditure and sacrifice.

Turning up the oven and preparing to roast

Added to the problems described, and undermining the robustness of society as well as the '*robustness* of ecosystems', are the scary effects of climate change and sea-level rise. Both are happening right now. What's more, all but staunch diehards – you could say 'ostriches' – are opening their eyes to a glaringly obvious fact: that too much carbon dioxide pumping out into the atmosphere, from an increasingly industrial world, is largely to blame. (So, too, ironically, is methane from agriculture.) Perhaps when coal-power fired up textile machinery and other industries back in the 1800s, the Luddites were worried about more than losing their jobs. For this was the time of the Industrial Revolution, when modernity began, unwittingly but quite literally, to fry the planet.

The Maldivian government, for one, recognizes the hazards of global warming and sea-level rise. Since the islands stand barely two metres above sea level, it has a vested interest in ensuring that the nation's foundations remain as robust as possible; not surprisingly, the people themselves – hoteliers, fishermen and shopkeepers alike – share these sentiments. It is the same for the Pacific's Marshall Islands and other low-lying tropical islands. The stark reality is that the continued physical and economic existence of such countries depends on a healthy and actively growing coral reef platform, on which the islands delicately perch. On top of that, the reefs act as a ring of natural physical defence, buffering the forces of waves and storms.

In the case of the Maldives, one problem militating against coral growth, and keeping pace with sea-level rise, is extensive coastal land-filling and reclamation in and around shallow coral areas. This has occurred most vigorously around the main island, Malé. Formerly oval, it is now almost square. Reclaiming once shallow coastal areas provided much needed space for housing and infrastructures, in the nation's pursuit of economic growth for greater '*efficiency* of industry and development'. It was done partly to create space for housing for local people, partly to service tourism.

In many ways, reclamation was an understandable solution, given the population growth, and that tourism is now the biggest generator of national revenue. Sure enough, though, reef loss and damage greatly diminished the reefs' ability to fend off blows from nature and defend Malé. One testament to this was the terrific storm of 1991. Widespread destruction followed, including damage to more than 3,000 dwellings and around 200,000 trees.

What followed was the need for an artificial breakwater on the south of the island for protection against flooding. This high-tech fix, costing 12 million dollars, or 8,000 dollars per linear metre, would not have been necessary had the possible adverse environmental consequences of undercutting natural coastal protection been considered more seriously.

Pressures for economic growth and development in Malé had, effectively, diminished the island's power to defend itself and its dependencies against bad storms. All of a sudden, in the aftermath of a really big one, it became clear that the island's natural robustness had become squeezed out, so had to be replaced artificially. Building houses and hotels vertically, instead of spreading horizontally – as in Singapore – might have created an eyesore. But it could have been a more robust solution.

When coral reefs get damaged, or worn out, the knock-on effects can be more alarming still, especially against a background of rising sea levels. The fact is that the calcium carbonate material that builds islands such as the Maldives actually originates from coral – their calcareous skeleton – in the first place. So unless the rate of coral growth and reef building (involving, paradoxically, the work of microscopic coral animals) remains greater than the rate of erosion, the structure of reefs begin to weaken. And so, too, does the robustness of the islands themselves.

On some islands the land is washing away, quite literally, from beneath the islanders' feet: for no coral means no sand and no island, or at least a disappearing island. This is not just theoretical fantasy, but reality: it is already happening, for example in the Pacific islands of Tuvalu. People are already beginning evacuation to more robust physical surroundings, like New Zealand. And, of course, even if an island gets only partial swamping, salt water and spray is extremely damaging to crops and soil.

Simply put, global warming and sea-level rise – made worse by more direct human activities – are beginning to weaken many terrestrial and marine ecosystems. For societies on many tropical islands, and many other areas, too, this new state of affairs does not bode well.

The good news, though, is that robustness in the form of self-correction (so-called 'negative feedback') operates in natural ecosystems and, to a degree, helps fend off unexpected blows, including climatic disturbances. It turns out that one vital cog in the works is natural vegetation, on land and (through microscopic phytoplankton) in the sea. For pastures green, indirectly, help create low clouds, which in turn have a cooling effect on climate.

Simply put, this dampening of conditions by natural systems is what helps them (and us) to keep going, when the oven is turned up, or when the going gets tough in other ways. The buffering ability of ecosystems is the normal state of affairs. It amounts to species 'getting it together' with their physical surroundings (not intentionally, of course) – an invaluable double act if ever there was one. It is part and parcel of the earth's proper functioning, and the essence of James Lovelock's Gaia hypothesis. It amounts to self-regulation, an important signature of robustness, in many different systems. As if by magic, this operates locally and at the planetary level. Push things too far, though, past the 'tipping point', and a system can easily flip to an altered state and positive feedback can take over.

Positive feedback does precisely the opposite of negative feedback: it reduces robustness. It is a symptom of a fevered environment or planet, and of fragility in many other systems; positive feedback is something that global warming seems to be accelerating. Worldwide increase in temperature, from rising carbon dioxide levels, is hastening the release of methane from the Arctic tundra. Within this permafrost, vast quantities of planetary methane reside – normally locked up and unavailable. Methane, although far less abundant than carbon dioxide, is a greenhouse gas about twenty times more potent, molecule for molecule. The trouble is that methane release (as a result of warming) causes further temperature rise, and so on . . . leading to a 'runaway' and unstable state. All of a sudden, robustness of the earth-climate system can begin to diminish; it is what is happening right now. (If the new state, itself, turns out to be 'robust', though, then we really are in trouble.)

Individual developing countries, like the Maldives and the Marshall Islands, feel, understandably, that they can do little to make industrial nations reduce their energy inputs and greenhouse gas outputs. For the nations who are largely responsible have been show to change. As testament to this, look no further than countries like the USA, China and India. All are now major emitters and contributors to global warming, and they seem to be unstoppable.

At one level, of course, small island states are right: their voices are little more than a weak echo shimmering across the oceans, which seldom reaches the ears of the drivers of global warming, those in the hot-seat of power. Yet there is something they can do. Given the prevailing climate, their best bet is a local environmental insurance policy; one based on simple, no-nonsense biological principles, but which helps ensure '*robustness* of ecosystems'.

First, atolls and coral reefs are not static, but living structures and have the ability for vertical growth; and, second, healthy coral reefs have a greater chance of coping with (by responding to) sea level rise and other disturbances than degraded, worn-out reefs, for example as a result of direct exposure to heavy sewage and sedimentation levels – or from being in the line of fire from other hasty development actions.

The premium for this insurance is the cost of environmental management – not discharging sewage on all the reefs; cutting down sedimentation; and not mining excessive quantities of coral for building material, or destroying reefs to make way for coast-to-coast hotels. Collectively, these measures can work wonders and help cut down reef deterioration. The simple expedient of retaining the '*robustness* of ecosystems' provides an invaluable buffer against the unwanted effects of economic development, especially as we are now entering an increasingly greenhouse world.

It would be a mistake, though, to suppose that weakened life and business support systems are a symptom only of modernity. It is true that the Incas, and a good many civilizations before them, left a relatively low footprint on the environment. So, too, did a number of coastal societies with traditional, self-imposed measures to regulate use of resources, as in parts of South East Asia and the Pacific. The environmental legacy, however, was not always quite so benign.

Wisdom from history

A sobering fact is that so many societies and civilizations are ephemeral: here today, gone tomorrow. Like species, they come and go. This, according to Jared Diamond, author of *Collapse: How Societies Choose to Fail or*

Succeed, is one of the disturbing facts of history. In the case of the Incas, environmental caretakers and innovators par excellence, they left the New World, and the only world they knew, quite suddenly. One decisive factor, as an aside, was gunpowder: Inca warriors were simply no match for the guns (and horses) of the Spanish conquistadors. The Inca civilization was robust up to the tipping point; then all of a sudden, it became fragile. In 1533 up to 3,000 Incas were killed within thirty minutes, and it was not long until the Incas' entire army – some 40,000 strong – was defeated.

Much more surprising, especially to politicians, is that a primary cause of collapse of societies is destruction of the environmental resources on which they depended. Not all societies, of course, have gone this way. But what Diamond's book tells us is that, when societies have collapsed – and not just in ancient times – environmental degradation has often played a decisive role.

This stark revelation, long suspected by environmentalists, is the thrust of Jared Diamond's arguments in *Collapse*. For otherwise dissimilar societies that have crumbled, or entered a 'parallel universe', the pattern turns out to be remarkably similar: before the downfall, a downward spiral of environmental decline, whether we're talking of human populations in Easter Island in the South Pacific or Greenland in the Atlantic's cold northern waters.

Over-consumption of resources, of course, is only one part of a wider disturbance created; what we're talking of here is collateral damage, to both land and sea – an impact that invariably accompanies heavy resource use and other developmental activities. Sooner or later, the flow of free environmental goods and services begins to slow; put another way, the '*robustness* of ecosystems' will eventually falter.

The problem, according to Diamond, is that diminished environmental robustness has a knock-on effect, and that is what has a destabilizing action on society – especially when accompanied by climate change, disease, or opportunistic neighbours quick to seize on such weaknesses.

A tale of two 'tribes'

To put literary and technical flesh on the bones of his thesis, one summer Diamond visited two dairy farms, separated by thousands of miles. Both farms were highly advanced, technologically, and the most prosperous in the district. Each centred around a fine state-of-the-art barn for sheltering and milking cows. There were other similarities, too: for example, cows were left outdoors on lush pasture over summer, the two farms and barns were of comparable size, and both were situated in areas of outstanding natural beauty, attracting tourists from far and wide. On top of that, the owners of distant farms were seen as leading figures of their societies.

Besides shared strengths, there were shared risks. Both farms were at high latitudes, so the summer growing season was limited, and on top of that came the ravages of drought, cold and other climatic instabilities. In addition, both farms were distant from population centres and a marketing outlet, putting both at a relative competitive disadvantage.

Those were the shared strengths and weaknesses. On both counts the two farms – one belonging to the Huls family in Montana, in the USA, the other the former manor farm of the Norse bishop Gardar, in south-western Greenland – had much in common. But, as Diamond revealed, there was an even bigger difference, so marked in fact that it completely eclipsed any features the farms had in common: their current status. The Huls farm, it turned out, is currently prospering (and an exemplary model and inspiration for neighbouring farms). In contrast, the Gardar farm does not operate at all; it is, and has long been, defunct. It was, in fact, abandoned 500 years ago. In its heyday, of course, the collapse of the Gardar farm must have seemed just as unlikely as would the decline of the Huls farm today in, what is, still, the most powerful country in the world.

It was not just the decline in that farm, though, it was also goodbye to the whole of Norse Greenland society. Not one soul remained. One way or another, Diamond explains, its thousands of people perished, perhaps from starvation, conflicts with an enemy, or social dislocation.

Or perhaps the inhabitants simply moved on – or, more likely, were shoved on – to pastures yonder. A major trigger early on, though, was almost certainly environmental damage, by over-grazing, soil erosion, turf-collecting and more invasive vegetation clearance. Deforestation and shortage of lumber were particularly problematic, for the Norse could no longer make houses, boats and barrels as they had once done. One thing led to another and, with key resources depleted, Norse military acumen was no match for the Inuit, who were eager for an ever-greater share of the land.

The environment-a-luxury myth

All too often today's politicians are, at best, dismissive of these sorts of tales – of any suggestion that decline in environmental robustness might foreshadow social decline or collapse. In their eyes, the environment is like any other inconvenient issue, merely something blocking economic progress; hardly a reason for the collapse of a society. Those in power proclaim, instead, that development is what is needed right now. As they see things, the environment simply cannot be, nor does it need to be, a priority.

On many counts their priorities are reasonable. Developing countries, after all, crave the technology and the comforts that many in more affluent nations enjoy. Yet non-sustainable resource use was often one big nail in the collective coffin; it is unlikely to be different for present and future civilizations. '*Robustness* of ecosystems' is what is needed to stand up to the threats, especially in a world so besotted and driven by '*efficiency* of industry and development'. As Diamond argues, dismissing the environment as an 'issue', just like any other, is actually wide of the mark on several counts.

For one thing, he tells us, there is a widely held misperception that we must decide between the environment *or* development. What the Aswan Dam in Egypt delivered, and did not deliver, revealed just how misguided that view of development is. In fact it is a delusion. Whatever the level of sophistication of society, prosperity and well-being lie, ultimately, in healthy natural resources, and keeping them that way. In fact, it boils down to '*efficiency* of industry and development' through assured '*robustness* of ecosystems', rather than alternatives to one another. It is a view consistent with enlightened thinking and traditional principles – not just the view of muddle-headed Greenies. Even in an era of globalization, that's what helps ensure the smooth running of economic and environmental cogs. So treating the environment as a 'sacrificial anode' (chunks of zinc bolted on to the underside of a steel ship to prevent wasting of the hull) is highly risky; doubly so when one is talking of the anchor-roots of society.

The second myth Diamond exposes is our misplaced blind faith in technology as a means of getting society out of the environmental quagmire – one, incidentally, that development so often puts it in in the first place. But it is a dodgy and flimsy assumption. Consider just one example, from agriculture: there is a groundswell of opinion that feels that GM crops and many other agricultural advances do not always best serve our needs; quite plainly, they can sometimes. One thing for sure, though, is that 'advanced' agri-technology seldom comes as a blemish-free, magical El Dorado. It turns out that high-tech can do as much (or more) to line the pockets of agribusiness as to support farmers and put wholesome food on the table. That, above all else, is needed to keep society on the path to well-being and prosperity.

Worse still, technology, in the words of Diamond: 'merely constitutes increased power, which produces changes that can be either for the better or for the worse. All of our current environmental problems are unanticipated harmful consequences of our existing technology.' Not only that, as one reviewer of Diamond's book explains: 'There is no basis for believing that technology will miraculously stop causing new and unanticipated problems while it is solving the problems that it previously produced.'

The third misconception, Diamond asserts, is that environmentalists are simply scaremongers, over-reacting, with a misplaced sense of cause-and-effect linkages between decay in '*robustness* of ecosystems' and the collapse of society. After all, sceptics contend, water still runs from our taps, supermarkets remain stocked and the fields are still green. However, while that remains the situation for lucky affluent nations, it is certainly not the status quo for at least one billion of the world's population. It also happens that areas of environmental despoliation often coincide with areas of political turmoil and, what's more, the fallout extends far beyond national boundaries.

To drive home what environmental and civil decay in distant lands can mean to Americans, Diamond calls for comparison of two lists of countries. For the first list, he proposes, ask an academic ecologist – preferably one with little or no savvy of current affairs – to list the main hotspot countries; that is, in terms of population pressure, resource over-use, pollution and so on. In all likelihood, the ecologist, in the words of Diamond, would respond: 'That's a no-brainer, it's obvious. Your list of environmentally stressed or over-populated countries should surely include Afghanistan, Bangladesh, Burundi, Haiti, Indonesia, Iraq, Nepal, Pakistan, the Philippines, Rwanda, the Solomon Islands, and Somalia, plus others.'

Then, Diamond suggests, ask a politician from the developed world, who neither understands the environment nor cares about it, to draw up a list of countries representing the world's hotspots, in terms of trouble areas: countries where state government is about to collapse or has already fallen, weakened by social unrest and civil war; and countries whose own troubles have affected affluent developed countries – influx of illegal immigrants, for example, or the need to quell rebellious uprisings, terrorist incursions, and so forth. The answer, Diamond proclaims, would be: 'That's a no-brainer, it's obvious. Your list of political trouble spots should surely include Afghanistan, Bangladesh, Burundi, Haiti, Indonesia, Iraq, Nepal, Pakistan, the Philippines, Rwanda, the Solomon Islands, and Somalia, plus others.'

The similarity between the two lists of nations is, of course, hardly coincidental. Just as environmental health helps create social stability, Diamond contends, environmental decay brought about by expanding populations, especially during earlier good times, is a precursor of social fragmentation and sometimes collapse. It seems to be a hallmark of many ancient societies that have collapsed and, it emerges, robustness squeezed out of ecosystems can lead to a chain of events that today's world is not immune to, either.

While in their ascendancy, it transpires, many societies have unwittingly set the seeds of their own destruction by undermining their environmental roots. Those mysterious abandonments generally happened, according to Diamond, in one or more of eight ways: habitat damage and forest clearance, soil problems (erosion, salt and fertility decline), water management problems, over-fishing, over-hunting, impacts of introduced species, human population growth and increased per-capita impact of people. By and large, this signifies a society or state becoming too big for its own environmental boots. Put another way, all these symptoms are interrelated indications of humanity becoming out of balance with its surroundings. Often it begins with diminished environmental robustness, then leads to social decline or collapse.

Many in power, of course, will have none of it: development is what's needed, right now – the environment cannot be a priority, nor, in their eyes, should it be a constraint to a prosperous future. On many counts their sentiments are logical; they chime with human nature, and the desire for progress. In the case of developing countries, you could say they are simply craving the technology and the comforts that many in developed nations now enjoy.

Advocates of unfettered economic growth brush aside modernity's dependence on a robust environment in all sorts of other ways, too. Superficially, at least, many of their arguments seem convincing. Ancient civilizations, or what's happening in the developing world, are one thing, they proclaim. For those societies, lacking sufficient technology or know-how, a precarious interdependence between the environment and development is only to be expected. But to extrapolate from those situations to somewhere like the US is, surely, going wide of the mark.

Do not be so sure, is Jared Diamond's message. Non-sustainable resource use was often one big nail in the collective coffin; it is unlikely to be any different for present and future civilizations than for those of bygone eras. Robustness is what is needed to stand up to the threats facing modernity and its descendants.

What happened to the Mayans could happen to us

It is sobering to recall, Diamond reminds us, '. . . the swift decline of the ancient Maya, who 1,200 years ago were, themselves, the most advanced society in the Western Hemisphere, and who, like us now, were then at the apex of their own power and numbers.' Consider what happened to them.

Heavy farming – probably involving double-cropping, decreased periods of land lying fallow in lowland areas – and movement of populations from the valleys to the hill slopes, formerly unoccupied and forested, was the start of the downhill slide of the Mayan civilization. But settlement on the slopes, by all accounts, was only brief. For what followed was forest clearance and erosion of the hill slopes, the soil becoming stripped of nutrients and lowering agricultural output. Not only that, hill soils, acidic from the (former) presence of the pine trees, washed down to the valley below. Archaeologists know this from painstaking detective work on material they unearthed from the foundations of buildings on the valley floor: that material was sediment containing tree pollen, which evidently got there during the eighth century.

The net effect of Mayan development was acute shortage of wood and fuel supplies, and creation of a 'man-made drought'. It is something that easily happens with massive deforestation. Analysis of skeletal remains points, unequivocally, to the deterioration of nutrition and health – over 200 years: from 650 to 850 AD.

It hardly takes agricultural science, or archaeological science – just plain common sense – to see that one thing leads to another. In the case of the Mayans, at least in the Copán area, once the hills became abandoned, through loss of soil or soil fertility, the extra population had to be fed from somewhere: that 'somewhere' was, according to Diamond, just one square mile of productive land in the valley below. This increased, of course, the competition for food grown there. Fighting to retain or access the most productive farmland would surely have followed. Because the king could no longer guarantee rains or prosperity, Diamond goes on to explain, it was an 'exit-only' visa for him: he was, quite literally, the agricultural and political scapegoat for failed harvests. After 822 AD, allegedly, no king ever appeared on the scene again and, to crown it all, the royal palace was razed to the ground less than thirty years later.

That, essentially, is what befell the inhabitants of Copán, a former Mayan city whose ruins now lie in present-day Western Honduras. How are the mighty fallen, indeed. From an initial and steep rise in numbers around 400 AD, Copán's population peaked some time between 750 and 900 AD to about 27,000, only to fall back to about 15,000 by 950 AD. By 1235, though, virtually no one remained in the valley, an assertion confirmed, through analysis of pollen remains, by the re-emergence of forest trees. With too much robustness driven out of the land, it was a downhill spiral and a state of fragility for the Maya themselves.

How are the mighty fallen

As this former Mayan stronghold demonstrates, so unnervingly, cities stumble and crumble in much the same way as the societies and larger civilizations of which they are so much a part. Robustness, it turns out, can also help us understand what makes them buzz or stagnate. Of course, it would be simplistic and naïve, in fact plain absurd, to suppose that the environment is the only driving force; cities, like the societies attracted to them, flourish and weaken for all sorts of reasons, frequently social and economic. Yet over-stretching and neglecting the environment, by trading robustness for corner-cutting and over-ambitious development, invariably backfires. It is, in fact, tantamount to lighting the fuse of a firework and expecting no sparks or any explosive fallout;

and we are not talking here of just the environment inside the city walls; or merely the natural environment, either.

Seen in this light, cities and towns are perfect parasites. Not only do they consume more food and water than they produce, they also produce more sewage than they know what to do with. And cities bury more people than they produce. Those are just some of the revelations in John Reader's recent book *Cities*. It is certainly the case for present-day London and New York today; and the same was probably true for classical Athens, Rome and other former centres of power, classical architecture and learning which, as an aside, happened to influence the Western world in so many ways.

Although cities say what goes, they are, ironically, vulnerable to unanticipated side-effects. A city fouling its groundwater with refinery wastes, or ignoring plate tectonics' warning groans, is likely to come tumbling down. The fact is that robustness of natural systems matters in all sorts of ways, even when it comes to the built environment. By building roads just wide enough to transport the wheat it needed – for cost-saving and greater 'efficiency' – many an ancient city perished once the population grew too large. But playing safe through some overkill, or over-provision, can give enormous paybacks. An obvious example here would be deliberately making roads wider than at the time seemed necessary. After all, it only amounts to robustness thinking.

Even mighty Rome, as John Reader reminds us, depended on the larder, local at first, then global. As its borders bulged, provisioning became like feeding the five thousand. This feat was made possible only by the maintenance of a fleet of grain ships and newly invented (thermostatically regulated and insect-proof) grain silos – robust technology, by any reckoning. Expansion of society also called for the construction of a new harbour and the appropriation of crops from faraway Egypt. But Rome outgrew even this remarkable supply chain and collapsed along with her empire.

As Lawrence Norfolk once said in a review of *Cities*, 'An industrious infancy followed by middle-aged spread, leading to a gluttonous old age and sudden death by starvation would seem to be the life-cycle of the city.' Sooner or later cities, like other systems, can reach the tipping point. You could call it over-consumption and environmental neglect, through and through. No one in their right mind would pretend that '*robustness* of ecosystems' is all that is needed to fuel cities and make them buzz. The really bizarre thing, it turns out, is that tolerance to immigrants and gays can instil that vital robustness that just helps keep cities going.

Bills to recover robustness are mounting

It does not require huge leaps of imagination, or fancy science, to realize that over-consumption, and the damage clean-up needed in its aftermath, can be crippling to societies in the modern world. Consider, as Jared Diamond does, the case of the US, a country now having to foot some truly colossal bills. With the American chestnut and the Grand Banks cod fishery gone, and the topsoil going, too, it is more than a serious blow to the economy.

On top of that come hefty toxic clean-up costs, for example in the Hudson River and Chesapeake. Then there is the cost of combating zebra mussels, water hyacinth and hundreds of other destructive and unwelcome visitors. Trying to combat 'alien invasive species' now costs billions of dollars annually: a colossal burden, even for the USA. It is little wonder that its economy (and American patience) is starting to wear thin. Some might even contend that bills of this magnitude could foreshadow the start of an eroded power base.

The bleak reality, in the words of Diamond, is that 'The cost of our homegrown environmental problems adds up to a large fraction of our gross national product'; and that completely ignores additional expenditure created by environmental problems overseas, military operations, and so on. Seen in the light of a plethora of recurrent costs, you do not need to be a pessimist to sense that a gradual economic decline might not be that far away; it happened, after all, to the Roman and British empires. According to many, Diamond included, the writing is already on the wall: increasing national debt and government budget deficit, widening unemployment, and fall in value of many pension funds.

Technology may help but, paradoxically, it can be as much a problem as a panacea. Difficulties societies face often seem to be the result of ill-conceived, high-tech projects and activities – followed by equally high-tech rescue operations hoping, but often failing, to provide a cure. Globalization, many now hold, works the same way. It is easy to be enamoured by the business benefits, of which there are plainly many. Yet we seem oblivious to its down-side; as a transnational enterprise, globalization is double-edged and sharp. On the one hand, the developing world is a great outlet for McDonald's burgers and other US exports which, without globalization, would not easily happen. With relaxed trade barriers, though, come Aids, other diseases and terrorism, too, as well as immigrant species.

Jared Diamond is, of course, not alone in realizing that unmistakable cracks are beginning to open up in society from fissures in the natural systems needed to fuel them; and in the robustness needed to maintain them. In their recent book, *Resilience Thinking: Sustaining Ecosystems and People in a Changing World*, Brian Walker and David Salt drive home the same point. Drawing on recent findings from resilience/robustness theory, they demonstrate that society and the environment really are, or at least should be, part of the same integrated system; that is our best bet for a better and more secure world. Their take-home message is that land managers and planners need to look beyond control, intensification and greater efficiency for sustainability solutions.

What is needed is an expanded horizon – not, of course, through chopping down all the trees, but by 'homelands' and ecological rangelands being treated and remaining as one. They base their proclamation not just on theory, for they also present five lively case histories, ranging from the Everglades in Florida to Sweden's Kristianstad Vattenrike.

Robustness (resilience, in the parlance used in their book and by many other ecologists), Walker and Salt point out, explains why greater efficiency alone cannot solve resource and other environmental problems.

Stretching things, you could say that robustness, just like the Holy Grail, holds miraculous powers and, it seems, is the key to a greener and rosier future. Thomas Homer-Dixon at the University of Toronto is another singing from the same hymnsheet. As technologies become more complex and interconnected, he tells us, major system failures are becoming ever more likely – especially as events in one place increasingly cause collateral damage, with fallout from one nation's borders ricocheting across to another. That is the core message behind his book *The Upside of Down: Catastrophe, Creativity and the Renewal of Civilization*, along with how to imbue society with greater vigour in the face of such environmental and social dislocations.

The long view

Immediacy and the quick fix, whether for city development or in other human endeavours, might seem the best way forward or even the only solution for progress, efficiency and satisfaction. That would be a reasonable conclusion, at least from a broad scan of modernity in action; whether in things it creates, or simply what it does for leisure. As one of a litany of reminders, look no further than the engineered flood walls constructed to shield New Orleans against hurricanes. Since these were replacements of natural defences, ones which were in many ways superior – but which got sacrificed for hasty, poorly regulated town planning – it would be hard to think otherwise.

Examples like this certainly point towards short-term vision as being the norm; an inevitable state of affairs, driven by eagerness for '*efficiency* of industry and development', even if that means kissing goodbye to insurance provided by '*robustness* of ecosystems' along the way. That would be a reasonable deduction, from the prevalence of efficiency-at-all-costs mentality, and the many other forms of here-and-now behaviour already described.

On closer inspection, though, human nature can be quite different. It is actually incorrect to suppose that immediacy and impermanence is the only normal condition. Quite plainly, shortsightedness has *not* always prevailed through the ages, strange as that might seem in the light of the corporate brainwashing and hoodwinking which now envelop us. As testament to this, we need look no further than the Huls farm in the USA, or the Incas several hundred years earlier. In the case of the Incas, it is sobering to recall that driving away environmental robustness was not what led to their downfall – nor, in fact, was any other here-and-now behaviour responsible: the collapse of their civilization was due to something entirely different, and quite unexpected.

Throughout history, many societies have taken the long view. Chinese dynasties, for one, bear testament to this state of affairs. Several dynasties continued, relatively unchanged, for many hundreds of years; some of their policies lasted even longer. It was the same in Ancient Egypt: their civilizations just went on and on; and if they stumbled – for example through outside intervention – they were often robust enough for life to return, more or less, to what it had once been.

The truth is that a longer-term approach to life could be just as natural a state of affairs as the here-and-now. It is just that for the last 100 to 200 years, by and large, we've taken a different tack. But that's not to say we are driven or programmed, genetically, to behave that way in everything we do. As a demonstration of one society refusing to fast-forward, one that has stood well the test of time, go to the Middle East and carefully observe the Bedouin; or, if you don't have the time or inclination, simply check out the many accounts by explorers and writers, and you'll see that they (like my father) have opted for the long haul and robustness, as if their lives depended on it.

Masters of the desert: a foot in two centuries

It would be short-sighted to underestimate the wisdom of the Bedouin – traditional 'occupiers' of desert lands since time immemorial. The region we are referring to is, of is course, the heartland of Arabia and northern Africa. One illustration after another leads to the same conclusion: that knowledge held by these people about sustainable living still provides salutary lessons, to modern conservation scientists, aid agencies and politicians alike. For development to work, as the Bedouin see things, trading environmental robustness for modern trappings and quick fixes will invariably come back and haunt you.

One extraordinary tale of Bedouin ways, in Southern Sinai, carries a simple message. Yet its profoundness echoes beyond its desert borders. The story comes from French coastal manager Alain Jeudy de Grissac, formerly working in Southern Sinai and recently in charge of an international conservation and biodiversity project in Eritrea. What he recounted, one summer's day in 2006, was something very down-to-earth, but so insightful I'll never forget it.

The tale related to wood – still the mainstay fuel for cooking and heating deep inside Southern Sinai and, in fact, in most of the world's desert environments. The problem is that, in any arid land, wood is invariably a scarce resource, especially following a lengthy drought; the harsh reality is that users can easily, and quickly, outstrip the capacity of trees to regenerate.

A curious fact, an Egyptian Bedouin once explained to Jeudy de Grissac, is that trees and bushes in the desert often appear dead but actually can still be alive. Because the practice is non-sustainable, the Bedouin generally avoid cutting wood from live trees; to be sure a tree is really dead, however, they wait (voluntarily, though, not through any modern environmental legislation imposed from on high) until it has been rained on and received water; in fact, *five* times, no less. In the searing interior of the Sinai Peninsula, as any visitor can attest, that can be a gruelling test of patience indeed. If that does not revive the tree, the chances are it really is dead. So using the wood as fuel then would not constitute unsustainable use of something so crucial.

That's not the end of the tale, though. Back in 1951, Jeudy de Grissac added, one violator of this long-standing tradition was made to relinquish – again not by any law, but by fellow tribesmen – three camels for his misdemeanour. It might seem like a trivial penalty for under-cutting environmental robustness; but allowing for inflation, Jeudy de Grissac calculated, the penalty today would be equivalent to the price of three Mercedes cars.

The behaviour he described on this occasion concerns the Bedouin use of raw materials, here wood from trees: something that can easily switch from being renewable to become non-renewable – creating a fragile, lifeless environment instead of a robust one that normally provides an uninterrupted supply of bio-fuel and other service. But Bedouin wisdom extends far beyond nurturing the living environment. We are talking here of the built environment, in fact a key natural ingredient for it. The material in question, sand – the basis of cement and concrete (and desert 'soil'), is of course something in far greater supply than anything living, or renewable, especially in such an inhospitable desert setting as Southern Sinai.

For dependable buildings and structures, the construction industry relies (unsurprisingly) on quality sand. In many areas, it turned out from Jeudy de Grissac's tale, unscrupulous construction owners – those eager to build new developments, one after the other, with the cheapest materials possible – took a short cut. The obvious choice was sea sand, beach sand or sand within reach of sea spray; there is, after all, plenty of it around, especially if you happen to live near the coast. The problem, though, as any chemistry student knows, is that cement and concrete made from salt-laden sand lacks robustness. It soon crumbles, as do structures made from it. As testament to this spectacle, the casual onlooker may not have failed to notice many collapsed restaurants and other buildings near the shore. This was especially prevalent during the 1970s and 80s, when businesses were experiencing a real bonanza boom; we are not just talking of Southern Sinai, though, for the same thing happened across much of the Middle East and quite possibly elsewhere, too.

Fortunately for those who had commissioned building work, there were also some scrupulous individuals within the construction industry. Among these were a number of Bedouin. Recognizing the importance of robustness in all matters relating to the environment, their solution boiled down to a mix of common sense, time and patience: using beach sand, or sea sand (assuming inland sand is not available or affordable) for building is OK, but only if it has been left for three years – a time span normally sufficient for the rains to wash away every last trace of salt.

In many ways this tale of the Bedouin was reminiscent of the earlier one describing their traditional approaches to the use of wood. At least one individual practising what he preached about resistant materials, Jeudy de Grissac recounted, was a Bedouin and desert dweller through and through. Yet he was equally at home in the modern world, for he also happened to be manager of a lucrative construction company in Southern Sinai.

Once good ideas catch on, they can spread like wildfire, from one place to another, even across the desert, and that is precisely what has happened. Because many Bedouin still wander freely across the desert – from inland areas to the coast – technical 'breakthroughs', old-fashioned approaches to wood conservation, or simply new ideas, can quickly reach new areas. You could even say that the protected area system in Southern Sinai, of which the Bedouin are an integral part, has helped create a more solid business environment, as well as a healthy and robust natural environment.

The Rashaida, perhaps even more so than other Bedouin, are a tightly knit desert group that chooses to live, simultaneously, in a slow-tech and a high-tech world. With no national allegiance, yet generally holders of three different passports – Saudi Arabian, Sudanese and Eritrean – the Rashaida don't care a jot for national frontiers. Most still live in tents, they retain long-standing tribal customs and they have impressive knowledge of the desert environment. Just to stay alive, and survive the tough desert environment, means thorough robustness thinking.

Just as for other desert pastoralists, camels are the backbone of the Rashaida's economy, culture and existence. In the 1960s, aid programmes in Sudan instigated a large-scale programme of mechanized sorghum crop production. Under the scheme, large plots of land were leased, mainly to urban entrepreneurs. The trouble was that the land was disc-ploughed and seeded, stripping it of its natural vegetation; with its robustness excised, not surprisingly, it became virtually useless for cultivation and as grazing ground. Among the pastoralists whose lands were encroached upon were the Rashaida.

As relative latecomers to Sudan, as it happened, the Rashaida had only tenuous territorial rights. On the face of it, the uncertainty led to disenfranchisement and did not augur well. Yet, paradoxically, the Rashaida adapted surprisingly well to the expansion of sorghum cultivation, even though it extended across their grazing lands. In fact, not only do sorghum by-products – *durra* stalks – tide the Rashaida's camel herds over the difficult months, but the feeding of camels has positive fertilizing effects on the soil. On top of that, camels help reduce soil erosion, since their soft-padded feet do not churn up the soil as the hooves of small ruminants would, were they able to survive there.

What is so amazing here is that camels have stepped, quite literally, into a precarious ecological niche, created artificially by mechanized agriculture; and they have been the only domestic animals able to do so. You could say, then, that the Rashaida are not only masters of the desert, but they are also custodians of environmental robustness, the anchor-roots of life and sustenance, especially in a harsh desert setting.

But to think of the Rashaida purely as environmentalists, or desert folk – more at home in the nineteenth and twentieth century than rubbing shoulders with modernity – would be to downplay their true nature. For the Rashaida also happen to be business entrepreneurs like no other. Besides camels, they have other assets and wealth in extraordinary abundance. In fact, many other pastoralists, and the sedentary population, too, view their ways with considerable envy.

More surprising still is that the Rashaida simply adore silicon, and here we are not talking just sand. For they are seriously into high-tech, too. If you are out in a remote desert village in Sudan – as I was in 1994 – and happen to want a recent Microsoft Windows computer upgrade, the Rashaida are likely to be your best (and only) bet. Unrushed they may be, but the wanderings of these desert nomads even take the Rashaida to Jeddah, one of many 'New Yorks' in the Middle East; a source of all sorts of electronic gizmos, and much more besides.

Drivers of civilizations: a political risk adviser's view

What makes civilizations succeed or fall depends on a host of factors, as we've seen. It is something about which many books have been written; it is a subject that continues to engage the minds of historians, sociologists, ecologists and even firms specializing in political risk. In his recent book *The J Curve: A New Way to Understand Why Nations Rise and Fall*, Ian Bremmer puts societies under the spotlight, highlighting the various factors that exert a major control over their robustness. He shows that one key driver is, effectively, the '*robustness* of ecosystems'.

Bremmer gives an old curve new meaning, here relating to robustness. For his central message, he draws on a mathematical relationship known for donkeys' years: the so-called 'J-curve'. The normal application of this graceful squiggle depicts the slow, initial rise of a population – of, say, flies or bacteria – up to the point when growth, quite suddenly, becomes explosive, as if out of control. Thereafter, the population simply keeps on growing at an ever greater rate. Here, of course, we're talking of ideal and rarely encountered conditions, with no constraints on population growth – shortage of food, space, competition and the like. The J-curve, in fact, holds good for any unrestrained population, of humans too. What you see on the graph is what you get: change numbers of organisms (the vertical axis) over time (the horizontal axis).

That's the background, where Bremmer is coming from, although he himself happens to be founder of Eurasia Group, a US firm advising on political risk, not a population biologist – the sort of person normally excited by J-curves. What he has done, though, in a streak of ingenious lateral thinking, is something completely different. Instead of depicting changes in population size, he showed that the J-curve can reveal insights into the ups and downs of human societies. He shows that among the key drivers, one of these is the 'openness' of society and another is, effectively, the 'robustness of ecosystems'.

What Bremmer is saying is that that very same curve, but used in a novel and very different way, can also reveal the forces that shape society, binding it together or destabilizing it, even causing it to split apart. Here, instead of time, the lower, X-axis on the J-curve represents openness of a society. This, according to Bremmer, is a measure of the extent to which 'a nation is in harmony with the crosscurrents of globalization. Simply put, this is the process by which people, ideas, information, goods, and services cross international borders at unprecedented speed' – for example, the extent of foreign direct investment entering a country, the proportion of people with access to global news, and so on. The Y-axis of the curve represents stability, in other words a state's capacity to withstand and to avoid producing shocks, a state echoing several important features of robustness. Openness of society, then, is one big driver of how robust it is likely to be; that is Bremmer's novel slant, the meaning of the X-axis. But it is by no means the only governing factor.

Intact natural resources – a major deliverable from robust natural ecosystems – plus other key assets, not surprisingly, help slide a nation further up the graph (or Y-axis), increasing social cohesion. That is another take-home message from Bremmer's book. Tsunamis and earthquakes (together with many social factors, such as economic sanctions), on the other hand, drag it back down, through their destabilizing action. So, too, Bremmer implies, can the unrestrained pursuit of '*efficiency* of industry and development', which, directly or indirectly, often leads to environmental decay; in other words, to the '*robustness* of ecosystems' going on the blink.

Like many good ideas, Bremmer's application of the J-curve – normally used to portray growth of 'lowly' organisms – is beautifully simple, incisive and intuitive. What's more, it seems to provide a fresh approach to explaining how the '*robustness* of ecosystems', combined with social and economic drivers, makes societies ebb and flow.

As the fate of the Maya in Yucatán and the Norse of Greenland remind us, non-sustainable resource use can so easily be one big nail hammered into the collective coffin. Just as tsunamis, earthquakes and other unfavourable natural events reduce robustness of a society, so too do over-consumption of resources, and the other forms of environmental corrosion that this sets in motion.

CHAPTER 2 CORPORATE COLLATERAL

Globalization and the efficiency delusion

Phantom of the global opera

Beginning in the 1950s, or even before that, according to John Gray, Emeritus Professor of European Thought at the London School of Economics, an insidious and incredibly powerful force started to shape the world like never before. This creeping black magic was globalization: essentially, the process of social, economic and also environmental change, brought about by increasing integration and interdependence of the world's nations. You could say that globalization is a powerful wave, the boundless spread of market imperatives, carrying with it the fate of many corporations – as well as the environment and the many individuals caught up in its wake.

During the second half of the twentieth century the world economy grew from $6.7 to a staggering $42 trillion, as capitalist economies flourished. At the same time many national trade barriers opened, allowing globalization to advance from a trickle to a flood.

Yet what it means, in one sense, is that we are moving from capitalist market economies run by nation states and their elected governments to a world controlled by global institutions. Among the big players, it is not hard to see, are the World Bank, the International Monetary Fund and the World Trade Organization (WTO). Big banks and transnational corporations, of course, are becoming increasingly influential, too. The WTO, for example, was granted extraordinary powers by most countries in 1995 to create and enforce regulations to facilitate the free flow of economic goods and services from one state to another.

Enthusiasts of WTO, as the umbrella organization for globalization, see this as a grand utopian mechanism for wealth creation and distribution. Widespread economic stimulation, they contend, will follow, bringing with it greater prosperity and cheaper consumer goods for everyone. And, of course, in many ways it has. The price of computers and high-fi equipment, for example, continues to fall, year after year. Not only that, human and environmental health should also rise markedly in developing countries.

In the eyes of critics, though, such sentiments are lopsided and miss out what is at stake. They believe that globalization can easily weaken, not improve, economic efficiency and robustness; that is, if you dig beneath the surface. Globalization – something advocates believe should promote '*efficiency* of industry and development' – leads instead to precisely the opposite: erosion of a nation state's economic, social and environmental policies. This could easily occur if, for example, national interests conflicted with those of the big transnationals. More effective and robust, the sceptics feel, would be regional free trade through smaller-scale networks – involving local communities and diverse, small and medium-sized enterprises. This, not global free trade, they assert, is our best bet for boosting business. Keeping things more local – not out-and-out self-sufficiency, but a step in that direction – also helps safeguard jobs, especially those of low wage-earners in developing countries.

The truth is that the vast economic empires worry little about community level affairs. Besides, globalization inevitably leads to uniformity, not only economically but also culturally and at the community level. In the case of agriculture, the world's food production systems are becoming more homogeneous and standardized. As many examples reveal, they are becoming less robust, too, much to our detriment. In the main, this has come about because globalization gains an ever greater economic stronghold on the harvests we reap.

In *False Dawn*, John Gray takes us through some of globalization's darker alleyways. He makes the case that globalization and free markets are not a natural state of affairs; quite the contrary, he argues, for they are a rare situation imposed by political interference. In the UK, for instance, free markets arose in mid-Victorian times, which happened to be a period of exceptionally favourable circumstances. Moreover, he shows that democracy and free markets, again contrary to prevailing wisdom, are competitors, not companions. What's more, as Gray reveals, global free markets have been used as a way of launching particular values (of the US most notably) across the world. Yet, in reality and pradoxically, this very act puts US national defence at grave risk. Witness, as one case in point, the events of 11 September 2001, which Gray believes is not what created the imbalances and conflicts, but rather reflects (grimmer) consequences of globalization that were previously overlooked.

Global capitalism and free laissez-faire markets are, Gray concludes, inherently unstable. They erode economic and political robustness, creating a system that is more fragile and very likely to break down in the near future; an ephemeral and flawed political experiment, if ever there was one, not a cast iron law of historical development. Ultimately, it may prove to be something short-lived: the mere twinkling of the corporate eye. Worse still, Gray asserts, globalization is something even more disruptive 'than the *belle époque* of 1870 to 1914' which 'ended in the trenches of the Great War'.

Not all, of course, agree. Many will not hear a bad word said against globalization, especially those with a vested interest in '*efficiency* of industry and development'. They firmly believe there is no viable alternative to regionalization and globalization. Besides, acolytes point out, few of us would happily cast the frills of modernity completely aside, with little more than a 'thanks, but no thanks'; especially those enjoying overseas travel and other affordable (at least to some) luxuries and products that globalization brings. Undeniably, goods from beyond the borders can and do bring enormous rewards and satisfaction.

But unless massive reforms can somehow restore global robustness, the real pessimists contend, the world economy stands to severely fragment, in a replay of the social and political upheavals of the 1930s – and in a spectacle far more tragic and depressing than Shakespeare's *King Lear*.

Not only that, ecologists are quick to retort, but opening up the sluice gates to trade has also allowed the influx of unwanted biological visitors. This, it turns out, is another of many forces disrupting the normal flow of nature's free goods and services; and an extremely costly one, too. Globalization does not, of course, halt the movement altogether. Rather, it swerves it in another direction, often not to our liking. Put another way, globalization makes the '*robustness* of ecosystems' increasingly precarious. On any count the downstream effects, particularly disaster management and its costs, are enormous. This can make economies far less sure-footed than political leaders care to admit. That's why so much is at stake.

One problem is that globalization protects us from the signals and early symptoms that normally remind us when humanity is out of kilter with its surroundings; for example, the outstripping of local food supplies, from heavy consumption. People of developing countries feel these built-in warning systems acutely. Through tight feedback loops, as Brian Walker and David Salt explain in *Resilience Thinking*, they instil social-environmental systems with robustness. For people of the developed world, though, things are different. With heavy reliance on food imports and other products of globalization, feedback loops loosen, signals weaken, and alarm bells may ring only when it is too late.

Aliens unwelcome

Like colonialism a century earlier, globalization has changed the face of the world, ecologically and economically, for ever. It is not difficult to see why. The wave of European colonialism in the nineteenth and early twentieth centuries helped set the seeds for globalization, and it happened to be a period of plant exploration; many of the newly acquired species were taken back home.

But, as Jeffrey McNeely, chief conservation scientist at IUCN – the International Union for Conservation of Nature – remarked in the journal *Euphytica* in 2006: 'The invasive characteristics of the newly introduced species often came as a complete surprise, because those responsible for the introduction were unaware of the possible negative ecological ramifications of the species involved.' Compared with the time when Europeans first arrived there, for example, New Zealand today has twice as many plants; so it is not just a question of the imports into the UK, but rather the role of the empire in homogenizing the world's flora – and, on top of that, often making the surroundings less robust, too; and we're not just talking environment, either.

Through globalization and colonialism, the world has effectively shrunk, hastening the spread of biological invasions from a trickle to a flood. For hitch-hiker species can now spread at the same speed as the trucks, ships, containers and aircraft which give them a free ride. To be even-handed, the tales begin on an upbeat note; how non-native species have nourished society, for example through many important food crops.

But we should not let this bamboozle us into overlooking the darker side of assisted biological migrations, of the sort mentioned above. What we are referring to here is 'invasive alien species'. This is ecologists' jargon for species that establish themselves in a new area, and then spread by out-competing resident flora and fauna. As testament to the hazards of immigrants, the website of the Convention on Biological Diversity pronounces: 'Alien species that become invasive are considered to be a main direct driver of biodiversity loss across the globe. In addition, alien species have been estimated to have cost our economies hundreds of billions of dollars.' Here, incontestably, invasives have cut right into the 'robustness of ecosystems'. On top of that, they have militated against the 'efficiency of industry and development' by dealing it a very powerful blow.

Even before the 1800s, and probably long before then, travellers sometimes collected plants from far-off lands. Just like coffee, sugar, tea, rubber and others that (for better or worse) helped build the British Empire, many imported species were money-spinners and hot property, too. In the early years at Kew Gardens, as Jane Owen and Diarmuid Gavin explain in *Gardens Through Time*, visitors actually had to be policed 'one-on-one' by gardeners, to make sure they didn't steal plants. One tale recalls the plight of a nursery manager who, after evading his minders, was accused and tried for taking introductions of new plants (though he was acquitted on a technicality); this 'green gold', the man knew, was something for which fashionable gardeners and botanists would pay a fortune.

Many more species, of course, enter new geographical regions and suit us because they provide food or game, while we bring in others to help control pests in their new surroundings. Besides, fish naturally colonize new seas and, without a helping hand, plants can gain a stronghold in new lands; species come and go simply as part of the normal course of events.

Yet it would be wide of the mark to suppose – as pathogenic bacteria disturbingly remind us – that 'biodiversity' is universally welcome, in all its guises. It is the same whether we are talking of the arrival of unwanted species through natural influx, human-assisted migration or an explosion in the population of species already present. Undeniably, nature's bounty of untold riches brings enormous benefits. On the other hand, for a good many species deliberately introduced – and for others slipping, inadvertently, through the net at border controls – any benefits are often eclipsed by the increased fragility of the environment, which brings huge collateral costs.

Consider, first, wildlife that is brought in intentionally. The kudzu plant, for example, was imported from Japan and planted in south-eastern states of the USA in the last century. It seemed the miracle cure for soil erosion, and in many ways it was. The trouble, though, is that the vine is so prolific and hardy that it engulfs almost anything in its path: hills, trees, roadsides, even houses. With global warming in full swing – higher temperatures, for example, inducing growth spurts and accelerating propagation – some believe it might even reach the Great Lakes of North America by 2040. Goats and herbicides, as agents of biological and chemical control, might seem an easy solution to slow the march of this green alien. Both are far from ideal remedies, though, because of the damage they themselves can wreak.

Curiously, though, kudzu is important for more reasons than

controlling soil erosion. It turns out that its increasing stranglehold everywhere it takes root may, on balance, prove to be no bad thing. Kudzu starch, for example, is much sought after for beverages, gourmet confections and herbal remedies; it can even cut down alcohol consumption. In fact, so sought after is kudzu starch in Japan – where demand exceeds supply – that a Japanese firm has built a processing plant in Alabama and will ship the extracted starch back to Japan. The kudzu vine has other direct benefits, too. Nancy Basket, originally from Washington State, is one entrepreneur who is actually using the kudzu vine, to make tree-free notecards, and baskets. An even more ironic twist to the kudzu vine tale is that, by engulfing trees, the plant may help, 'sacrificially', to save trees from loggers: cynics might contend that it is the revenge of nature against commercial enterprise over-dependent on technology.

In other cases, though – especially when it comes to accidentally introduced species – it is quite another matter; the effects can be far more detrimental and clear-cut. As an arrival into Florida from Latin America in 1884, the water hyacinth is a plant that is prolific like no other. This plant can double its population in just a fortnight, so it is hardly surprising that it has taken over many waterways in Florida and other south-eastern states of the USA. What has happened is that water hyacinths have displaced many local plants, clogging ponds and aquatic thoroughfares. Problems are not just confined to the USA, either: economic devastation caused by the plant in seven African countries amounts to a cost of 20 to 50 million US dollars annually. Manatees, or 'sea cows' – a slow-tech solution, if ever there was one – seem better at controlling the plant than mechanical or chemical approaches; the problem, though, is that there are simply not enough manatees around to do the job. Like its close relative, the dugong in the Indo-Pacific, this massive herbivore faces a dodgy future in the global arena. For this reason conservationists have classified these gentle giants as 'vulnerable'.

Then there are the non-native animal invaders. One of the most infamous of these must be the zebra mussel – a species originally from the Caspian and Black Sea region. Discharged with water from a transatlantic ship near Detroit, between Lake Erie and Lake Huron, biologists believe, this mollusc made its debut appearance in the USA in 1988. It is a true by-product of the increasing trade that accompanies globalization. With no known enemies, the zebra mussel competes for food with native Great Lakes species. Worse still, it clogs intake systems for power plants and water supplies; it fouls beaches and, in great masses, populations encrust boat piers and ships' hulls. The cumulative costs of damage and attempts to deal with zebra mussels between 1989 and 2000 were at least 750 million dollars, possibly even 1 billion. What's more, these costs don't include the damage caused by the quagga mussel, a bigger and potentially more destructive species that arrived in the Great Lakes in about 1991.

Like it or not, introduced alien species (including many disease organisms) are one down-side of globalization, often an extremely disagreeable one, too. Increases in international trade unavoidably pave the way for free-riders – many of them opportunists, that prove to be robust, even far from their native land; like the big transnationals themselves, introduced species can quickly take over and monopolize a region. Over the years as many as 50,000 species may have been introduced from around the world to the USA alone. Recently, David Pimentel, at Cornell University's Department of Entomology, Systematics and Ecology, estimated that invasive species may cost the USA a staggering 137 *billion* dollars per year.

The scale and cost of trying to outsmart nature's free-riders defy belief, as the above figures testify. In this respect, trying to control the influx of invasive species is no different from conservation and environmental maintenance more generally. As an economist working in the Maldives once remarked, 'Conservation does not come free, a fact that environmental scientists often seem to overlook.'

Yet neglecting conservation, especially preventive measures, can be even costlier, especially given the devastating effects of introduced alien species. After all, annual bills exceeding 100 billion to combat them – largely through crisis management and other remedial actions – hurt economies, even that of a country like the USA. Worse still, invasive aliens are but one of many unwanted by-products arising from unfettered globalization, in the quest for greater '*efficiency* of industry and development'.

Surprisingly, common-sense measures can often be remarkably effective, against at least some introduced species, even in the midst of global forces. Just as judicious border control can help a country keep out foot-and-mouth disease, so too can simple vigilance and prudent action go some way towards controlling unwanted species – when it comes to total aliens, or naturally occurring organisms we would rather do without. Either way, simple, minimal-tech measures can help instil at least some security and robustness into the environment to guard against harmful incursions, and thereby benefit society.

Consider, as one example, a tale reported by Thailand's National Biological Control Research Centre in 2004. The outcome was successful, yet what happened in the combat amounted to little more than attentive monitoring and swift follow-up action:

> A classical case on the timely management of insects was witnessed in Thailand in May 2003 in Bangkok when over 500 nymphs and adults of the Madagascar hissing cockroach were confiscated from a pet shop, the shopkeeper fined, and the cockroaches incinerated by virtue of the announcement of the Ministry of Public Health. The cockroaches were smuggled into the country, reared and sold as 'pet' animals. It was believed to be an insect vector and an intermediate host of several medical and public health pathogenic agents.

In itself, of course, this isolated and rather obscure example carries little clout. It would be pure fantasy to suppose that small-scale acts of vigilance are enough to tackle, nationally let alone globally, the unnatural spread of species. When it comes to hitch-hiking species attached to the hulls of ships and smaller boats, or in ballast water (to keep empty oil tankers and cargo ships stable), the world has a very serious job on its hands; the zebra mussel's arrival in the Great Lakes is one reminder of this. Here a whole raft of measures is needed, and even then slowing the flow might still be like stemming a strong tide – a challenge for modernity indeed.

Yet in cases like the Thai example mentioned, onward transmission of pathogens, in the absence of cockroach control, could have very nasty health consequences. So thinking and acting small can have surprisingly big effects. Who knows if, in the case chronicled above, outbreaks of cockroaches and the pathogen would have directly threatened environmental robustness; but human health could certainly have been put on the line.

Marching to the beat of the corporate drum

Trading robustness for rapid returns is a risky business in more ways than one, whether we're talking impact from globalization or from local enterprises. It is a principle the Bedouin, for instance, have been quick to grasp, in their dealings with both the natural and the built environment. Wearing robes that have changed little over the centuries, they might look far behind the times. Yet 'going with the flow' – instead of always trying to fight nature, and subdue it – is actually forward-thinking.

Choosing to be blind about what might happen tomorrow, to the environment and then to us, modernity has trodden a very different pathway. Sceptics might even call such short-sighted exploits, invariably assisted by high-technology, fast-backwards. However dressed up, modernity's mission statement usually boils down to preoccupation with the here-and-now, corner-cutting – with little thought for who else and what else might bear the brunt.

It's the same whether we're talking about fallout on the environment, sometimes quite literally, or collateral on anything else not within our immediate vision. That's the danger when drivers of 'efficiency of industry and development', with insufficient checks and balances, are at the wheel.

In some ways, this mentality is hardly surprising. With such ruthless cut-and-thrust needed nowadays just to balance company books, streamlining for business efficiency is the name of the game. Going for big profits, of course, puts the squeeze on even more. Ditching unproductive baggage, after all, is little more than common sense and good economic sense, at least on the face of it: no company boss in his or her right mind wants 'superfluous slack'.

Besides, it is not as if capitalism and modernity are trying, deliberately – as if through some conspiracy – to force decay of the environment; it is just one of many unfortunate spin-offs. Consider, for example, the marinas, malls and condominiums in and around New Orleans. They were hardly built, in the pre-Katrina decades, in a wilful attempt to sabotage the environment, even less so city life or the tourist industry. It was simply that wetlands and a string of developments together made for an overcrowded marriage, at least in the eyes of the town planners and engineers; something had to play second fiddle and go; and it was not going to be economic development. It was the 'robustness of ecosystems' instead.

In such a bloodthirsty and competitive world, retaining anything inessential, or doing anything remotely avoidable (like worrying too much about the environment), is simply wishful thinking. Many company bosses would see such action as tantamount to commercial suicide. To see the cutting-edge corporate mindset in action, consider the way one really big global giant goes about earning its daily crust; things are little different, though, when it comes to firms just trying to survive – let alone hoping to make it big time. Focusing on the job in hand, what really counts, is the name of the game. Performance and profits, and allegiance to shareholders rather than to the 'robustness of ecosystems', are what really count.

With a recent annual turnover of 35 billion dollars, Dell Computers is a model company, and one of the world's largest personal computer manufacturers. Part of its financial whiz lies in its build-to-order ethos: customers get exactly the machine and add-ons they want. Dell also believes that the 'most efficient path to the customer' is a direct one, with no intermediaries. To maximize profits, Dell – like most other well-run businesses – adopts a strategy of minimizing operational redundancy; put another way, it keeps slack in the system down to the bare minimum. At one level, Dell nearly gets a free byte: customers pay Dell before parts are ordered from suppliers, but Dell itself has a month to settle up with the supplier.

In the corporate world, as Dell demonstrates, adopting a just-in-time ethos is all about lean supply chains. An inescapable fact is that keeping excessive stock on the shelves is an inefficient and dangerous strategy, one which, for any company, can be the kiss of death. Yet squeezing out everything that seems expendable – in other words, minimizing redundancy – can also be risky business; to the business itself, of course, aside from any knock-on effects 'downstream'. By keeping stock to a minimum (about four days' worth at Dell), problems with a vital – and often distant – producer or supplier can restrict or even hold up production; so too can failure of a vital component, or something critical within the company's own intricate network. With virtually all spare capacity squeezed out, when some unexpected hitch occurs a company's efficiency, and the boss's job, can be on the line.

Consider Dell's own performance. Its second quarter profits tumbled from fractionally over 1 billion dollars in 2006 to 502 million dollars for the same period the previous year. The company, not surprisingly, took steps to boost business by improving prices and investing in technical support. Part of the problem, paradoxically, lay in the computers' power pack. Because of a potential fire risk, 4 million batteries had to be recalled. Whatever else had caused profits to slip, adverse publicity – from an unforeseen hardware glitch – undoubtedly made matters worse.

When it comes to fighting for your corporate life, or even having to/choosing to operate with supply chains only half as lean as Dell's, it is hardly surprising that the boss's antennae cannot be tuned into anything as remote as 'worthless swamps'; or into any other ecosystems for that matter. That is not say that firms, or development corporations, are neccessarily irresponsible or negligent, when it comes to the environment. BP and several other companies, as mentioned, have a firm commitment to environmental sustainability. In fact, Dell itself is committing to greener hardware. It has announced that it will remove key toxic chemicals from its PCs, laptops and other products, to make them more environmentally friendly and to tackle the mounting crisis of 'toxic e-waste'.

By and large, though, bowing purely to the dictates of '*efficiency* of industry and development' (and company shareholders) easily leads to the loss of robustness. This damage may extend to the environment, to business or both; that is the bitter truth and irony. Sometimes, admittedly, it is a case of trickle-down effects, which can be difficult to predict. Often, though, that is not the case. It hardly takes rocket science, for example, to figure out that once developers landfill and obliterate a shallow shrimp-breeding area to make way for something like a port, or a housing complex, it will no longer remain a productive natural system. It is hardly surprising that more than robustness drains away from the area. Once devoid of resident flora and fauna and covered in concrete, the area is unlikely ever again to revert to its former 'free-for-all' state; at least not without deliberate ecological restoration.

Worse still, perhaps, through heavy-handed coastal tinkering in one place, other buildings and structures downstream also stand to collapse, or become seriously undermined by the new patterns of erosion. In fact, as already mentioned, that is precisely what has happened in parts of the Red Sea and the Arabian/Persian Gulf; and we're not just talking isolated examples, here or elsewhere, either.

So we don't only mean here the perils of losing ecosystem robustness, through short-sighted development, and what this means to fishermen and others directly or indirectly reliant on it. That, of course, is bad enough. But business itself can also suffer, because the built environment stands to weaken, too. An environment in which modern, high-tech infrastructures start to crumble is hardly one that is conducive to business or investor confidence, after all.

Scale these sorts of things up to what modernity is doing in, and to, the wider world, and it is not hard to imagine what else might be lurking round the corner, awaiting our society. All of a sudden, being too overwound can lead to catastrophic failure – in the things we do and create as well as in nature. Gradually, even a few politicians are waking up to the fact. It is hardly surprising, either, given all that is happening right now, before our very eyes. Former US presidential candidate Al Gore is one of these. Deep down, perhaps many more are secretly thinking, but still daren't come out and admit it: the '*efficiency* of industry and development' aspiration, unchecked, is proving to be a delusion. It is a state of affairs the Luddites certainly would have made no bones about.

Origins of efficiency and the efficiency trap

One might suppose that corporate collateral damage, a by-product of today's rat race, is something that began only in the last century. It was certainly in full swing then. But to understand its true origins we must fast-backwards to the 1800s. This was a period in English history when the Luddites destroyed their weaving looms and tried to call the shots at their workplace. They were worried that new textile machinery, brought in to help cut costs for greater efficiency, would make them superfluous to requirements.

We are referring here to the beginnings of a movement and of modernity: the Industrial Revolution, a powerful forward march heavily reliant on machinery. It was something the Luddites were violently opposed to, which was why they destroyed the looms.

Corner-cutting to boost efficiency began ruthlessly in nineteenth-century industrial Europe and America, when society became seduced by profit through cheaper workforce, competition and automation. This was the time when the '*efficiency* of industry and development' movement really launched itself. Once efficiency gained a stronghold, it became cast in stone and iron – silicon chips not being around then. Frederick Winslow Taylor, an American pioneer of 'scientific management', and the first acclaimed efficiency expert, was particularly influential. He measured factory and office tasks with stopwatch precision and argued that productivity could be boosted if workers performed them more efficiently. Taylor's thinking and actions began the process that drove us into the efficiency trap we are in today. Directly or indirectly, he encouraged behaviour that accelerated the breakdown in ecosystem (and business) robustness in a way never seen before.

Best known for his high-speed steel, Taylor fused the efficiency of the lathes and the men who operated them into 'the one best way'. For those witnessing the red-hot tools slicing tubes of steel at the Paris Exposition of 1900, it was the instant when, as Robert Kanigel put it, 'they watched the world speed up before their eyes'. He achieved such unprecedented efficiency by stripping down every job into its components, breaking down the layout of our kitchens and even the way our libraries are organized into their constituent parts, then pruning, tuning and timing them. This reduced by half or more the labour needed by ordinary folk to achieve a particular goal. Relentless melding of humans and machines into a streamlined production system set the pace for the industrialists of the twentieth century. It was a system where no materials, energy, effort or time were put in if it could possibly be avoided.

Some even argue that Taylor ranks with Darwin and Freud as a maker of the modern world; directly or indirectly, all certainly had a huge impact on the environment, though of course in radically different ways. Like a pervasive afterglow from the Industrial Revolution's 'big clang', 'Taylorism' set worldwide standards for efficiency that remain with us today – besides, many Victorians considered it a virtue to 'waste not, want not'.

The trouble with Taylorism, or efficiency at all costs, though, is that the various checks, balances and shock-absorbers that keep the output flowing come second to such ruthlessness. Undeniably, the industrial magnets of the USA, Europe and others Taylor influenced had a handle on efficiency. But it was only superficial efficiency, in that it was often at the expense of welfare, the environment and everything else considered secondary to maximizing profits.

Efficiency is a slippery concept. Just as Lewis Caroll's character Alice discovered when peering through the looking-glass: 'The more you look, the less it is there.' Funnily enough, inefficiency can stand out more than efficiency itself. One thing for sure, though, is that with a mindset focused exclusively on '*efficiency* of industry and development', with scant regard for the '*robustness* of ecosystems', the meaning of efficiency is too narrowly focused.

'Efficiency', often little more than cost reduction for the boss, has become the holy grail of performance measures in the modern world: the rallying cry of a quasi-moral crusade. But there's a catch: efficiency, just as we saw, is often ambiguous. The questions 'Efficiency for whom?', 'Efficiency at what cost?' and 'Efficiency over what time?' are seldom asked. As a source of light, a normal bulb, for example, is surprisingly inefficient. Yet as a heater it is very efficient – especially in a sealed box.

Efficiency is the ratio of output to input, a concept engineers love. Actually, though, the concept has far humbler origins than engineering, or than Frederick Taylor for that matter. Going further back in time than the nineteenth century, it is clear that even the Church, paradoxically, was quite partial to efficiency, at least when it came to getting things done in a reasonably timely manner.

Fast-backwards fourteen centuries and we witness Benedictine monks living, not surprisingly, less frenetic lives than masters and fathers of business efficiency. Nevertheless, the monks rose early, watched the stars, turned hourglasses and used water-clocks. As foreign affairs journalist and author Carl Honoré tells us, 'Using primitive clocks, they rang bells at regular intervals throughout the day and night, to hurry each other from one task to the next, from prayer to study to farming to rest, and back to prayer again.' Suggesting that monks 'hurry' might be over-stretching things; but you could call their ways forward planning, or simple time management.

Curiously, though, long before Benedictine monks practised time management, philosophers had begun unpicking the threads of efficiency. To Aristotle and others, including Sir Francis Bacon, the 'Father of Modern Science', efficiency was merely any cause that produces an effect.

But thinking moved on, and efficiency began to capture aspects of the performance in a machine or other system.

In power stations, for example, energy efficiency is a measurement of energy exported compared to energy released by the fuel. Just as an aside, inefficient power plants achieve only around 35 per cent efficiency; most of the energy disappears, quite literally, as puffs of wasted heat. The efficiency of better plants can climb to around 60 per cent. Ecologists also like to measure efficiency. Net productivity – the amount of organic material produced in a given area per unit of time, after allowing for energy going in, like respiration – is one way of measuring efficiency for ecosystems.

But efficiency also carries a second, more subjective meaning, resonating with desirability: the performance of a system against how well it *should* be performing. You could say, in the words of Herbert Simon, American polymath and researcher in cognitive psychology and computer science: 'In its broadest sense, to be efficient simply means to take the shortest path, the cheapest means, toward the attainment of the desired goals.'

Desirability and low cost were precisely what drove efficiency of machines, mining and the textile industry throughout the Industrial Revolution; in the case of textile machinery their introduction, of course, is what led the Luddites to revolt. Beginning in England in the mid-1700s, the Industrial Revolution spread a century later to the USA – the home of Frederick Taylor. Much of our current preoccupation with cheapness at all costs, profits at all costs and 'efficiency at all costs' has its roots in the Industrial Revolution, and particularly in Taylorism. Even before Darwin formulated the idea of 'survival of the fittest', society had been seduced by profit through cheaper workforce, competition and automation.

Efficiency, however measured, embodies the quest for getting more from less, or even something for nothing; that is, of course, when your thinking is so focused it only stretches to '*efficiency* of industry and development' and conveniently chooses to brush aside the '*robustness* of ecosystems', or other inconveniences that have to be sacrificed en route.

73

The 80/20 principle: forget what does not count

Highly selective (or blinkered) thinking, and doing only what 'counts', is one trademark of modernity, especially in the corporate world. It turns out that around 80 per cent of results flow from only 20 per cent of the causes or effort: the so-called 80/20 principle. As business expert Richard Koch points out, 20 per cent of products account for 80 per cent of sales, as do 20 per cent of customers. The relative proportions are not always the same, but the imbalance between cause and effect seems to hold true.

Discovered long ago by the Italian economist Vilfredo Pareto (1848–1923), this predictable imbalance is becoming a defining and indelible inscription of highly effective individuals and organizations. Applying the 80/20 principle too rigorously, though, can be a risky business. What the principle rests on is perfect knowledge of that disproportionately valuable 20 per cent; being able to identify what it is and where it lies. And, equally, ensuring that in the process of homing in on the critical 20 per cent something else, perhaps more valuable, does not go by the wayside. And that is all the more likely if this happens to be not a product at all, but something intangible like the '*robustness* of ecosystems'.

Yet most adherents of the 80/20 principle, especially in the corporate world, care little for the intangible. In their eyes, unremitting targeting of the tangible is all that counts, especially when the financial stakes are high. As with Taylorism, though, if you take a broader sweep of the horizon it becomes clear that the efficiency produced is only superficial. That is the trouble when modernity follows, too unswervingly, the 80/20 principle. In the process, it may trade (often unwittingly) welfare, the environment and everything else standing in efficiency's way, including, paradoxically, human health and robustness.

Consider, as a prime case in point, the fate of Kamei Shuji, a grand master of Japanese efficiency. As a high-flying broker during the stock-market boom of the 1980s, his performance was unrivalled. Shuji's ninety-hour weeks, Carl Honoré explains in *In Praise of Slow*, more than paid dividends. To his boss he was the gold standard to which all other staff in the company should aspire. Like Taylor before him, but quite unlike the Benedictine monks, Kamei Shuji strove for efficiency at all costs. So much so that when Japan's economy bubble burst in 1989 he worked even harder to make up the losses. The following year, at the age of twenty-six, Shuji died suddenly of a heart attack. The Japanese Labour Ministry statistics reported thirty cases of victims dying of overwork, or *karoshi* in 1989. By 1990, however, a council of attorneys estimated that over 10,000 people were dying from *karoshi* each year. And the situation extends far beyond Japan.

Kamei Shuji's efficiency was short-lived. Burn-out took him and his wealth to an early grave. Directly or indirectly, he probably knew about and followed the 80/20 principle: he was certainly a highly focused individual. Of course, Kamei's fate, and *karoshi* more generally, is an extreme circumstance, affecting a relatively small proportion of the human population, even of the business population. Nevertheless, it epitomizes the ends to which some individuals – and powerful organizations, to which they swear allegiance – are prepared to go in ruthless pursuit of a goal. As many examples demonstrate, one goal is invariably a strong appetite for greater '*efficiency* of industry and development'. Besides self-interest, much of it seems to hang on satisfying a product-hungry society, with little worry about wider repercussions.

From these and many other examples, one would be right in supposing that there is a disagreeable, rather austere side to efficiency, in virtually every sphere of life. From the stock market to publishing to 'e.commerce', efficiency is one-sided: only the winner or winners count. Whether under the spell of Taylorism, or the 80/20 principle (or both), modernity is a lopsided, here-and-now culture; never mind any inconvenient collateral damage happening tomorrow. With this sort of behaviour, it is hardly surprising that the '*robustness* of ecosystems' gets eclipsed so often by the '*efficiency* of industry and development' alternative.

Too big for the national boots

So-called economic prowess and efficiency can be a short-term delusion for other reasons, too. Consider, for example, gross domestic product, a metric brandished and flaunted by some 'like there is no tomorrow'. In fact, that is why, quite literally, they are so wide of the mark. Environmental and other problems that accompany economic performance are simply not captured in these sorts of yardsticks: that is their down-side. As the world's biggest superpower, the USA undeniably enjoys exceptional standards of living, with outstanding institutions and an open society; unbridled capitalism, many believe, has brought unrivalled economic performance. Since 1950, for example, its economy has soared to unprecedented heights on the wings of efficiency – and with little sign of altitude sickness, at least if you are taken in by the figures for GDP. Between then and the late 1990s GDP grew from 10,000 billion dollars to nearly 30,000 billion dollars.

Yet recent balance-of-payments deficits of 430 billion dollars, stock-market losses of around 1,000 trillion dollars, and rising inequity point to something rather different: an economy (and a society) showing signs of fragility. For sure, the USA has gargantuan earning power and, claim optimists, the capacity to sustain colossal deficits because of the sheer size of its economy. But some analysts, such as Will Hutton, are less certain. Decline in investor confidence, for example, might just burst the fiscal bubble, as gloomy events in 2008 began to reveal.

Over-zealous reading of the economic pulse, perhaps not surprisingly, is partly to blame for the optimism about US power and international standing. From 1950, its GDP grew almost 300 per cent in five decades. For political expediency, of course, governments and business leaders are quick to seize on figures revealing even a hint of economic growth and efficiency. Yet GDP (and GNP) were never intended as indices of economic health, or of human well-being. As many economists themselves admit, these sorts of macro-economic, national wealth yardsticks are shallow on several counts.

For one thing, there is no dip in national GDP following overuse or misuse of its natural resources – which, for the many reasons described, can actually weaken a nation state. Worse still, money spent on activities such as oil spill and air pollution clean-up, ironically, counts as a positive gain; these expenditures actually create an increase in GDP. We might argue that this is reasonable, since clean-up is preferable to pollution; but critics contend that many problems are preventable, and that dealing with them should therefore be reflected negatively in a nation's economic balance sheets.

On top of that, the innumerable and invaluable non-monetary transactions or services, such as coastal defence and protection, performed by natural systems, are not reflected in performance records, GDP and other national accounts; this is partly because their economic value is so difficult to pin down precisely. What sand dunes, salt marshes, reefs and other natural systems actually contribute to development, though, is far from trivial – even if conventional economic indicators fail to recognize and capture it. Strangely enough, it is a spectacle resonating with services to society in the form of voluntary and other unpaid work. Only when they're not there do we appreciate just how precious they can be.

Economic reality checks

As Will Hutton points out, there are all sorts of reasons for 'the state we're in' – expounded in his book, thus titled, and in a later one, *The World We're In*. A fundamental problem, though, is that economists cannot even agree on what makes financial systems tick. Both conventional economists and ecological economists concede that national and global wealth depends, ultimately, on natural resources. Thereafter, the two schools think differently.

People have infinite potential and capacity for finding new solutions, conventional economists argue, through new ideas and technologies, as the need arises. Whether optimists, or realists, these economists see the achievement of ever greater economic performance through the use of less energy and resources, and by finding substitutes for these. And all this will happen, presumably, in the blind hope that the '*robustness* of ecosystems' does not topple during modernity's quest for '*efficiency* of industry and development' in more thoughtful ways.

Consider, as a manifesto for this ethos, the long-term forecast of the late Julian Simon, former Professor of Economics at the University of Maryland. What he said encapsulates what many traditional economists believe the future holds for human society: 'This is my long-term forecast in brief: The material conditions of life will continue to get better for most countries, most of the time, indefinitely. Within a century or two, all nations and most of humanity will be at or above today's Western living standards. I also speculate, however, that many people will continue to think and say that the conditions of life are getting worse.'

In contrast, ecological economists hold that there are no substitutes for many natural resources. These include air and water and, in particular, living resources such as soil, fishery stocks and biodiversity. They point out that many current economic and development activities seriously downgrade and undermine the robustness of these renewable resources. But instead of tapping into them for just the interest – a notion of prudence, and perhaps also efficiency, which should resonate with all economists – an undeniable fact is that human activities increasingly erode the capital. Sooner or later, renewable resources transform, unsurprisingly, into something that fails to replenish itself. Consider, as an illustration, what has happened to North Sea cod and, more worrying still, to most of the world's major commercial fish stocks, too.

Besides fish and other free goods, though, comes the multiple flow of free services provided by ecosystems, i.e. natural capital; even in the modern world this, after all, is what underpins the whole of society. Robert Costanza and colleagues have estimated that these are worth, globally, a staggering $17–54 trillion annually. The best estimate is $36 trillion, which, interestingly, closely approximates the world's total annual 'economic' output of around $40 trillion.

Costanza's approach, as might be expected, precipitated much debate, and still does. Some argue that these sorts of figures cannot possibly accommodate the wide-ranging cultural thinking about what resources are actually worth. Quite possibly so, though it has to be said that the figures were not drawn, arbitrarily, from Costanza's hat, or from any other individual's; they arose from an extensive trawl of the global technical literature. Others, though, argue that trying to put any figure at all on natural systems is too simplistic and unrealistic, and necessarily undervalues what essentially is invaluable.

The real point here is that nature has to be worth far more than merely the value of timber, fish and other products sold in the local market, or the supermarket. And if, in addition to goods, modernity does bother about the '*robustness* of ecosystems', or other useful services, it seems to be over a remarkably short time period. Advocates of '*efficiency* of industry and development' do not seem worried about the long-term value of our economy, either. We consider an economy or country robust because of how much money it makes, and how many services/items it produces, rather than how productive it may be in the long term. This view of robustness is incomplete, for it does not allow for longevity – robustness *over time*, which, of course, is precisely what the concept is supposed to capture.

Corporate compensation to offset collateral

When it comes to corporate interests, the USA is ahead of the game. Yet, curiously, this is in more ways than one. As a society, the USA loves litigation like no other, something newspaper reports, TV, and Americans themselves make no bones about. If someone, or something, is harmed then someone should be made to pay the consequences. What's more, it is a principle that now extends, perhaps unexpectedly, to the environment; and the USA is by no means alone in taking this stance.

Perhaps it hails a new dawn, the beginnings of modernity awakening from its complacent slumber: realization that environmental systems really do matter; they provide our surroundings with an indispensable 'buffer' against buckling from sea level rise, climate change and many other disturbances imposed by our society or nature itself. It is perhaps a faint signal that politicians are beginning to see that a healthy and robust environment helps their countries fulfil not just their conservation commitments, but their economic and development aspirations too. You could say that having to provide compensation, as a principle and in practice, encourages more sustainable development – that environmental damage created should not be 'free'.

It is a message beginning to resonate far and wide (though not nearly as fast as many would wish). Qatar, for example, is one of several Gulf States recognizing that without environmental compensation its and the region's natural systems could soon face almost total collapse. Given that more than 50 per cent of the coast is now developed – a euphemism for 'artificial' (concrete instead of natural) – trying to re-instil ecosystem robustness is a refreshing change. The Gulf might be a young sea, but with these and many other incursions, including plans to dam its entrance (which may not be so fanciful as one might wish), it could soon be heading for terminal decline.

For the most part, as many examples demonstrate, the erasure of nature is a process that is not easy to reverse. We are not just talking the Gulf here, either. Yet, for decades, in the interests of unfettered '*efficiency* of industry and development', forcing modernity to reduce its tempo has been an uphill struggle. Therein lies one colossal burden modernity continues to bear, as, too, will the next generation.

Naturally, if construction teams can avoid sacrificing the environment in the first place, in the process of development, so much the better. But for damage that cannot be avoided, the Qatar government, for one, typically insists on environmental projects costing 3 to 5 per cent of the development project budget, as a form of financial compensation. The system in Qatar, a newly emerging modern state, is still in its infancy. That is hardly surprising. For example, it is not yet entirely clear if Qatar's chosen levy of 3 to 5 per cent is too much, too little or reasonable. From experiences in other countries it turns out, in fact, that the link between levels of financial compensation (based on any flat or percentage rates) and impact is relatively weak, as are incentives for the developer to reduce impact.

Nevertheless, even the sceptics, those of us who have witnessed at first-hand the colossal collateral damage inflicted on the Gulf's environment as its States 'modernize', must admit that environmental compensation as a cost for 'fast-forward' is at least a step in the right direction. We're not talking here, naturally, of totally suppressing economic growth – undoubtedly the wish of hard-core environmentalists – but of at least subduing modernity's passion and zest for '*efficiency* of industry and development'.

What's more, incentives to reduce environmental impacts are becoming better and better, through a system that tries to scale and tune compensation to the level of disturbance created. Approaches are becoming increasingly sophisticated, going far beyond developers simply having to cough up financial compensation, to help offset environmental injury. Following practices in the West, for example, Qatar is considering proposals for providing the developer with the option for compensation through preservation or re-creation of the same ecosystem that is damaged, instead of the compensation percentage (dollars) approach. Here, though, we are talking of something more than simply a hectare gained for a hectare lost. The jargon used for how much ecosystem must be *restored*, relative to the amount likely to be *injured* following the construction and operation of a development, is 'environmental mitigation ratios', or 'offsets'.

This requires the developer, or independent party, to estimate first the types of ecosystems affected and their area. Then, for each hectare (or other spatial unit) of ecosystem affected, the developer would be required to protect or enhance, for example, two or three hectares of similar ecosystem – or some other mitigation or compensation ratio. As this example demonstrates, more compensatory hectares are required than affected hectares: this acts as a buffer, providing added robustness in the event that the environmental protection or enhancement projects is less successful than expected.

Environmental restoration projects can involve the preservation or re-creation of the same ecosystem, preferably nearby; ideally, also, in advance of development, to compensate for forthcoming incursions, likely to follow, for example, from the construction of ports, towns or sports complexes. Environmental compensation can be either for complete loss of ecosystems and species, or for partial loss of them.

Of course, like the financial compensation system, environmental compensation through mitigation ratios/offsets is not ideal, either. It assumes, implicitly, equivalence between the ecosystems injured in one area and the ecosystems restored somewhere else. In reality, of course, some areas contain outstanding examples of an ecosystem: they may, in fact, be highly distinctive and unique, not replaceable or simply transferable elsewhere as a means of compensation. Equally fundamental, of course, is that enough suitable environmental restoration projects have been designed and are actually available.

By and large, though, environmental compensation and restoration helps reverse the steady decay of ecosystem robustness – or, more seriously, of ecosystems themselves – as modernity marches on unflinching.

In the USA the European Union, the Arabian Gulf and increasingly elsewhere, too, more finely tuned compensation techniques are being brought to bear; for example, to provide stronger links between compensation and the impact a development leaves behind. This takes into account more factors than used in mitigation offsets, in particular: the type, severity, duration and extent or area of environmental impact. These and other factors are what help determine, more precisely, how big the environmental project (as compensation) should be.

Let's just suppose, for sake of argument, that sedimentation from dredging a port (or some other coastal construction project) is expected to cut biological productivity by 50 per cent, in twenty hectares of ecosystems on the seabed over the three-year construction period. In approximate terms, the method ('habitat equivalency analysis') would identify the need for compensation in the form of thirty hectare-years of ecosystem loss to this project (20 hectares x 50 per cent loss x 3 years of impact).

Hence, the developer would be required to put into action a restoration project, most commonly by footing the bill, which is esti-mated to provide at least thirty hectare-years of ecosystem benefit to comparable natural systems. This obligation could be met in many ways; for example, improving six hectares of the ecosystem by 50 per cent for ten years (perhaps by dredging high levels of contamination present in targeted sediments) could be sufficient. Alternatively, the same overall compensation could result from providing funds to expand a nearby protected area by an additional six hectares for five years. Either way, and at the end of the day, the net end compensation (30 hectare-years) should be more or less equivalent.

Whether injury compensation is calculated from habitat equivalency analysis, environmental mitigation ratios, or some other mathematical sophistry, the end product is similar: compensation in the form of priority environmental projects. Sometimes these are referred to as an 'environmental mitigation bank'. In practice, developers are generally required to purchase 'credits' sufficient to offset the impacts caused by their shopping malls, marinas and so forth. The price of credits is based on the cost of the underlying compensation project.

Increasingly, credits can be bought and sold, even on international markets. You could say, with only slight exaggeration, that they are being traded like hot potatoes. Use and trading of carbon credits in an attempt to alleviate climate change is, in fact, an extension of these very same principles. This is now all the rage, in the news and on TV, big-time. Put another way, it is an attempt to put the brakes on modernity as nature's heat-sensitive amplifiers kick into action and start to warm us up. Restraining modernity, through environmental compensation, is something the Luddites would surely have revelled in, perhaps even killed for.

In the case of carbon credits, laudable though the scheme is, it seems to be fraught with difficulties. For one, in many cases the cutting of carbon emissions can actually occur in the absence of trading. Climate Care, for example, one of the UK's biggest off-setters, has distributed some 10,000 energy-efficient light bulbs in a township in South Africa. Although well-meaning, it turned out that an energy company has also been doing the same thing, free, to loads of customers, including its own township. So the saving on electricity, and hence greenhouse emissions, would have happened anyway.

Then there is the challenge of calculating emissions in the first place. Greenpeace claims to have a gold standard, to ensure that emissions reductions are 'verified, additional and consistent with sustainable development'. It is a far cry from many other schemes on the market, though. As Manchester journalist Dan Welch put it while investigating off-setters for *Ethical Consumer* magazine: 'Offsets are an imaginary commodity created by deducting what you hope happens from what you guess would have happened.' Perhaps there is no real substitute for holding back. The need to cut greenhouse gas emissions seems incontestable, especially given that the benefits of tree planting, as a means of mopping up surplus carbon dioxide, turn out to be far less assured than generally acclaimed.

Small can be beautiful

Though clearly peanuts in comparison to what shopping malls, marinas and other big developments are now doing, or should be doing, to compensate for environmental collateral, small enterprises can also do their bit to preserve the '*robustness* of ecosystems'. But then, of course, they tend not to create such environmental havoc in the first place. Some enterprises, although small-scale and modest, have been surprisingly innovative in coming up with ways of keeping a low environmental footprint.

More than 200 miles north of London is Danby Dale, one of a series of valleys extending south from the river Esk to the North York Moors. Once traversed by Rosedale monks and later inhabited by Quaker families, the dale remains an oasis of tranquillity. Yet it is something more, for Danby Dale today is the site of Botton Village, the first ever Camphill adult community for people with special needs. Established in 1955, you could say than Botton is a 'cooperative' with a difference.

Influenced by the Austrian-born philosopher Rudolf Steiner (1861–

1925) and the Viennese paediatric doctor Karl König, Camphill communities integrate people with special needs with others in the community, with whom they live, work and interact on a daily basis. In terms of food security, and in other ways too, Camphill systems seem remarkably robust, at least up to a point.

Despite its ups and downs, Botton and its various self-support systems have stood the test of time and kept going remarkably well. Camphill communities, and the Steiner schools, are best known for their ideas on human well-being and educational needs. Yet it is not only these ideas that go far beyond mainstream thinking. For one thing, no one 'earns' at Botton. Residents do not individually own a car, a TV, their house or other everyday items; instead, there is a pool system. It all works, not through any financial transaction, but through needs being recognized.

Resource-sharing, understandably, promotes cost efficiency – which is important, since Botton's funding still has to come from somewhere (largely donations and grants, for which the community is accountable). In today's business and managerial jargon, the pool system creates the right economy of scale. But there are far wider spin-offs from resource-sharing, ones that extend to nurturing the environment, for example by helping to cut carbon emissions. With rocketing fuel prices, what's more, car pools are now catching on in mainstream European society, and beyond. Far from 'backward-looking', when it comes to environmental management you could say Botton is actually ahead of its time.

Botton is surprisingly forward-looking in other ways, too. For over 300 people – co-workers and their families, assistants and individuals with special needs – five farms, various workshops including a printing press, as well as crop production and extensive gardens, come together as one more or less autonomous and robust unit. Like resource-sharing, self-sufficiency helps cut transport and hence energy needs and, with it, wear and tear on the environment. Through a sense of balance, and forward-looking vision, the Botton community and the setting in which it chooses to operate, have achieved a remarkable level of robustness.

According to conventional wisdom, self-sufficiency is an unlikely gateway to prosperity in the modern world, or so advocates of globalization would have us believe. Yet through over-reliance on outside supplies, modernity's lean supply chains, we can easily become victims of an unexpected shortage, or an economic squeeze. In many ways, self-sufficiency is precisely what has helped shield the village and its residents from uncontrollable outside events.

On the other hand, not even Botton Village or its farms – however isolated, organic or self-sufficient they may be – are immune to some events, such as the side-effects of 'mad cow' disease (BSE) or the 2001/2 outbreak of foot-and-mouth disease. The cattle herd at one Camphill farm in Scotland, for example, had to be slaughtered when adjacent farms became infected by foot-and-mouth. Yet, curiously, on another Camphill farm in Gloucestershire, in a similar situation, they were spared. Botton's herds, it turns out, narrowly escaped slaughter when farms in the neighbouring dale were affected. Just as robustness theory tells us, through the 'robust yet fragile' paradox, no system can be immune against every assault, not even Botton, though, one way or another, it manages to keep operating despite its fair share of challenges.

The continued existence of Botton and its sister communities – their sustainability – depends, as mentioned, ultimately on outside financial support. That is a practical issue that Botton has always had to face. It is difficult or impossible, after all, for any society to go it alone one hundred per cent. Another inescapable fact is that Botton as a system only functions socially, financially, environmentally – and robustly – because of traditional principles: group needs override self needs.

Throughout much of Britain and the Western world, in complete contrast, priorities could not be more different. For the individual, and the here-and-now, is what seems to count most; that was certainly the mindset of Thatcherite Britain back in the 1970s and 80s, and also an ethos that modernity still seems reluctant to relinquish; no wonder, then, that there has been so much collateral damage. Clearly, though, principles are not always put into practice. We might find at least some of the outcomes from Botton appealing; but fully embracing its ethos and the day-to-day 'nitty-gritty' – some might say sacrifices – that are needed to produce them might be quite another matter.

Not a trace left behind: the travelling journeyman

Even for the modern world, it turns out, there can be simple ways of reducing collateral damage; so much so, in fact, that environmental compensation after 'the act', of development or operating, is not even necessary, because problems do not arise in the first place. Consider, as a case in point, an old-fashioned, unrushed yet surprisingly effective approach to business: the travelling journeyman.

On the face of it, nothing could be more bizarre and out of kilter with modernity. One also has to admit that travelling journeymen are hardly going to feature as the central chapter in any *A to Z Guide to Productive Organizations*, either. Yet the 'movement' is now enjoying something of a revival, as *Guardian* writer Stephanie Boucher explains.

In a recent article, Boucher told a tale of a blacksmith, Julian Coode, and his assistant. One winter's afternoon, after a tea break, the two were suddenly greeted by a young man, totally unannounced: Sebastian Reichlin, of Swiss-German nationality. So weird was Reichlin's attire – dungarees with mother-of-pearl buttons and an earring bearing a little key – that he could have stepped in from a different century and planet, not just another country.

For Reichlin was a craftsman, but one of an unusual sort: a travelling journeyman, who had served his time as an apprentice and now wished, as tradition holds, to benefit from an acclaimed master – even if finding him meant shunning cars, public transport, or any transport for that matter, and slowly wandering beyond national borders.

A centuries-old tradition that once prevailed in Britain, the travelling journeyman seems to have survived in Germany, France and some other parts of Europe. This peculiar behaviour and approach to business may have prevailed during medieval times, remarks Stephanie Boucher, when skilled workers travelled far and wide across Europe, including Britain, to help build the great cathedrals. But, as she also explains, 'young tradesmen and, increasingly, young tradeswomen are reviving the custom of journeying to far-flung masters of the trade to build on their skills'.

A journeyman, it seems, was a transition between the apprentice, fast-disappearing, at least in the UK, and the fully-fledged master. In fact 'journeyman' may well come from the French word, *journée*, meaning paid a daily rate, for which travelling (on foot) was part of the deal.

Besides getting fit while on the hoof, travelling *à pied* means, of course, leaving virtually no environmental footprint, not a trace left behind – whether we're talking down-to-earth effects on ecosystems, or carbon footprints in the sky – since walking creates virtually zero carbon dioxide emissions, and no other, more obvious forms of pollution. In fact, it is hard to imagine a greener way to travel to work, to do one's bit to help assure the '*robustness* of ecosystems'.

As anyone any with any business savvy will be quick to point out, though, going slow and going green is all well and good for the environment. Anyone suggesting, though, that travelling journeymen might still have any place in the corporate world, or any serious organization for that matter, would be totally off their rocker, completely out of their mind. In a world increasingly driven by '*efficiency* of industry and development', such incredulity would hardly be surprising, either.

Walking to work, quite plainly, is hardly a realistic alternative for city slickers (though some do cycle) or, in fact, for most of modernity. It hardly takes an MBA from Harvard or Stanford to see that most businesses would quickly come to a grinding halt, if most of the day – or week, or longer still – was simply blown away by part of the workforce as it slowly meandered to work, drifting from one town to another, or from one national border to another.

If you really think about it, the snail-pace of the travelling journeyman, with all the time in the world, could not be more different from the slickness of the just-in-time style of operations – increasingly a corporate signature of business prowess and efficiency. Prolonged journeying on foot might keep the journeyman trim. But it is hardly the same thing as keeping the supply chains of Dell Computers and the like lean for a productive present and prosperous future. So if company bosses cannot even be sure who will turn up to work each day, the prospects of cutting-edge performance and productivity would seem little more than zilch with travelling journeymen on the payroll.

If you imagine, then, that the travelling journeyman is simply an anachronism – and went the way of the Dodo, or the Luddites – there would, admittedly, be more than a grain of truth in your reaction. But you would be only partly right.

What is so remarkable, and so surprising, is that such a simple, old-fashioned way of going about work can actually add robustness to business, as well as to the environment; that is, aside, of course, from any enhancement of career prospects for the journeyman, or other perks of the profession. The truth is that travelling journeymen do not necessarily slow businesses down and hold them back, which, on the face of it, one would expect them to do. France, for example, boasts three such organizations, allegedly of medieval descent, operating across the whole country. Part of the young tradesmen's time is spent learning crafts and living communally, but travelling is what the journeymen also do. The largest of these, L'Association Ouvrière des Compagnons du Devoir, puts young incomers, quite literally, through their paces. Between residential centres is the travelling phase, remarks Boucher, known immodestly as the Tour de France. Speed may not be its branding, but there are other pay-offs.

And as the marketing manager of one English engineering firm, Total Maintenance and Engineering, once remarked, when a French journeyman suddenly turned up: 'We accepted him, in our broken French, because we needed workers. Then we discovered that his skills, at twenty-one years of age, were far superior to our own workers.' Another *compagnon*-trained journeyman followed, essentially because they were more versatile, had a positive work ethic and seemed at home in any social situation. What a far cry from its home-grown apprentices, TME felt. Not only that, Boucher points out, the firm's clients actually began requesting 'the French kids'.

These and other tales of travelling journeymen, of course, would be music to the ears of Luddites, were they around to witness such examples of business expediency combined with environmental responsibility.

High tempo, low footprint

The travelling journeyman echoes, in an indirect way, how cutting a deal on the high seas once came about. Here, though, the tempo was greater – not just because of the wilder conditions, but more because getting business was, quite literally, a race against time; a very different sense of urgency compared to the unrushed approach of Sebastian Reichlin, and his predecessors, on land. Nevertheless, both at sea and in the case of travelling journeymen, you could say it was entrepreneurs relying on their wits and devices, to seek their fortunes – or even just work away from home turf.

Like the travelling journeyman, wheeling and dealing at sea was an industry that created negligible disturbance on the environment and global climate. That is because, up to about a century ago, trade was driven more by the power of the wind than the power of petroleum. Just like the even slower meanderings of the travelling journeyman, propulsion was carbon neutral. (Of course, timber had to be used to build the ships, so their overall carbon footprint was not actually zero.) Yet, curiously, it turns out there was some pretty lively business, too.

Consider, as a prime example, the old Bristol Channel pilot cutters. Around the beginning of the twentieth century, these fine sturdy craft ventured, on modest sorties, from the UK's sheltered waters for the open Atlantic; the epitome of maritime robustness, as mentioned, and leaving barely any environmental footprint at all. Their purpose: to escort incoming shipping through the hazardous shallow waters to the safety of port, winter or summer. Crack pilots, like Lewis Alexander of Barry, could reputedly make £1,500, a princely sum for a year's work at the time of World War I. The problem, though, was that it was first come, first served. Latecomers never got a bean, at least not from that ship; they would have to wait for the next, which might pay less, so it was slimmer pickings. The rivalry was intense, as Tom Cunliffe points out; so there were some very fast pilot cutters 'driven hard by some really desperate characters'. What's more, to get the best prize this often meant venturing westward far into the Atlantic.

Actually, timber for shipbuilding 90 was used in unsustainable quantities, causing the deforestation of much of Europe through the middle ages and later

Wind power might have been fine, of course, back then, since little else was available, especially for the likes of pilot cutters. Few, if any, would have had engines, so it was sail there or don't get there. Besides, ships nowadays have sophisticated navigational equipment: they hardly need escorting or molly-coddling far out at sea – at most only a pilot and tug when nearing port or dangerous coastal shallows. But that's not all, as efficiency seekers would quickly remind us. Sailing in today's world is all well and good for Admiral's Cup contestants, or the likes of British yachtswoman Ellen McArthur in her trans-ocean sprints. But that's purely sport, doing things for fun.

Even the very image of cargo-laden sailing ships traipsing across the seas is the very opposite of what modernity, and its love for '*efficiency of industry and development*', aspires to. We are talking, after all, about the movement of merchandise for a product-hungry world, in a very commercial world; the very spice of globalization. What is needed here, surely, is quick and reliable transport, not antiquated vessels, or even modern ships, driven by the vagaries of the winds.

As in the case of travelling journeymen, then, one can easily be bamboozled into thinking that sail power could never have a serious place in ocean transport today, especially in an era of container freight so reliant on high-tech. Reduced or zero oil pollution and carbon emissions might be one thing, but surely nowadays sail power could never get even a sideways glance, let alone a serious look-in.

Perhaps not; yet with rocketing fuel prices, cynics should not feel so sure-footed. Ports and cargo terminals, after all, are where hold-ups mostly occur. Lack of speed during transit is generally not where the problem lies. Who knows, then: we might just see resurgence in sailing vessels, at least for the transport of non-perishable freight.

Commercial sail power was, in fact, considered seriously at the time of the OPEC fuel crises in the 1970s, when per barrel petroleum costs shot through the sky. The same happened again in 2008, when the price escalated to way over $100 per barrel. This might precipitate similar scares and interest once again. And modern Luddites will be quick to remind us of something else: wind carries no extraction costs, it is free at delivery and (still) tax free. Besides, global warming was not in the forefront of everyone's mind three or four decades ago. Times have changed. So perhaps the days of commercial sail are not over for good.

What is really surprising is that the old sailing ships were not necessarily slouches, either. Take the clipper ships, like the *Cutty Sark*; her turn of speed was legendary. Between 1883 and 1895, for example, she made twelve round trips from Australia, and won the wool race year after year, and broke record after record. In one famous incident the *Cutty Sark*, initially lolloping along in light winds in 1889, was overtaken by the new mail steamer *Britannia* – reputedly one of the world's fastest ships. In the night, though, the wind freshened, *Britannia*'s distant smokestack drew nearer, and the *Cutty Sark* finally passed the steamship and beat her back to port.

Of course, if sail power should once again bring merchandise to our shores, it will almost certainly not be in the holds of clipper ships, as much as the likes of my father might wish. Instead it will be in something decidedly more high-tech – perhaps in sail-assisted ships. Nor should one suppose, either, that transport and escort are the only useful maritime industries that can be undertaken in green ways, as another trip down memory lane reminds us.

Perhaps even greater entrepreneurs than the owners and masters of pilot cutters, or tea clippers, were the purveyors of a service industry founded on other traditional sailing craft: the Falmouth quay punts. As the nineteenth century slipped into the twentieth, these vessels performed a rather different role from that of the pilot cutters. For the quay punts, and the men on them, serviced the needs of incoming vessels through provision of mail, tailoring and other ship-to-ship services. Like the pilot cutters, though, these boats were seaworthy and fast, robust and – for their day, at least – efficient transport; they had to be, in an enterprise where the stakes were so high. What's more, like other sailing vessels, they were environmentally friendly: green through and through.

One particularly creative and thoughtful soul was chaplain James Badger. The skipper of the goodly and godly Falmouth quay punt

Clarice, Badger was a maritime missionary who set about spreading the gospel. If any enterprise smacks of opportunism, perhaps there is no finer example than the goods and services reliant on these fine traditional craft, and the journeys they made to secure a good deal.

So remarkable, in fact, are the sea-keeping and other qualities (including speed) of the traditional workboats that they are making a comeback; both the originals, and a new production live in replica form, in a boatyard in Falmouth; a reprieve, perhaps, but still it is a breath of new life. The truth is that versatility and old-fashioned robustness still have a place today.

Who knows, though, old packhorses may once again have their commercial use, especially given their impeccable green and carbon-neutral credentials (in comparison with modern ships). In today's climate, it is a credential any service industry, in its right mind, might envy. Greater use of sail power would also be a move the Luddites would endorse, especially if it created extra jobs, were they here to witness the state that lust for '*efficiency* of industry and development' has put society in.

CHAPTER 3 THE LIE OF THE LAND

Seeds of fortune and destruction

A double-edged plough

In Western Pakistan lies the Harappan Desert, a habitat too dry and inhospitable for people to live in. Four to five thousand years ago, a major Harappan–Indus civilization began and flourished, not in the desert itself, but in and around the river Indus and its tributaries. Parts of the region at that time were richly forested, and the monsoons provided rainfall like a free gift from heaven. It was a prime example of a self-adjusting, robust (eco)system, largely because of its intact forest.

Just as a robust landscape, with intact trees and soil, was essential for this ancient civilization, so the same is true for our society today; not, though, solely for the future of forest people, but for the future of the earth and quality of air.

In the case of the Harappan–Indus civilization, robustness of the land began to diminish when peasant farmers replaced the forest with scrub and grass, as grazing for cattle and goats; changes in river courses and other natural events may also have played their part. As half the forest was intact and the rains kept on coming, things were fine. But beyond the 'tipping point', as James Lovelock explains, the region turned arid: the rains simply stopped. What did remain of the forest perished; today it supports but a fraction of the population that once was there.

Lovelock's tale is a Catch 22, if ever there was one. Agriculture is precisely what has always nurtured and sustained society; it has been its mainstay for at least 10,000 years. Yet, according to him, the practice – now more of an industry – is linked to two of the world's three deadly

Cs: cars, cattle and chainsaws. Damage to trees (often for agriculture, not just for timber) from chainsaws is obvious and almost goes without saying, as does impact from cars, something that of course agriculture cannot be blamed for. As an aside, it may be added that car emissions have contributed both to global warming, and to acid deposition – contamination of the atmosphere and, eventually, forests and lakes too.

Harm caused by cattle, the middle 'C' in the trio, is also serious. For when natural forests are replaced by cattle farms and food crops, apart from the loss of trees and natural vegetation we greatly diminish the land's power to regulate the climate. If that were not enough, the greenhouse gas methane is an unavoidable product from cows (whose populations are on the increase) – from both ends, as a result of eating grass. One dairy cow generates 50–150 litres of methane daily, equivalent, if burned, to the energy of 200 litres of gasoline; wetland agriculture also generates methane. What's more, methane delivers a double whammy to the atmosphere: for it happens to be both a power-ful greenhouse gas and a depleter of ozone up in the stratosphere; and ozone, at least when high up, acts as a natural 'Factor 50' sun shield against harmful incoming ultra-violet radiation. As Australians, for example, are aware, too much UV easily leads to skin cancer.

Clearly the world's three deadly Cs, such vital ingredients for modernity's 'efficiency of industry and development', can hardly be banned, but their moderation is clearly of the utmost urgency. Painful as the fact may be, in Lovelock's eyes – and he is not alone in this view – agriculture has to be the number one threat to the 'robustness of ecosystems', and hence to earth and humanity. It is hard to imagine a greater irony.

Changes to the Harappan forests, although only a tiny region, echo a wider problem, in that agriculture, globally, has now stripped away some two-thirds of forest and other natural terrestrial ecosystems. What we are left with in the place of rich, complex natural systems – imbued with spare capacity and other forms of robustness – is something radically different: simplified, substitute ecosystems, increasingly for the short-term benefits of agribusiness, rather than jobs for farmers and wholesome food for everyone. Not only that, once transformed into an 'artificial' system their constituents become more prone to diseases, and they are more fragile in other ways, too.

Media coverage and documentaries constantly remind us of the many valuable products provided by trees, and the devastating effects of deforestation – whether to fuel agribusinesses, or the '*efficiency* of industry and development' more generally. More serious than the loss of materials and products, though, is the loss of planetary ecosystem services, in particular the disruption of natural climate regulation. Forests are a big player in this. All too easily we focus our attention on pollution of soils, air and the sea. Serious as this may be, we seem blind to something graver: the removal of forests, marshes and other wetlands, and turning them over to the plough, but in order to feed hungry businesses as much as hungry mouths. By replacing too much of natural systems with food crops, and particularly with cattle, we undermine the earth's natural robustness, perhaps most seriously by weakening the ability of the land surface to control its own climate.

The truth is that rain and clouds, particularly in the tropics, are not (surprising though it may seem) the status quo – not simply something to be taken for granted as modernity 'advances' in a forward quick-march. Things are that way because, through their leaves, trees put out millions of litres of water annually. Water vapour rises in the atmosphere, condenses, and clouds form. Clouds are the origin of rain, allowing trees to grow, which in turn binds soil into the life-sustaining material it is. Replace forests with insensitive farming, though, and the cycle gets broken. As a result of our efforts, what's more, more than 20 billion tonnes of topsoil wash away or get blown away each year. Forests are one of the checks and balances that control soil loss and erosion. With an area of forest the equivalent of 200 football fields destroyed in Brazil in less than one hour, though, it is hardly so surprising modernity has a few problems on its plate.

Exfoliation, according to James Lovelock – someone you could call a 'planetary physician' – is effectively destroying the earth's living skin. Just as in human medicine few people can survive the loss of more than

70 per cent of the skin by severe burns, so too is the outer protective barrier vital to the earth system. We are now close to, if not beyond, losing 70 per cent of natural surface land cover. For a scary reminder of what's at stake, recall the tale of the Harappan–Indus region and what unsustainable farming by its ancient civilization led to there.

Most living systems, in fact, have considerable over-provision or redundancy, an invaluable and indispensable form of robustness; rather like our old racing Bentley with its twin fuel pumps, plus a back-up petrol delivery system just in case both pumps failed. Forests and other terrestrial ecosystems are no different; that's the reassuring news. It is what enables them to recover from fires, diseases and destruction – even from replacement, up to a point, by so-called efficiently farmed ecosystems. After all, a human can do quite well with only one kidney. As Lovelock remarks, though, it would be quite another matter, with one organ missing, to attempt a crossing of a hot desert by foot. Precisely the same arguments apply to plant systems: for forests and clouds go hand in hand, and over-conversion of 'inessential' natural ecosystems to farmland comes at our peril. Superfluous to requirements, if you think about it, is a sentiment that could not be further from the truth.

As a simple illustration, yet with more than a grain of truth in it, Lovelock likens the great forests of Amazonia to a super air-conditioner. Suppose, he explains, forests reduce the sun's heat arriving in the canopy by just 1 per cent. To achieve the same effect from engineering, each hectare of forest would require a refrigerator with a cooling power of 6 kilowatts. Even assuming no capital cost, and that the operation was completely efficient, annual cooling costs would be around $1,300 per hectare. And those were Lovelock's figures more than ten years ago; since then (1991) fuel prices have rocketed.

For comparison, Lovelock explains that clearing one hectare of tropical forest to rear beef cattle might produce sufficient meat to go into 1,850 (give or take) hamburgers. Putting it another way, five square metres of land, for example forest, is what is needed to produce just one hamburger, equivalent to stripping away a refrigeration service that would cost $65 to do artificially. On this basis, Lovelock contends, the value of refrigeration services of 'Amazonia Inc.', in its unfettered state of natural robustness, that is, stands at around $150 trillion. On top of that, its dividends and shares are not just for local customers, local forest dwellers, but extend to the entire world.

But without more sensitive and enlightened agriculture, the loss of central services brought about by enterprises more hungry for finance than for food is something likely to continue; and with it a shower of unexpected hazards. Loss of Amazonia's super air-conditioning services, and other knock-on effects, provide a graphic illustration of agriculture-driven devastation; here, chillingly, because a climate of efficiency and profit forces choices in favour of short-term gain rather than long-term robustness.

In the case of cattle, curiously, research suggests that methane production can be lowered by changing to feeds rich in forage legumes. This and similar measures might help, though it is hardly a substitute for the root of the problem: rising population of cows, and their spread to 'unnatural' habitats like forests converted to grasslands.

Gone with the wind

The effects of losing the earth's living skin extend, of course, far beyond disrupting the atmosphere and climate; what happened to the Harappan–Indus civilization was bad enough, as is climatic disturbance from laying waste to Amazonia and other forest wilderness areas today. (That's aside, of course, from the global warming caused by burning of fossil fuels.) But we're referring here to an equally serious tragedy: loss and erosion of soil.

Fast-backwards almost one century to North America, to witness how the making of a new life and a new land, geared more towards *efficiency of industry and development*' than the *'robustness* of ecosystems', completely transformed the environment. As Geoff Sites of Oklahoma University neatly put it, 'agricultural profits clouded the minds of the farmers'. What happened was the work of the new farmers, supposedly for the good of the community; in the name of progress, at least that was the intention. Yet what actually followed, from events beginning in the 1930s, was devastation on such a scale that it spread across at least five mid-western US states and into the next century. Put another way, the seeds of agricultural capitalism had been sown.

Damage from expansion of agriculture, in fact, began much earlier. But what we're talking of here is the creation (unintentionally, of course) of the infamous dust bowl. For it illustrates the calamitous knock-on effects that can arise from over-zealous agriculture, not only for agriculture itself, but also for the wider society. Here the root of the problem, quite literally, lay in the soil, for it soon began blowing in the wind. How this came about was through a combination of bad luck and insufficient attention to soil robustness – basically, as a result of farmers hoping for a better return than the land could possibly provide.

Before the 1600s, when settlers arrived in North America in their droves and began planting crops and grazing livestock, the vegetation was quite different. Native perennial grasses, their roots penetrating deep into the soil, were what dominated the prairie grasslands then. At no cost, these grasses held the fertile topsoil firmly in place. Not knowing what lay ahead, the farmers ploughed and uprooted these grasses, replacing them with annual crops. The problem was that these had a less extensive root system than the native plants; so the soil became more fragile. Over-grazing followed, thereby denuding the soil of its now shallow-rooted crops and exposing it to the ravages of high winds.

Added to the problem were major droughts in 1890, 1910 and between 1926 and 1934. During the 1930s, in particular, windstorms created gigantic dust clouds. A gargantuan aerosol of mainly brown topsoil would be one way of describing the unexpected state of affairs. At least one of these covered the entire eastern half of the USA. Several darkened the sky at midday; not unlike the spectacle in Kuwait following the conflagration of hundreds of oil wells during the 'first' Gulf War in 1991.

Vast areas of US cropland became severely eroded, stripped of topsoil and unproductive. Not only loss of soil followed, but also death of birds, rabbits and other wildlife that haplessly ingested soil-laden air. With agricultural production and the economy now undermined, thousands of families became displaced and migrated to California or industrial parts of the mid-west and elsewhere in search of work. But because of the Great Depression, few managed to find jobs. This downward spiral of events led in 1935 to the US Soil Erosion Act. One outcome was the formation of soil conservation districts and other environmental measures.

There is now evidence of natural two-year drought cycles, superimposed on longer, two-to-four-decade cycles, and perhaps others; this, of course, exacerbates soil erosion. While we can probably do little to control those natural processes, we nevertheless do have the power to regulate what has sustained and nourished farming and human society for at least 10,000 years: soil and the environment. Yet, as Colin Tudge starkly reminds us in *So Shall We Reap*, we seem blind to the self-evident: that humans are a species, and the earth is its habitat. Whether we are a poet or a bricklayer, religious or atheist, forgetting our biological origins is something we do at our peril. Yet as modernity chases and jumps on to the corporate and industrial bandwagon, nothing, it seems, could be further from its collective mind.

Until the catastrophic events just described, the settlers' efforts in America would have paid good dividends. Improved crop and animal production helped boost agricultural efficiency. But with droughts, coupled with poor cultivation practices, came both unsustainability and reduced efficiency. As is now clear, overproduction was encouraged at the expense of the environment. Costs of helping to rectify the problem are ongoing to this day. Following public concern about the impact of topsoil loss and ineffective farm subsidy schemes, the US Congress instigated the Conservation Reserve Programme in 1986. Through economic incentives amounting to $120 per hectare per year, farmers were encouraged to convert cropland back to grassland or forest to help reverse ongoing resource degradation. By 1990 some 14 million hectares – only one-quarter of the land requiring conservation to halt soil erosion

– had entered the programme.

The simple truth is that soil loss is a plague that won't go away, and one that is increasingly fuelled by modern agriculture. Like fossil fuels, without care and restraint soil easily disappears more quickly than the time it takes to form: development of the upper 2.5cm of topsoil, for example, generally takes from 220 to 1,000 years. The problem, though, is that annual erosion rates on many agricultural lands are around 20–100 times the average rate of topsoil formation.

Figures vary from place to place, and are updated from time to time. Yet even with adjustments here and there the arithmetic makes disquieting reading. By the mid-1990s, for example, topsoil was eroding faster than its rate of formation on about one-third of the world's croplands, representing a staggering 85 per cent of total land degradation. With such heavy erosion of the soil, and of ecosystem robustness, it is no wonder that so much of agriculture has become unsustainable; and, at the same time, has put some indigenous tribes at risk of extinction. Yet one official Brazilian agency, at one time known, ironically, as the Indian Protective Services, declared tracts of rainforest to be empty of indigenous populations, when they were not, simply to accelerate the development of those regions.

Growth at all costs

Agriculture presents modernity with extraordinary opportunities for manipulating nature for what it can extract from it – in an ideal world, mainly for food but, in reality increasingly for finance and in unsustainable ways. What has happened to soil over the decades bears testament to this. It is not merely a matter, though, of '*efficiency* of industry and development' carrying more clout than what, on the face of it, is the opposing '*robustness* of ecosystems' lobby. The real irony is that maximizing farming output, instead of optimizing it, carries enormous costs; and we're not just talking here about the health of agriculture, but human health, too.

In the case of organic food, some of course claim that organic actually tastes better and is more healthy. Opinion is still fiercely divided. But the real advantages of organic and free-range may lie not so much in the product as in the underlying process, i.e. in farming itself. Whether for eggs, chicken meat or other produce, organic farming adopts sound ecological principles; that, after all, is part of its ethos, what it is setting out to accomplish. It is an approach that contrasts markedly with so much of high-tech farming. But then it is hardly surprising for an industry that bows, increasingly, to the dictates of agricultural capitalism.

As Colin Tudge reminds us, though, we should not be fooled into supposing that organic is a glorious panacea, either. In *So Shall We Reap*, he exposes some of the pitfalls of getting on the organic bandwagon. He tells a tale of one truck, the size of a warship, seen in his local market town; it sported the logo 'Fresh Organic Produce': fine in principle, but, as he remarked: 'such quantities, dished out from some central clearing-house, are not in the spirit of the thing': it is hardly a spectacle that true organic producers would be proud of. Naturally, large quantities of food in the UK, just as in any other country, are needed to feed everyone; that is reasonable and is common sense. But less commendable is putting an organic dressing on food production purely for economic expediency (since organic stuff generally costs more).

To be fair and even-handed, though, neither, too, is the routine dishing out of antibiotics by intensive farming commendable, or necessarily the best way forward. An inescapable fact is that modern agriculture, not just medicine, is a big driver of bacterial resistance and the need for new antibiotics. One such case is the unexpected down-side of using an antibiotic called avoparcin to control and treat (enterococcal) bacterial infections in hens, pigs and other farm animals. Banned in Europe in 1997, through fears about human health, Roche Vitamins made a decision no longer to manufacture avoparcin. This is leading to its worldwide withdrawal; yet its legacy remains with us.

The problem is that farmers administered avoparcin routinely, albeit in tiny concentrations (less than ten parts per million), in animal feeds and water; not so surprisingly, perhaps, bacterial resistance followed.

* It is certainly less unhealthy. The "scientists" who claim pesticide products are safe are in the pay of the profit-maker. And research into dangers does not get funded

Directly or indirectly, avoparcin-resistant strains of enterococcal bacteria entered the human food chain. Because avoparcin's chemistry is similar to that of a related antibiotic, vancomycin, bacterial resistance to the latter followed: VRE (vancomycin resistant *Enterococcus*) was first discovered, interestingly, in the guts of farmers.

What's more, it is thought that the vancomycin resistance gene may have transferred from *Enterococcus* into *Staphylococcus aureus*, producing intermediate level vancomycin resistance. As vancomycin is one of the most important antibiotics used to treat MRSA (methicillin-resistant *Staphylococcus aureus*) in humans, this is particularly worrying. More alarming still is something reported in the medical journal the *Lancet* by scientists Bruno González-Zorn and Patrice Courvalin, in 2003: the occurrence in the USA of strains of MRSA that were also resistant even to high concentrations of vancomycin.

As agriculture expert Jules Pretty states in the opening paragraphs of his book *Agri-Culture*, despite great progress in stepping up food production 'industrialized agricultural systems as currently configured are flawed'. In the case of antibiotics, he notes that in the UK alone 1,200 tonnes are used annually: only 40 per cent are for humans, while 60 per cent are used for farm animals, horses and domestic pets.

Yet only one-fifth of the antibiotics and other antimicrobials used in modern agriculture are for disease treatment; a staggering four-fifths are used either for growth promotion or for disease prevention. It is hardly surprising, then, that antibiotic resistance is becoming so widespread. Even when it comes to providing our most basic needs, though, there has been enormous collateral damage. Many now believe that growth enhancers and other antibiotics are building up to alarmingly high concentrations in the food chain.

As just one of the antibiotics used in farming, avoparcin, demonstrates, unbridled enthusiasm for production at all costs can deliver a powerful double whammy: to agriculture, because routine use of one antibiotic leads to resistance and an arms race – a relentless hunt for another antibiotic, in which resistance has not yet built up – and it is also bad news for human health, as build-up of resistance to an agricultural antibiotic can, paradoxically and unfortunately, lead to resistance to closely related antibiotics that happen to be vital in combating deadly infections such as MRSA. That is one reason why the dishing out of these drugs as if they were Smarties, or candy bars, is such risky business.

The practice already causes deaths and could cause them in huge numbers.

Food for thought

Few, if any, food-related issues in recent years have been condemned and defended so fervently as genetically modified organisms (GMOs). Like agriculture itself, GM technology is not just about science and technical solutions to farming, but also about wider issues: potential environmental and health risks, as well as the ethics and matters of practicality and corporate interests surrounding this branch of biotechnology.

As with many technologies, some benefits undeniably follow from GM technology. To whom, for how long and at what costs, though, are issues – rather like the small print on a contract or agreement – that we should also be mindful of, preferably sooner rather than later. Given what's at stake, and the public's growing distrust of large corporations, that is precisely what is happening. That's why society is still unwilling to give biotech companies carte blanche to infuse genetically modified organisms into whatever, wherever and whenever they choose.

Genetic studies and selective breeding done by Gregor Mendel in the 1800s, and by traditional farmers long before him, are what has led to agriculture's high-tech zenith; but GMOs and cross-breeding are not exactly the same. While the latter works on the same or similar species, over several generations, genetic engineering permits the one-off transfer of genes between species – even if one is wheat and the other a cow – to the extent that an organism may contain genes from many others. As the century progresses, designer organisms seem increasingly possible and, what's more, the order of the day.

No one in their right mind would deny that we desperately need plants that are more resistant to drought, floods, disease, salty conditions and much more besides. Genetic engineering is certainly a prime candidate, Colin Tudge points out, for providing the genes for super-robustness in the crop sorghum – the staple crop in much of sub-Saharan Africa. The problem is that intensive searches for these genes in naturally occurring close relatives have so far proved fruitless.

An alternative approach is to try to insert particular hardiness genes from groundnuts, that is from a completely different species and family (legumes). But the technology needed to create the genetically modified organism is proving a hard nut to crack. However, scientists from the International Crops Research Institute for the Semi-Arid Tropics are hoping the idea can be made to work. If it can, for the poor people in an environment as harsh as sub-Saharan Africa the sorghum–groundnut transgenic organism would be little short of a miracle; or, in the words of biologist Lyall Watson, 'gifts of unknown things'. Assisted by 17 million dollars of support from the Bill and Linda Gates Foundation, African scientists are also looking to GM technology as a way of making sorghum more drought-tolerant, as well as a more fortifying food – richer in vitamins A and E, certain nutrients and protein.

Besides sorghum, one potentially valuable application of GM technology is to keep pests off plants, by using genes that do not kill them, but instead (and more naturally) give pests a dose, quite literally, of their own medicine. Pheromones are signalling chemicals used, for example, by aphid insects to warn others of impending danger. Since they are highly specific, they would not deter more desirable insects such as butterflies and bees. One study took place in a lab at Cornell University, and in the field, to check out the theory. The experiments involved genetically modified maize fitted with a gene to make its pollen kill insect pests. There was concern that wild monarch butterflies – a non-target species – might also get the kiss of death. Yet, as it happened, there was negligible risk. Nevertheless, as other examples confirm, genetic modification is not without legitimate concerns. That is why cynics are so worried by the prospects of modernity unleashing GMOs and perhaps leading, ultimately, to the unfettered greening of our fields by this technology.

Part of the problem lies in the nature of the genetic code. In one sense, it is digital, as each bit of DNA – or gene – corresponds to a specific piece of information. A better analogy, as Colin Tudge explains, is language, where specific genes become more like words. As we all know, the meaning of language comes not just from individual words, but also through grammar and syntax; how they are strung together into phrases, sentences and chapters into something as rich and diverse as Tolstoy's *War and Peace*. In a word, language is context dependent, and genes – with all the evolutionary and historical baggage they carry – are no different. Hence, the possibility of all sorts of problems, not just opportunities, potentially lies open in a transgenic organism created from newly introduced genes. We might like to think that '*efficiency* of industry and development' will always bring untold benefits, but the question is at what cost to the '*robustness* of ecosystems' and, what's more, to human health.

Consider, for example, potatoes. Although not toxic themselves, many of their wild ancestors are. Through selective breeding, the toxicity has been removed; the genes may still reside, but are simply repressed. However, a novel gene introduced to produce a better potato variety might inadvertently knock out the repressor, or otherwise allow the 'dormant' gene to be expressed. We can of course test for toxic effects. However, by further (conventional) cross-breeding, the novel gene could become incorporated into different crop varieties, each of which has a different genetic milieu. Hence a gene, malignant when introduced, could have harmful effects in different strains after several generations.

It would be quite wrong, then, simply to brush aside concerns of Greenies and cast them as scaremongers, stirring up trouble for no legitimate reason. An undeniable fact is that we live in times when GM and other biotechnology should be an aid. In one sense it is, but the worrying thing is that in many instances there stand to be as many losers as winners.

Colin Tudge, for one, acknowledges in *So Shall We Reap* the potential application of GM technology to animals, but more for medicine than for agriculture. For agriculture, then, society has every right to be cautious and not bamboozled and bulldozed by corporate interests. Definitely undesirable, too, Tudge and many others believe, is the insertion of novel genes into animal livestock, especially if the purpose is merely faster growth and greater commercial profit. For this can bring with it practical problems: genetically engineered bovine growth hormone to raise milk production, for instance, increases udder infections and hence the need for antibiotics – contributing to their ever greater resistance and the biological 'arms race'. But such concerns – you could say unavoidable and unfortunate collateral – may well not be in the forefront of the minds of bosses in big corporations, especially when annual profits are the order of the day. *Carcinogenic meat – who cares?*

Another worry, this time an indirect one, yet now taken seriously, is animal welfare: does society really like the idea, Tudge asks, of the featherless chicken (featured on UK TV in 2002) or, worse still, brainless chickens – something considered seriously by some agricultural biologists? What's more, he adds, 'a gene dropped into an established genome can throw the entire organism off course'. Unlike civil engineering projects, which carry a blueprint of operations, natural or created genetic systems come with no such master plan. What happens when they run is far less predictable. What's more, if a GMO happens to run wild (something perhaps more likely in plants than in animals), it may prove to be more robust than its unmodified relatives. Particularly nerve-racking is that we cannot be sure if that would suit most of us, or not. The cynically inclined would not bank on it.

When it comes to what GM food might bring, the public, certainly in the UK, is increasingly sceptical, even to the point of refusing to buy such products. As James Surowiecki points out in *The Wisdom of Crowds*, public opinion often has extraordinary collective insight into issues about which experts, curiously, can be way off the mark. He tells a tale of statistician and geneticist Francis Galton. Walking through an exhibition one day, about 100 years ago, Galton came across a weight-guessing competition: a fat ox had been selected and the gathering crowd had to wager their bets on the animal's weight. There were butchers and farmers, as well as people with no special knowledge of farming. Until then, Galton's observations and experiments had convinced him that faith in experts, not public ignorance, was where our hope for a better society lay. What came out of the guessing competition, though, he could scarcely believe. From 787 guesses, the average weight of the ox came out at 1,197 pounds, a value remarkably close to its actual weight of 1,198 pounds. Given the right circumstances, as Surowiecki explains, groups can be smarter than individuals – even when they include experts.

Genetic modification and many other biotechnology issues are, admittedly, far more complex than simply estimating the weight of a slaughtered farm animal at a country exhibition. Here, solid technical knowledge is clearly essential for any informed 'committee decisions' about GM foods, even if the public also has valuable opinions. As a case in point, an advisory body of leading scientists, ACRE (the Advisory Committee on Releases to the Environment), was set up to make decisions about GM technology in the UK. The Committee evaluated investigations to determine potential side-effects of GM oilseed rape, beet and maize on British farmland wildlife; it was the largest ever field trial in the world. In 2003, the scientists reported differences in wildlife abundance, compared with conventional, non-GM varieties of the crops. As a result of the study, GM maize was given the conditional green light, but the other three GM crops got a provisional 'thumbs down' – though approval might potentially be given if certain farming practices changed.

Jules Pretty, for one, believes that ACRE makes very good decisions about GM in the UK. As the above example demonstrates, approval is not automatically granted: advocates of slow-tech are not, then, necessarily wide of the mark with their caution. Trying to balance the risks, benefits and widely differing perceptions about using genetically modified organisms, though, is a tough call. One thing for sure is that without a wide sweep of the horizon – that is, evaluating how GMOs might affect the 'robustness of ecosystems' – any assessment of their effects on the 'efficiency' of industry and development' could be shallow on several counts.

If a field trial of GM plants 109 demonstrates dangers, how can that experiment be reversed? The genie's out of the bottle. This is unbelievably irresponsible.

Proponents of GM technology claim that farming and humanity can be saved from impending disaster by GM crops, if not livestock. And, many believe, the evidence is out there to prove it. As Colin Tudge points out, though, counter-evidence comes not just from nostalgic, muddle-headed Luddites. As he goes on to say: 'In reality, genetic engineering has so far contributed nothing that can truly be said to be of any significant use at all in feeding the world. Its contributions have purely to do with alleged ease of husbandry, and hence with reduction of costs.' Nor, for the world at large, is this likely in the next half-century, he adds, by which time the world population should have stabilized, to around 10 billion (though some UN projections suggest we will stop at 8.5 billion, and then numbers will actually fall).

While hyper-stress-resistant strains of sorghum are dearly needed in Africa – potentially through GM technology – this does not mean that failings of traditional husbandry have been the main problem more generally. Similarly, science and technology, with exceptions, are not what enabled populations to expand nor what propelled humanity through 10,000 years of rural development. Instead, it was the craft of agriculture. Only in the last seventy years, Tudge asserts, has science had a serious impact on agriculture and food production.

One unequivocal benefit of science for agriculture was the green revolutions around the middle of the last century, although, not all farmers benefited. But this was not a GM solution; it involved standard selective breeding. The triumph arose from the fact that wheat and rice, particularly on the Indian subcontinent, could not be grown in sufficient quantities to feed the rising population; adding fertilizer, it turned out, was not sufficient. The new genetic strains – semi-dwarf varieties – instead of merely growing taller and toppling over, produced greater yields when heavily fertilized. Despite the large input needed (of water and fertilizer), and the millions of poor farmers who could not afford them and who suffered, the green revolutions helped avert famine in Asia. But the rescue, as mentioned, came not from any newfangled technology like genetic engineering; for the revolution came about before the term had even been coined. Rather, it arose from traditional, old-fashioned plant-breeding techniques developed over the centuries.

Even where GMOs have been used, as in the case of golden rice – rich in carotene, a key input for vitamin A synthesis – it is hardly, asserts Colin Tudge, the gift so commonly ascribed. Tudge's argument centres on the fact that carotene is one of the commonest bio-molecules around; nature is simply full of it, not only in exotic and expensive fruits such as mango and papaya, but in all sorts of green leaves, too. What's more, carotene is something practitioners of traditional horticulture – 'farming with or without glass' – produce in abundance. Problems arise, though, in modern agriculture's switch from multiculture to monoculture – single species crops, often of relatively uniform genetic composition, which may lack certain of the key vitamins of their precursors and which are more prone to disease. In this sense, then, modernity's tinkering has led to diminished robustness.

Part of the problem, it would be fair to say, lies in what created the possible need for genetic modification in the first place. In the case of xerophthalmia – a common eye problem resulting from carotene and vitamin A deficiency – the need for golden rice is essentially one consequence of the erosion of horticulture. The problem arose through failure to recognize the extraordinary value of this traditional practice, until it had been pretty much eclipsed by rampant and relentless commercialism. Of course golden rice is a helpful solution, given the new undesirable state of affairs. Put another way, though, increased xerophthalmia is seen as unavoidable collateral damage, but may be more an illustration of traditional societies being duped (indirectly) by the imposition of Western economics.

Whichever side of the GM fence we sit, Jules Pretty for one believes we need to be much more balanced in our treatment of transgenic organisms (and other agricultural technologies). One key issue, he believes, is the process of technology development – not just the technology itself – as well as, of course, affordability; that is, if GM or other agricultural technologies are to become true allies in the alleviation of poverty and hunger. Not only that, Pretty points out, we are all too quick to treat GM as one thing, a 'cure-all'. But in reality, it is many things; it really needs to be treated on a case-by-case basis. Besides each GM product bringing different potential benefits for different stakeholders, he adds, each carries different health and environmental risks. Hence, '*robustness of ecosystems*' is a matter that should be taken as seriously as, or more seriously than, simply the '*efficiency* of industry and development' for the benefit of agri-capitalism.

Two key questions, in Pretty's eyes, should surface in any evaluation: first, does the new GM crop replace a technology that is more harmful to human health and the environment? One example of least a reserved 'yes' is insertion of a gene in cotton that has the same toxic effect on pests as commercial pesticides – and is no different from them, except that it is much less damaging to the environment. Following use of *B.t.* cotton (which contains the toxin through expression of a gene from the bacterium *Bacillus thuringiensis*) in China, for example, insecticide use fell by more than 60 per cent compared with levels of use in 2001. The outcome was considerable health and cost benefits for farmers; concern remains, though, over the potential for evolved insect resistance – either through the *B.t.* cotton itself, or through over-zealous spraying of insecticides in and around it.

The second cardinal question Jules Pretty believes we should ask when considering the use of genetic modification is: can the problem be solved using existing research and technology? One of several success stories he cites is GM technology leading to the development of new varieties resistant to yellow mottle virus in rice. Attempts to confer resistance in local varieties using conventional breeding had failed. Tests in five countries, however, revealed total resistance to the virus, which often reduces yields by 50 – 95 per cent. This is another case, then, when it would be wrong for purveyors of slow-tech, or anyone else for that matter, to dismiss the innovation purely on the grounds that it is GM technology, all of which in their eyes is a bad thing. Given the recent surges in food prices, and the ever-increasing number of mouths to feed, many are banking on GM crops as a rescue remedy.

Much GM research seems aimed at creating patent-able versions of basic foodstuffs as a source of revenue

The benefits, of course, are not always clear-cut, especially when judged against the risks; but then neither should there be an automatic 'thumbs down'. Part of the reason for such public opposition, Pretty believes, is that for first-generation technologies – beginning in the late 1990s – consumers could see no obvious benefits, for example, traits like herbicide tolerance and insect resistance. Perhaps newer technologies will be different, in applications already developed and tested but not commercially released: viral resistance in sweet potatoes, frost tolerance in strawberries – perhaps even varieties adapted to grow on contaminated or degraded land, and in other environments normally too hostile for food production. Looking ahead, we might well see GM crops with greater drought resistance, increased light/water/nutrient efficiency; possibly also 'designer plants' for producing plastics and other desirable compounds.

Experiments on complex systems like the natural world will always have unpredictable effects,

But technologies can turn in unexpected directions, and agriculture is no exception. An ironic twist to the GM tale is that a new cutting-edge technology might even supersede GM. Instead of gene-splicing and using transgenic organisms to improve crops, as Jeremy Rifkin, author of *The Biotech Century*, explains, scientists are achieving this through 'genomics' and 'marker-assisted-selection'. (MAS). It all sounds very high-tech, and in one sense it is.

Yet, paradoxically, it is actually a super-efficient way of accelerating the long-standing practice of classical breeding: searching for desirable traits in other varieties or wild relatives of crop plants, then cross-breeding these plants with existing commercial crops to go one step better. Using the technique, researchers have been able to cut down the time needed to develop new plant varieties by at least 50 per cent: little short of speeding things up but still using what is, fundamentally, slow-tech. It is as if high technology has gone round in full circle, ending up by simply dressing up old-fashioned plant-breeding techniques; you could call the inspirers of this amazing technology New Age designer outfitters.

Using the new technique, scientists in India and the UK have developed

this is scarcely likely to alleviate hunger.

and put on the market drought and mildew resistant strains of pearl millet. The European Union – whose public seems resolutely opposed to GM – is one admirer of MAS. Stavros Dimas, its environmental commissioner, remarked recently in a speech that the EU should not ignore the use of 'upgraded' conventional varieties as an alternative to GM crops. The fact is that GM, like any other technology, can never be a catch-all solution, a miracle cure for modernity; we need to consider it on a case-by-case basis, whether advocates of '*efficiency* for industry and development' like it or not. Despite undeniable potential, and some promising applications, overall benefits are still not convincing; especially, that is, if one takes an ecosystem's-eye view, and one that considers robustness above all else.

Net benefits or gross costs?

Despite all the efforts to alleviate hunger and poverty, agriculturally driven environmental damage is all too prevalent in the West and in the developing world. Consider, as an unnerving reminder, the down-side of antibiotics, or what we've done to the soil – something supposed to be there for growing the food that feeds us, not disappearing in a dust cloud or washing away down rivers. Boosting production through highly mechanized farming, come what may, seems to be one stamp of modern agriculture, and often an invasive one too. A much better bet, according to Jules Pretty and his colleagues, lies in resource-conserving technologies and practices – ones that produce net development benefits, instead of gross environmental costs; in other words, retaining the land's robustness for all to reap.

In a recent (2006) issue of *Environmental Science and Technology*, Pretty and colleagues demonstrate what happened during the early to mid-1990s following a number of mostly low-tech and slow-tech, relatively inexpensive interventions on over 12 million farms in fifty-seven poor countries across the world. Their findings seem astonishing. While they are not confident that such efforts towards greater sustainability are sufficient to meet global increases in food demands, few can deny that it is a step in the right direction.

First and foremost, average crop yields rose by a staggering 79 per cent and, on top of that, all crops showed improved water-use efficiency. But here is the real surprise: on over three-quarters of the farms, there was a decline in pesticide use by over 70 per cent, yet yields also improved substantially – in fact by 41 per cent. 'Best-tech', quite plainly, is not necessarily 'high-tech'. Remarkable benefits, it turns out, can follow from resource-conserving technologies, most of which are uncomplicated in principle and in practice yet carry very real benefits for food production. That, after all, is what agriculture should be all about.

Consider one of the eight packages adopted: integrated pest management. Here, farmers relied on biodiversity and *'robustness* of ecosystems': that was the approach for control of weeds, diseases and pests; and only when these options were ineffective did they resort to pesticides. Whether we're talking of non-chemical pest control, incorporating trees into farming systems, or livestock integration – for example, dairy cattle and poultry (including use of zero-grazing) – the outcomes are broadly similar: retaining robustness of the land's natural systems, and harnessing that to power agriculture from one year to the next.

It would be a mistake, though, to suppose that 'appropriate technology' is something that makes sense only for the world's rural poorest, in developing countries. In a very different setting, in western Europe, consider an approach and technology recently put in place that is equally low-tech. The strange thing is, it seems to be spreading almost like wildfire and can (unexpectedly) help fuel the *'efficiency* of development and industry'.

Lazy farming and other low-tech remedies

Philip Trevelyan, former London film-maker – now farmer, musician and entrepreneur – is a very different kind of incomer from the settlers in North America described in the opening section of the chapter. But his approach to the land resonates strongly with the enlightened agricultural measures just mentioned. Opting for life with a different tempo, in the 1970s he and his artist wife, Nelly, moved to Spaunton, a tiny village set in the North York Moors National Park. In 1997, still in creative mode, Trevelyan set up a new enterprise: the Lazy Dog Tool Company, to make hand tools for farmers and growers. What he created, though, turned out to be far more than a slow-tech reaction to weed control through spraying.

Modern agriculture generally involves extensive spraying. The problem is that this high-tech solution – combined with our obsession to erase Nature's natural stubble – is polluting, and it impoverishes the landscape. In the eyes of extreme environmentalists, chemical weed control is anything but effective and cost-efficient. Such sentiments may be rather harsh and wide of the mark, at least to some; tell this to farmers in the tropics, for example, who might lose their entire crop to a pest and thus starve, and see how they react. They do need pesticides from time to time. Yet many, except agricultural capitalists, believe that things have gone out of kilter: costs to the '*robustness* of ecosystems' are fast outweighing benefits to the '*efficiency* for (agro-)industry and development'. Most pesticides kill natural predators & create a need for

Something far more fundamental, though, is that many weeds – far more from pests – are actually beneficial, in all sorts of unexpected ways. In pest a recent issue of *Organic Farming*, John Zarb, an independent researcher icide in sustainable farming, explains just why. Farmers can use chickweed and groundsel, for example, as valuable green manure; fifty years ago New Age farmers and commentators, such as Newman Turner, practised and preached this and much more. Consider, for instance, weedy cereal stubble; far from being waste, this was valuable for over-wintering stock. And before the combine harvester entered the field, Turner would cut the weeds and unripe corn around the field edges as input to silage. It was added robustness, for the land and livestock alike.

These were the messages put out by Turner and others to a new generation of farmers seduced by the promise of an El Dorado from over-zealous agri-firms. The truth is that the latter were hungry for markets and anxious then, just as they are today, to sell chemicals and other products that rid farms of weeds at all costs – all in the name of '*efficiency* of development and industry', however shallow their benefits might turn out.

Undeniably, some weeds such as dock, ragwort, thistles and nettles are – quite literally – a pain, in any farmer's reckoning. In grassland and crop-growing areas, and especially in conservation areas, manual digging and pulling may be a better solution, though, than agro-chemicals; and, at the same time, one that helps retain ecosystem robustness. The problem, though, is that this is not just hard work; it is too costly and inefficient also. Or is it?

Not so, at least if you have the right tools, counters John Zarb, and Philip Trevelyan has demonstrated that an alternative approach is now at hand. The name of his company, Lazy Dog Tools, refers to the first tool produced: a fork for lifting and removing tap-roots such as those of spear-thistle, as well as ragwort and nettles. Other tools followed. Unlike most conventional tools, and a real bonus, is that the Lazy Dog operator works without the need to bend. This may sound only a trivial bonus. Yet many trials have shown, unequivocally, that operators can work for extensive periods with much less physical effort than with the conventional hand tools commonly used for farming and growing; so Trevelyan's slow technology is doing something far more than re-inventing what old-fashioned tillers of the land already had at hand long ago.

It may not be hands-free, but it is an agro-chemical-free method of weed control and eradication, extending far beyond the re-invention of traditional equipment: you could call it true innovation. As Zarb and Trevelyan reported in *Conservation Land Management*, 'Several years of trials led to the development of a range of robust, ergonomically designed hand tools.' It adopts technology that combines functionality and innovation, using ecological solutions to attack the root of the problem.

Far from being inefficient, backward technology, the new tools allow contract Lazy Dog operators, or 'gangs', to work for prolonged periods with minimal fatigue, in most weathers – in winter, early spring or late autumn, which on some farms are relatively slack periods. Use of

nettles don't have tap roots! and they make fine compost.

agricultural sprays, in contrast, can only be used in restricted conditions, adding inefficiency to operations – a matter, though, conveniently brushed aside in most performance evaluations. If it is blowing a gale, for example, neighbours may not appreciate a free dose of herbicide or pesticide falling on their land, or in their garden.

But what about efficiency in the case of lazy weeding; can this approach really be a viable alternative to the advanced farming technologies now so widely available? In a nutshell, it depends how we measure efficiency, but the bottom line, as suggested, is that it can.

Compared with herbicides, John Zarb argues, a 'lazy offensive' on weeds carries many advantages – some obvious, others hidden: for one, weeding, as mentioned, can take place when convenient, not just when the weather conditions happen to be right. Then there is the fact that moving livestock away is unnecessary, a time-consuming activity often required when farmers spray agrochemicals and, incidentally, something that should be accounted for in any proper assessment of efficiency and performance. Adding to Lazy Dog's cost-efficiency is the absence of high capital costs, overheads, recurrent and invisible outlays – an unavoidable down-side of pesticide equipment, especially if you take into account all the costs involved in spraying, and all the safety precautions that legislation now insists on.

Above all, though, Lazy Dog tools and techniques are environmentally friendly, which is undeniably a major plus. Not only that, material excavated can actually be used for composting, in the spirit of recyling, self-sufficiency and sustainability. Although valuable environmental and cost-saving measures, these sorts of issues seldom enter the balance sheets in agricultural capitalism's quest for year-on-year boosts in 'efficiency of industry and development'.

Added to all this, and the hallmark of Lazy Dog tools, is that the complete removal of a weed virtually prevents regrowth the following year, further increasing this slow-tech's efficiency and cost-effectiveness. Of course, you may not spot every weed. Nevertheless, in our orchard, for example, over three successive years, the number of thistles seen and mechanically removed went down from close on 1,000, to less than 100, to about ten. Nowadays, it is very rare to spot even one and, if we do, it is soon zapped with a 'chisel hoe'. Spraying with herbicides, in contrast, unless you use something really deadly (and completely unselective), like the innocuous-sounding 2,4-D or 2,4,5-T, generally needs to be done more frequently, something else conveniently overlooked in efficiency assessments for agro-chemicals.

Undeniably, herbicides and pesticides can be applied in no time at all – that is, of course, once the weather and other conditions are right. Dosing a three-hectare field with agrochemicals, for example to rid it of docks, would take only an hour, or even much less. Low-tech operations, admittedly, are a very much slower way of dealing with the same-sized area. One Lazy Dog trial, for example, was sponsored by Defra, the Department for Environment, Food and Rural Affairs. Between 27 April and 4 May 2004, John Zarb reported in *Organic Farming*, 'some 10,183 docks were removed from three hectares of pasture (used for spring grazing and hay) in 102 man-hours, at a cost of £206 per hectare (or £100 per acre)'. On top of that come the possible transport or accommodation costs of contract gangs, the capital costs of tools (unless work is done by Lazy Dog gangs), time for removal and burning or hot-composting of weeds, meal and refreshment breaks.

On the face of it, then, and compared with crop spraying, slow-tech weed removal is an approach that could not be more inefficient. As already suggested, though, to get a true picture of efficiency, the hidden costs and benefits also need to be unearthed.

In the case of agrochemicals, besides the costs already mentioned, there is another extremely worrying environmental down-side, and an economic one to deal with, that scarcely gets even a mention. The disquieting reality is that water companies have to remove pesticides from our drinking water, at a cost of around £120 million year. It was Jules Pretty and colleagues who put a price tag on those 'externalities'. But the real irony is the fact that water-board tenants in major water catchment areas actually spray docks and thistles routinely.

Clearly, no single farming approach, manual or chemical, can be a magical universal solution. On the one hand, the agro-industry seems unstoppable, given the mistaken belief of many on the payroll that its chemical cocktails are the perfect elixir for more productive land. Yet at the other extreme we see many farm workers still breaking their backs, using hand tools designed a century ago; even if they can afford better ones, they see no reason for change. Some might call that a Luddite approach to land management, and an even crazier one. Lazy Dog approaches to farming, on the other hand, simultaneously tap into both the traditional ('*robustness* of ecosystems') and the new ('*efficiency* of development and industry'). By drawing on both, it is an innovation that seems to be resonating with changing consumer demands. This also mirrors precisely, of course, the modern Luddite's mentality.

On top of that, Lazy Dog sales, perhaps unexpectedly, have taken off, both nationally and abroad. Support for New Age farming tools that value both robustness and efficiency has extended to national organizations, including the UK's environment and rural affairs department, Defra, and the national machinery 'ring organization'. This is a government scheme providing support to farmers through shared machines, computers and other facilities. This helps them improve efficiency through better economies of scale. National radio and TV have also celebrated Lazy Dog approaches. As testament to their benefits, slow-tech gangs have removed thistles and other weeds in many parts of the UK, including the estates of several English celebrities.

More surprising still, perhaps, is that agriculture can benefit from little more than wisdom alone, with virtually no technology. Ecologist Jake Weiner, now at the Royal Veterinary College in Copenhagen, recently explained how on Radio 4's *Learning from Nature*. Simply planting crops at high densities and in two-dimensional patterns, rather than rows, he explained, has the remarkable power to suppress weeds. At high densities, there can be adverse effects on the crops themselves, from overcrowding; so there is a trade-off. However, this arises only at very high crop densities. Hence, what amounts to spending a little extra time turns out to be a helpful, efficiency-promoting exercise in the long-run. What's more, it's an enlightened, no-tech approach to crop growing that minimizes the need for agrochemicals, and helps the land retains its natural robustness.

A step that goes beyond zero-technology or minimal-technology is, paradoxically, to do absolutely nothing at all. Across much of Europe, a forward-looking scheme is now in place which places an obligation on farmers to hold back on production; to retain and conserve a certain percentage of farmland biomass or productivity annually – not just crop it all. The amount that has to be kept unused – a de facto 'protected area' – is assessed on an individual farm basis, depending on local ecological conditions. Any surplus above this level, effectively a production quota, a farmer may harvest and sell.

In some ways, it is an approach that resonates with letting fields 'lie fallow'. It is a long-known farming strategy to rest land after a prolonged period of heavy growing; a traditional way of doing agri-business, and one in operation long before the Luddites arose, and rose up, in the nineteenth century. One way or another, these are low-tech schemes that aim to *optimize*, not *maximize*, harvests. They all help to encourage farmers to become good or better custodians of the environment. By embedding principles of ecological robustness into habitat and land, holding back will benefit conservation; and, at the same time, it will help foster farming efficiency, equity and sustainability over the longer term; in other words, a win-win situation, for farmers and ecologists alike.

Gardens of Eden

Tending the land in ways that retain or re-instil robustness might be one thing. But in our quest to produce more and more, to squeeze everything to the limit, green agricultural technologies in themselves are not sufficient – especially against a backdrop of urban creep, industrialization, and now climate change, too. The land has simply become too overwound, and that's not just the view of hard-headed environmentalists.

As IUCN (the International Union for Conservation of Nature) and other organizations recognize, we need ecosystem protection in varying degrees; and here, we're not just talking about farmland, nor just isolated areas here and there. IUCN offers different categories of protected area, depending on management requirement. Strict nature reserves and national parks, for example, protect more rigorously against consumptive human activities; others, such as protected landscapes (or seascapes) and managed resource protected areas, allow for the sustainable use of natural resources and certain types of intervention.

A further point is that new protected areas are being designed to help alleviate poverty. As Jeffrey McNeely (chief conservation scientist at IUCN), Lea Scherl and colleagues remarked in a report in 2004; 'A healthy environment is not sufficient in itself to alleviate poverty, but equally, any attempt at poverty alleviation that ignores environmental realities will soon be undermined.' An inescapable fact is that the '*robustness* of ecosystems' is not something that can simply be brushed aside when it comes to society's basic needs.

Protected areas of countryside, curiously, have not always been for public benefit; that is if one takes a historical perspective. Many acres of England's forests and other lands, for example, were once 'no-go' areas protected by, and for, its monarchs once they had seized them. One famous area, Sherwood, became a Royal hunting forest after the Norman invasion of 1066, and was popular with many Norman kings, including King John. 'Forest' was actually a legal term, and meant 'an area subject to special Royal laws designed to protect the valuable resources of timber and game'. These laws were strictly and severely imposed by Crown-employed foresters, wardens and rangers; and woe betide unwelcome intruders.

For modernity, though, the state of affairs is generally very different: nowadays, protected areas are put in place more for the benefit of citizens than of rulers. What's more, they provide a time-tested, human-dominated solution (but by no means the only one) for dealing with our overwound world. Not just to alleviate poverty either, for protected areas also provide a buffer, or insurance, against modernity's insistence on greater '*efficiency* of industry and development', whatever the cost.

Enlightened conservation, after all, is something that comes down to sense and sensibility, combined with best scientific practice; it is about sustainable harvests, without undermining the very systems responsible for their production in the first place. Ultimately, protected areas work by retaining or regenerating the '*robustness* of ecosystems'.

Another enlightened, yet long-standing remedy for getting the best out of nature is horticulture. It is an activity, as Colin Tudge points out in *So Shall We Reap*, which amounts to gardening, with or without glass. At its simplest, horticulture is little more than tending plants where they stand. Yet, as Tudge also remarks, horticulture spans the complete spectrum of technical innovation, from the simple right up to advanced hydroponics – crop production using water and nutrients, instead of soil.

What makes even low-tech systems so valuable is that the benefits extend far beyond the production of plants for food, profit and decoration.

A bookshop-cum-coffee shop, where anti-slave papers would later be thrashed out, is an unlikely venue for the beginnings of the first Horticultural Society. But on 7 March 1804, botanist Sir Joseph Banks and six other gentlemen met at James Hatchard's bookshop, in London's Piccadilly, to form Britain's now 200-year-old society. With neither garden nor library, it simply had a mission: the improvement and practice of horticulture. Within twenty years, membership had climbed from a mere seven to 1,500, and it ran floral fêtes and conducted plant trials in a leased garden at Chiswick. What's more, the new society, in the words of Jane Owen and Diarmuid Gavin in *Gardens Through Time*, 'had identified and filled a gaping hole in the market: it had created a focus for the plant craze that was to reinvent the garden'.

The curious thing, though, is that garden fever has not only led to a passion for plants – whether ornamental and exotic species, fashionable plants or simply vegetables. Gardens, it turns out, are also a vital cog in the machinery of national and even international conservation. What they do is actually bolster the benefits of larger, protected areas set up by government and environmental organizations. However you look at it, tending the land through gardens and, of course, larger protected areas, helps re-inject life and robustness back into terrestrial environments. A (big or small) protected area is, after all, an identifiable area containing wildlife or other special features, separated from the harmful activities which undermine its persistence.

Hence a garden is much more than a paradise, or Garden of Eden. For what it can achieve is a safe haven echoing the very same aspirations as the Eden Again Project, in the real Garden of Eden. What I'm referring to here is Mesopotamia – the region in southern Iraq known today as the Tigris–Euphrates delta or Shatt-al-Arab. When Saddam Hussein drained its marshes in the early 1990s, this unbelievable act, coupled with upstream damming, displaced not only the Marsh Arabs but the area's fauna, too: around 90 per cent of the marshes became devoid of resident birds and other wildlife.

As a counterbalance to the harm inflicted, Eden Again and other projects are helping to reinvigorate these internationally famous wetlands, and their occupants, to their former glory. In 2003, for example, local farmers began blowing up earthen dams to restore the flow of water; far from destructive, these low-tech acts of restoration are encouraging the return of previously resident birds and other wildlife. The marbled teal, Basrah reed warbler and other rare birds, for example, were sighted during the 2005 census; not only that, salinities have dropped to levels that will support freshwater fish. Although the re-flooded soils have released noxious hydrogen sulphide and toxins from military ordinance, Joy Sedler, a restoration ecologist at the University of Wisconsin, is optimistic about the marshland's rehabilitation. Sedler served on the Eden Again International Technical Advisory Panel, a group of experts assisting the Iraq Foundation in dealing with what the UN has described as one of the world's worst environmental disasters.

The truth, though, is that much smaller Gardens of Eden – even the humble garden pond (which provides, for example, a breeding habitat for frogs and dwindling populations of other amphibians) – can play a surprisingly helpful role in the conservation of wild species and the maintenance of robustness in natural systems. It might be only low-tech, but in some ways it's a valuable antidote to the collateral that so often follows in the wake of modernity's push for greater '*efficiency* of industry and development'.

Consider, as one illustration, Charles Darwin's gardens at Down House in Kent, England. He might have used the 7.2 hectare estate for walks, inspiration and a test bed for his ideas on natural selection and evolution, but the grounds also harbour rare and unusual plants: among them the Comit Orchid, several 'red-listed' (globally threatened) species of grassland fungi, sweet chestnut and mulberry – trees which were mature even when Darwin was alive. The estate has survived, relatively unscathed, since his death in 1882 to the present day; one could say that the legacy left by Down House and its gardens is a safe haven for wildlife species, as well as a celebration of the great man's genius.

Yet it would be wrong to suppose that the grand gardens at Down House, the highly ambitious Eden Project in Cornwall and the Royal Botanic Gardens in Sydney are the only sort of gardens that can help stem the ebb of wildlife populations. Even a simple backyard garden, and urban green spaces, can play their part, too. In fact, some rare species of mammals, including many different bats, spend part of their lives more in cities than outside them.

The conservation benefit, naturally, comes not so much from each individual garden or green space, but from the collective network, or mosaic, that arises. Each small garden, or pond, helps create larger ecological corridors. These provide life-sustaining avenues along which, as Jakub Szaki at Warsaw's Institute of Physical Planning of Municipal Economy explains, much can happen: animals can travel, migrate and meet mates; plants can propagate; genetic interchange may take place (although this may not always be a good thing); individuals can re-colonize habitats where local extinction has taken place; and organisms can move in response to local disturbances and disasters.

In the case of disturbance, ecological corridors can help combat the effects of large-scale as well as local events. In an increasingly greenhouse world, for example, movement to the cooler or wetter regions (north and west in the UK), or to higher altitudes (approximately 170 metres altitude per degree centigrade rise) is the natural response of plant communities. Besides the right environmental conditions, though, migration to more equable climes requires a continuum of suitable habitats; and this is just what many small gardens, as a network, help to provide.

Like plants, many animals, of course, will also migrate as a result of hotter summers; the distribution of several birds and butterflies, in fact, is already showing a general northward migration – mirroring, presumably, the opposite trend in the southern hemisphere. Nevertheless nature, like business, is full of trade-offs. One disagreeable fact is that ecological corridors smooth the passage for unwelcome insects, pests and diseases, as well as resident species, particularly when the steam really starts to rise with a vengeance.

In fact, as Richard Bisgrove and Paul Hadley, at the University of Reading's Centre for Horticulture and Landscape, reported recently, termites have already been found in Cornwall; similarly, in the USA, where summer temperatures are appreciably higher than in the UK, pests such as the Japanese beetle are now making the cultivation of many garden plants difficult. On the other hand, it also has to be said, pest control is precisely what gardeners try to do, often quite successfully, in their painstaking attempts to modify and manicure a natural habitat into a miniature Garden of Eden.

Whether your garden is in the backyard, on a rooftop or somewhere bigger (or you don't have one at all), one thing is for sure: this timeless, time-consuming pursuit extends beyond greening the home and providing an oasis of tranquillity for the tired and overworked. It is also something far more than what Francis Bacon considered a garden to represent back in 1625: an art form and the hallmark of a civilized society. For it achieves something even greater, as Bisgrove and Hadley suggest in their 2002 report, *Gardening in the Global Greenhouse*: 'The role of gardens and parks as innumerable components in a green web, supporting and at times replacing the fragile network of natural ecosystems, has been little explored . . .' Not only that, they add, 'these millions of landscapes, large and small, will have a vital role to play in reinforcing a system of ecological corridors through which wildlife can migrate in response to climate change'. Simply put, it is a common-sense remedy for planting robustness, where it counts most.

What's more, Bisgrove and Hadley conclude, 'the beneficial effects of good soil management and maintenance of a healthy plant cover in coping with climatic extremes in gardens provide a model which, if followed on a national and international scale, will do much to slow the pace of climate change and to reduce its impacts'; and that is aside from giving future generations the chance of experiencing the simple pleasure of sitting under a tree that could easily be Darwin's age, were he still alive.

It would, of course, be a mistake to view gardens and bigger areas of protection only through rose-tinted spectacles; opening the door to pests, as mentioned, is one less agreeable characteristic. There is another issue, too. Some of these areas, at least on the surface, might seem unduly large and wasteful of space; areas that we could put to better use in other ways, for example under the plough – or simply to fuel the *'efficiency of industry and development'* – rather than stifling it by cutting down or cutting out use. Some might call the insurance and over-provision instilled by protected areas as unnecessary and 'inefficient', rather like the principles of robustness, through over-engineering, used in our Bentley back in the 1930s.

That view of protected areas, though, is very shallow and wide of the mark. By and large, the movement of species to new areas through gardens and larger national parks has been beneficial. Green areas, quite plainly, provide modernity with multiple benefits and services which flow beyond their borders. They might seem old-fashioned, but they are an effective, time-tested approach to land management and development.

Opening up the gateways for disease transmission

Not shutting down so many abattoirs is another common-sense, low-tech measure that might have gone a long way towards containing the 2001/2 foot-and-mouth epidemic in Britain. Of course, no one can pretend that this so-called efficiency measure for the livestock industry was the only decisive factor in triggering the outbreak and influencing its spread. Border controls, livestock culling policies and decisions on vaccination played a major part, too. An undeniable fact, though, is that closure of so many abattoirs did not prove to be such a great service to the '*efficiency* of industry and development' after all. Prior to the 2001/2 epidemic, for example, the last foot-and-mouth outbreak in England was in 1969, but was confined more or less to Cheshire, in the north-west of the country. Back then, though, slaughtering took place locally in abattoirs; animals did not travel right across the country, the perfect vehicle for disease transmission and spread. As Colin Tudge points out, the past sixty years have seen a steady decline in the number of Britain's abattoirs, and a corresponding need for longer journeys. By the 1990s, about three-quarters of those remaining had been closed. Between then and the close of 2000, numbers had dropped from about 1,300 to little more than 300.

More frequent and longer journeys (usually a matter of hours) – coupled with a short incubation period – happen to be what is needed to get foot-and-mouth disease off to a sporting start. And that is precisely what the virus did: it got going at full throttle. Instead, as Tudge explains, the very opposite is what should happen: 'In general, animals should travel as little as possible in the course of their brief lives, and should be slaughtered locally.' If this pushes up the cost, Tudge and many others feel it is a price worth paying for meat that is produced more safely and humanely.

But that is not the end of this tale. Not shutting down so many abattoirs might well have helped maintain the health of a completely different industry, too. For the devastating blow that England's tourism industry suffered at the dawn of the new millennium was not through a fall in the national or international economy, nor better deals on offer elsewhere, nor the impact of terrorism. The unprecedented downturn in tourism revenue that followed actually arose from something linked to farming and the food chain: the 2001/2 foot-and-mouth outbreak. Because in order to control the spread of infection much of the countryside became off limits, tourists (and residents) were not free to travel wherever they wished.

You could say that modern agriculture, just like the manufacture of computers, is all about lean supply chains. It can be a hazardous gamble, though; a bit like playing Russian roulette – not just for the industry itself, but also because of the collateral damage, the unanticipated knock-on effects from agriculture to other industries. Without a doubt, greater attention to the '*robustness* of ecosystems' makes the environment more buoyant and productive. Not only that, and added to the bargain, comes greater '*efficiency* of industry and development': in other words, a deal too good for modernity to miss out on.

Nature's shakers and breakers

Delve deeply into what counts and it turns out that the real makers of the world are species, the products of nature's own assembly line. Ultimately, they are what influences the robustness of the land (and the sea) – and the economies dependent upon them – as modernity marches to the beat of the corporate drum. That is why they matter so much, whether we're talking agribusiness, or anything else driven by and benefiting from the '*efficiency* of development and industry'.

Quite plainly, not all species count equally; at least not from our own perspective. Take potatoes, rice, wheat and other crops, which together make up the global larder. These species are of disproportionate economic and cultural importance in comparison with the small handful represented; the same is true for the organisms currently exploited for drugs and other useful compounds. Since these are species indispensable for life and prosperity, modernity should try to avoid development activities that harm them and erode robustness of natural systems underlying their production.

Yet other species we would happily do without. Consider, as a prime example, the zebra mussel, and the ecological and economic damage that tiny hitch-hiker wreaked around the Great Lakes in little more than a decade. Back in its natural habitat and local ecosystem, of course, this mollusc is likely to be quite an important species. So it is not so much a question of its existence, as a question of where it is invading. The problem is, zebra mussels are just one of a growing number of invasive alien species now plaguing our waters and lands – and quite a different kettle of fish from simply 'non-native' species like tomatoes introduced into, for example, Europe.

Besides species harming the environment and human interests, the reverse, of course, is equally true: collateral damage from development activities is often detrimental to species, sometimes including humans. Consider, as just one poignant reminder already mentioned, the indiscriminate use of antibiotics in agriculture. Besides resistance brought on by routine use, detrimental effects on human health may also follow – for example, as are have seen, in the wake of the use of the antibiotic avoparcin, once administered on farms to control and treat livestock infections.

How greatly species in combination – their collective biodiversity – matters, though, is still far from settled; that is something very different from individual species, and it continues to engage the minds of theoretical ecologists and conservation scientists alike. Which cogs in nature's machinery are redundant, surplus to needs, is the million-dollar question. But as Jeff McNeely at IUCN once remarked: 'I would certainly find it difficult to come up with any species that is redundant, and that we could do without. Any time I feel that I have identified such a species, I immediately start wondering whether I truly understand the role of that species in its ecosystem. I sometimes wonder whether we are being arrogant even to pose such a question.'

Certainly few scientists today would deny that the accelerating erosion of species from many areas (and the world overall) is hugely damaging.

Similarly, the addition of species – at least alien invasive ones – has become an ever greater threat to ecosystems and economies. The tremendous mixing or homogenization of species, accelerated by globalization, will result in some species becoming more abundant, while others will decline in numbers – some perhaps to the point of extinction. Either way, it can be bad news economically. Even a single species can wreak havoc: in the Western USA, for example, loss of ecosystem services as the salt cedar replaced native species caused impact amounting to an estimated 7 to 16 *billion* dollars loss over fifty-five years.

One way of keeping nature more intact – retaining its robustness – is a simple, low-tech solution known long ago: through protected areas, to safeguard critical 'hotspots', the places and species that really count. That seems our best bet for buffering the power of a high-tech world, which is eroding natural capital so rapidly. Another undeniable fact is that high-tech is by no means a sure fix for getting the environment and society out of the state both are now in – partly, or largely, through globalization, pushed along by the World Trade Organization. Yet this same organization, together with the Convention on Biological Diversity and other international agreements, could, ironically, be invaluable instruments for regulating the ebb and flow of species. Even in today's world, species remain a mainspring of the global economy, aside from their more fundamental role in stocking the global larder.

CHAPTER 4 FROM COAST TO COAST

Overwound and in need of repair

Rise and fall of coral reefs

Maintaining a robust system that caters for the expectations of conservation and economic development is a tough call, anywhere in the world, and nowhere is it more challenging than on the coast. Around 60 per cent of the world's population – close on 4 billion people – now lives within sixty kilometres of the sea, and this number is increasing rapidly due to a combination of population growth, migration and urbanization.

The unrestrained pursuit of diverse human activities seeking exclusive use of coastal areas inevitably leads to competition for finite resources, environmental degradation, economic and social disruption. One growing problem is the fallout from industries eager for a slice of action on the coast, yet often unaware or unconcerned about any accompanying environmental damage. The consequences can be catastrophic. As evidence, witness the increasing toll of lives, property and investment lost as a result of erosion, coastal storms and other episodic events.

Coastal scenes like this border on a nightmare. It would naturally be naïve to place all the blame for this sort of fallout with modernity, or simply heavy population pressures. After all, the wake of destruction after nature strikes a mighty blow seems to be beyond our control, whatever we have done or not done to the coast beforehand. On closer inspection, though, it turns out that the havoc wreaked is invariably made worse by modernity turning its back on the 'robustness of ecosystems'. It is one inevitable outcome of unfettered development of our coasts. This is bad news for development and, of course, damaging for ecosystems too. One ecosystem often caught in the line of fire, one now receiving shrapnel from all directions – sea, land and air – is coral reefs.

When intact and robust, coral reefs represent one of the greatest manifestations of life on earth, dwarfing even the most ambitious engineering structures of humankind. What is so extraordinary is that they represent the work of such tiny animals – coral 'polyps' (related to sea anemones) – assisted by microscopic algae called zooxanthellae; these organisms, it has long been known, are vital to coral health. The sheer size of reefs, and how nature achieves this, makes Australia's Great Barrier Reef, in particular, one of the great wonders of the world.

Considered one way, coral reefs are nature's own solar-powered, aquatic 'food factories'; throughout the tropics, their complex habitat and high biological productivity provide the basis for major fisheries, and the livelihood of coastal communities. Aside from fish, though, reefs harbour a bewildering variety of organisms – in fact they are home to more than 25 per cent of all marine life.

In engineering terms, reefs function as self-repairing breakwaters; that is because they are renewable, like other living resources. Provided they remain robust and in healthy condition, and do not become too degraded, they go on perpetuating themselves, year-on-year, offering free natural protection against storms and wave action. That is one reason why yachtsmen, for one, love them as well as fear them (the latter, because of the navigational hazard they present). The fact is that, even a small, semi-submerged patch reef can provide a calm anchorage – with nothing but the reef, barely visible, separating the yacht from breaking waves and 2,000 miles of open ocean.

As TV documentaries, the press and research are discovering, coral reefs – which have been in the seas for around 200 million years, and are something we've always taken for granted – are disappearing; and it is happening in the mere twinkling of a geological eye. Most reefs today are between 5,000 and 10,000 years old. Yet what has taken nature centuries to build can be destroyed, or seriously degraded, more or less instantly.

One recent study in the Caribbean, for example, points to a staggering 80 per cent decline in living coral over just thirty years. This bleak picture came from scientists Toby Gardner and Isabelle Côté and colleagues, then at the University of East Anglia, now working in Canada. They analyzed bucketfuls of data collected at more than 200 sites from sixty-five separate studies, publishing their findings in the journal *Science*; so the state the Caribbean reefs are reportedly in is hardly a one-off, unrepresentative snapshot.

The global situation seems little better, with 30 per cent of reefs already severely damaged and around 60 per cent predicted to go by 2030. It is not just reefs themselves that could be carrying a one-way ticket. Increasing numbers of reef-dependent species risk extinction too. Decline in coral, providers of a reef's many colours, may be a symptom of ill health; but what about the cause?

Reefs have always had their ups and downs, long before any human society arrived on our shores; that is undeniable. Hurricanes, tsunami strikes, disease and geological events have all been influential. In the past, the really big natural events shaping reefs have typically occurred over millennia. In contrast, the devastating effects from modernity, and expanding populations – even just eking out a living – in developing countries, have happened over a much more compressed time period: a matter of decades.

Furthermore, the wake of destruction following natural episodic events is a good deal worse once reefs and other coastal systems are already weakened by our own actions; especially those from short-sighted, ill-conceived development plans. Within only a brief spell of time, we have managed to carve a deeply ingrained imprint on reefs and leave an indelible legacy for future generations to inherit.

The fallout from chronic human activities is not always newsworthy, yet it is highly pervasive. For it can chip away at the 'robustness of ecosystems' as destructively as more eye-catching events like an oil spill.

It is just that it is less obvious and happens more gradually. Particularly destructive are coastal habitat loss, erosion and sedimentation; the by-products of dredging and creating artificial land. Often this is done in order to build new hotels, houses and marinas – or any other development features that someone has decided must go on the coast.

The squeeze from swelling human populations, as mentioned, puts the '*robustness* of ecosystems' on the line, too. Anyone who has witnessed, first-hand, the stretch of coastline south of Colombo in Sri Lanka will know how the sheer numbers of people, and sardine-packed dwellings, can create a very overwound environment. It is the same in much of South-east Asia and the Caribbean, too. As the human population rises, what's more, it is a problem that is hardly going to disappear.

From a global view, though, capitalism and corporate greed, development for short-term gain, has become an equal or even more powerful driving force. One insidious by-product of our wish for ever greater '*efficiency* of industry and development' is sedimentation. It is a problem, though, that results from poor management of the land, as well as from over-zealous construction and development along the coast. Particularly serious is deforestation, whether to satisfy a product-hungry society (for timber), hungry agribusinesses or other non-sustainable farming practices. Either way, downstream effects, quite literally, come as part of the package: we are talking, in particular, of soil erosion and transport of sediment down rivers. Once dumped in the sea, the fallout of suspended material smothers, damages and kills coral.

Added to sedimentation is increasing pollution from oil and other compounds that are far more harmful. One category, ironically, is the latest generation of 'lower toxicity' anti-fouling paints, used to keep the underneath of ships and smaller boats clean; these new compounds, containing so-called 'booster biocides' (herbicides), were produced in the aftermath of paints containing the deadly agent TBT (tributyl tin) – a synthetic compound hailed by many as the most toxic ever produced on the planet.

Nor should we overlook the crippling effects of warming sea temperatures on coral reef robustness. One consequence, and a problem increasingly linked to climate change, is coral bleaching. This is an ailment resulting from corals expelling their keepers, their guest microscopic algae (zooxanthellae). Remove, partially or completely, these residents from their coral host, as happens during coral bleaching, and the coral becomes pale and unhealthy, hence the term. Worse still, it may actually die; what you end up with then is a ghostly collection of whitened coral skeletons, sometimes reduced to a pile of rubble. It is a spectacle that could not be more different from the colourful marine cloak which is a reef's normal appearance and condition.

Following the 1998 El Niño Southern Oscillation (ENSO), which, like other El Niños, warmed up certain tropical seas, 90 per cent of corals in much of the Indian Ocean died. More worrying still, the road to recovery is a long haul. If that's not enough, we now know that 'booster biocides' can have a similar detrimental effect. These chemicals, even in tiny concentrations, can cause corals' resident algae, quite literally, to up sticks and 'leave home', too.

In the case of the Caribbean reefs, the good news is that some are recovering. But the bad news, as Toby Gardner, Isabelle Côté and collaborators explain, is that the new coral communities seem to be different from the old ones. The million-dollar question – and one not just confined to the Caribbean – is how well already weakened or altered reefs will be able to respond to warming sea temperatures and sea level rise linked to global climate change. Curiously, this is a process that began in Luddite times, kick-started by the Industrial Revolution, and has now kicked in with a vengeance.

Rising temperatures are not the only worrying effect, though. There is the problem of increasing acidification of the oceans, too. Like atmospheric and ocean warming, it is happening as a result of the large volumes of carbon dioxide being emitted into the atmosphere. The irony here is that a coral's skeleton is made up of limestone, in other words calcium carbonate – a substance comprising (besides calcium) carbon and oxygen atoms; so one might expect that atmospheric carbon dioxide, which has the same constituents, would be good for coral. Yet that is true only when the carbon dioxide is at an appropriate level, which today is being far exceeded.

As we enter an increasingly greenhouse world, more atmospheric carbon dioxide enters the oceans. This creates more acidic conditions, undermining the process of skeletal formation in corals; and to the detriment of their health, too. We have already gone from pre-Industrial Revolution concentrations of around 280 parts per million to present-day levels of some 380 parts per million. If the amount climbs to 500 parts per million, according to marine ecologists, calcification in virtually everything in the ocean will halt: not just in corals but in microscopic algae with a calcareous coating, too; one example is the armour-plated 'coccolithophores'. The fact that these organisms mop up carbon dioxide – including the vast amounts produced, on land, as greenhouse gas emissions – means that their loss would be bad enough. On top of that, however, these tiny but extremely abundant organisms produce a gas which, via other compounds, forms the 'seeds', or particles, that are so essential in the formation of low clouds across the open ocean. And low clouds have a major cooling effect on our climate. In many ways coccolithophores, like corals, exert a tremendous influence on the 'robustness of ecosystems'.

As the oceans warm up, this may also make the oceans slightly more acidic. (Additionally, warming makes carbon dioxide leak out of the oceans and weakens their ability to absorb surplus carbon dioxide in the atmosphere). However, overall, the effects of temperature on the ocean's acidity are far exceeded by the effects on increasing acidity driven by rising concentrations of atmospheric carbon dioxide levels in the ocean. This is now becoming very serious, as is the direct, 'cooking' effect of temperature, especially on coral reefs.

Perhaps less obviously, another human activity has also had devastating effects on coral reefs: fishing. But we are not just talking about the direct effects of removing too many fish, and leaving insufficient individuals behind to sustain the stocks; that is bad enough, and has happened right across the globe, not just on reefs, but more or less everywhere that people like to fish. On top of this, problems also arise from collateral damage inflicted through fishing. Believe it or not, fishing has become one of humanity's most heavy-handed, non-sustainable, extractive enterprises, on a par with deforestation on land. But it has happened in some unexpected ways.

Marine ecologists have long known that parrot-fish, although not the tastiest of fish, are something far more than attractive residents of coral reefs. Like other herbivores, parrot-fish are natural manicurists; by removing dead bits of coral and cropping algae, they help keep reefs sparkling, healthy and robust. Upsetting the balance by over-harvesting these herbivorous fish, though, can quickly result in something far more serious than loss of the daily cleaner; in a matter of decades, or less, the reef quickly turns from a colourful and productive system dominated by corals, to one overgrown by fleshy algae, followed by a population explosion of sea urchins. Eventually their rasping jaws may leave nothing but bare rock. This is something that could not be more different from a coral reef or, in fact, a natural ecosystem of any sort. Simply put, without care and attention, a reef can quickly lose robustness and flip into a changed state.

Scientists now realize that both the vulnerability and robustness of changed reef states hangs in the balance between different 'functional' herbivore groups; these are assemblages of animals dominated by parrot-fish and other fish, but include very different animals, including sea urchins. Ecologists David Bellwood and Terry Hughes at James Cook University in Australia classify these herbivores as 'bioeroders' (which remove dead corals, promoting the settlement of live ones); 'scrapers' (which remove algae and sediment); and 'grazers' (which remove seaweeds, preventing coral overgrowth and shading).

The problem, though, is that if their balance is upset and leads to a changed reef state, this invariably means an undesirable reef state. Sometimes it is business as usual: if, for example, loss of one species is compensated for by the actions of another; in other words, if there is redundancy. But loss of this redundancy can be costly, even though modernity often treats it as 'unproductive baggage', superfluous to requirements. Urchins and fish, for example, can substitute for each other to some degree, in that the manicuring service may well continue. The problem, though, is that the grazing power of urchins, and hence erosion, is generally far more destructive than that of fish. So if the balance shifts, allowing urchins to proliferate, it spells trouble ahead. Dislodged corals, degraded reefs and even destroyed reefs in the Galapagos bear testament to extraordinary mechanical power of urchins' jaws. When it comes to these animals it is, quite literally, strength in numbers.

To help prevent the deterioration of coral reefs (and other ecosystems) – whether from fishing or from more direct pressures – one solution is to let them do what they do naturally, if given half the chance: self-regulation, to help things keep going against the odds. This, of course, is one hallmark of robustness, that magical whiz which helps to 'empower' systems. Writing in a recent issue of *Trends in Ecology and Evolution*, Terry Hughes and colleagues highlight the invaluable role of resilience (the term often used for robustness in ecology). They consider it, essentially, as 'the extent to which ecosystems can absorb recurrent natural and human perturbations and continue to regenerate without slowly degrading or unexpectedly flipping into alternate states'.

The reality, though, as coral reef studies now confirm, is that without deliberately building in safeguards through 'diligent management' – something as important for nature as for businesses – ecosystems can easily shift between alternate stable states; the switch from a reef-dominated system to a non-living one, as mentioned, bears testament to this unwelcome spiral of decline leading to a fall in marine health.

It hardly takes rocket science, or marine science, to figure out that reducing the root cause of disturbance in the first place is the surest way of preventing catastrophic failure of reef robustness. Less obviously, though, it also hangs on the balance of its resident species, like parrot-fish and urchins – in other words, functional herbivore groups, and sometimes its non-residents, too. Knowing how many and which of the myriad species present are essential, though, and which may be superfluous to 'normal' requirements, is a very different matter. For ecology, in fact, it has been tantamount to cracking the Da Vinci Code.

Traditionally, a good many ecologists and conservationists have tuned their antennae to which species are present (or summary measures of biodiversity). They have focused on this as much as or more than on what species do for a living; and, as different herbivore groups demonstrate in the case of coral reefs, their balance is a big driver of reef fate and health. Interest, understandably, has concentrated on cod, turtles, dolphins and the like, as well other species of commercial or scientific importance, plus, of course, ones threatened with extinction – just as attention has been on tigers, elephants, and so on, on land.

Variety undoubtedly is the spice of life. It is starting to look, though, as if a purely species-oriented focus is insufficient. One reason is that it is proving remarkably difficult to know, for sure, whether high, intermediate or low levels of species richness confer greater 'robustness of ecosystems' – and help carry them through adversity, so that they come out of it still intact, or at least functioning; much, it turns out, hangs on whether species happen to be high or low in the food chain, and on much more besides.

A far safer bet, as Terry Hughes and colleagues point out, is a deeper understanding of the role of biodiversity in ecosystem processes. This acknowledges, as mentioned, the need to safeguard key functional groups of, for example, herbivorous fish and corals. In the case of corals, what really matters for reef functioning is the build-up of skeletal calcium carbonate and the provision of shelter – something governed at least partly by the shape of the coral colony, rather than by their particular biological identity.

It is also clear that, despite the cautionary caveats ecologists like to add, higher species richness *can* provide at least some ecological insurance against environmental (and scientific) uncertainty; evidence is accumulating, for example, that high-diversity marine ecosystems have greater levels of functional redundancy, and hence robustness, than their impoverished counterparts. On the other hand, as Hughes and colleagues point out, that is only half the story. For if all the species within a functional group react in the same way to a disturbance, such as pollution or overfishing, extra species do not lead to strength in numbers: just like a pack of cards, they can all fall together, when the chips are down. But if all species happen not to respond in the same way, it may be a case of 'the more the merrier', if robustness is what counts – especially when there is a mixed bag of environmental assaults or insults. Hence, in low diversity situations – coral reefs of the Arabian/Persian Gulf and Bermuda being classic examples – it is probably wise, for insurance, to hang on to as many species as possible, just in case.

Little short of a paradigm shift, delving into nature's inner workings using robustness as a tool is radically changing how we think about disturbance and recovery, even their very concepts. According to systems ecologist Magnus Nyström at Stockholm University, this broadens the perspective from recovery at the area disturbed to include the sources of robustness of surrounding areas that help keep reefs healthy, and in particular adorned by coral – rather than less agreeable organisms, or no organisms at all. Put another way, we need to assess and actively manage robustness, rather than merely symptoms of its loss, like decline in the amount of living coral carpeting a reef.

What we also need, as Bellwood and Hughes urge, are new ways to measure robustness, for better custodianship of ecosystems and to cope with uncertainty and surprise. At Warwick University's Department of Biological Sciences, we developed one recently in collaboration with Warwick mathematicians Matt Keeling and Ian Stewart. As a test case, we analysed a massive dataset on living coral collected from Thailand by British reef ecologist Barbara Brown over more than twenty-five years. Our 'index of robustness' adopts a probabilistic approach. On a scale of 0 to 1, it considers the likelihood of a reef or any other system feature remaining robust over time and at different localities, simultaneously, in the face of (as it happened) climatic disturbances and sedimentation. We are hopeful that applications of the index might extend to all sorts of other systems, perhaps to ones even outside biology.

But as Hughes and other researchers also point out, in the meantime, and in view of other uncertainties about coral reefs and fisheries, the creation of more and larger marine reserves – no-take areas – must be one of our highest priorities: we need to protect the '*robustness* of ecosystems', as well as measure it, and in this respect reefs are no different.

Part of the solution, one could say, is low-tech and is almost as simple as going out fishing: to stop harmful human activities, including fishing, in certain carefully selected areas. Just as no-take reserves maintain and actually boost fish stocks, so too marine protected areas offer good insurance for managing robustness in reefs and other ecosystems more generally; holding back, quite literally, gives undeniable paybacks, whether we are talking of the Caribbean, the Red Sea or the Galapagos Islands.

The Southern Sinai experience

On a small-scale map, Southern Sinai is a V-shaped piece of land forming, near enough, an equilateral triangle. The Gulf of Suez defines its western margin, the Gulf of Aqaba the eastern, while the lower apex tumbles abruptly over the reef crest into the Red Sea. The triangle's upper side merges with Northern Sinai. This continues northwards to the Mediterranean, where the Nile discharges what remains of its waters, sediment and life-promoting nutrients, following the high-risk bypass operation brought about by the Aswan Dam.

In reality, of course, Sinai is far greater than a geometric shape or grains of sand. Holiday brochures vividly portray what is on offer, and prospective travellers are lured by a land like no other: an exotic blend of Middle Eastern desert and the deep blue waters of the Red Sea. And if that is not enough, Southern Sinai is parcelled up into linked marine and terrestrial Protectorates. As the chapter reveals, though, the benefits extend far beyond the obvious role of conservation. Sinai is not actually a country at all; formerly Israeli, and the nearby Tiran Islands once the realm of Saudi Arabia, it is now Egyptian territory, and a national asset cherished by many as greatly as Tutankhamun and other bejewelled treasures.

It would be expecting too much for the coral reefs to be all yours, though the experience certainly is. Because of attractive holiday packages, some choice spots are nowadays subjected to more than 100,000 dives annually. It might seem like sardine-packing, and in a sense it is. But education and diving regulations to minimize damage and protect coral reef robustness are taken seriously. In heavily dived spots, for instance, it is 'drift dives' only; the boat simply tracks the divers, without need to anchor and damage the corals below, though many spots now have fixed moorings to prevent such disturbance.

Despite undeniable mass tourism, and very heavy demands placed on some reefs, the system seems to be holding up – remaining robust – that is, reef health, visitor numbers and the value of tourism investments. This happy circumstance has prevailed through a combination of ambitious plans and visionary thinking on the part of the Southern Sinai Protectorates Development Programme.

While prosperity and well-being have always been paramount in the Egyptian government's eyes, so too has conservation. The Protectorates are testament to this, covering a land and sea area of close on 10,000 square kilometres: this has made, in effect, Egypt's entire Gulf of Aqaba coast into a single, large protected area.

Unsually, though, it has been conservation *for* and *by* tourism development. Realizing that strict environmental regulation actually enhances the tourism product and, at the same, increases the value of their investments, many developers have turned a brighter shade of green. Put another way, they see the wisdom of '*robustness* of ecosystems' not as a stricture, but to benefit '*efficiency* of industry and development'. Through a vested interest in conservation the developers have, in effect, taken over several activities normally done by marine biologists and environmental scientists – checking reef condition, compliance with environmental controls, and so on. That's Southern Sinai's distinctive branding and, what's more, the driving force for all tourism and economic development activities in the whole region.

What the Egyptian authorities have done, curiously, is to expand tourism development at full throttle, but only in selected zones, and with numerous environmental safeguards and the strictest tourism regulations imaginable. Put slightly differently, 'holding back' is what has helped propel economic development forward. It is certainly counter-intuitive, but it seems to have worked. What's more (global politics permitting), tourism on Egypt's Red Sea Riviera is expected to continue long into the future.

Beginning with little more than 1,000 beds in 1988, for example, tourism capacity on the Gulf of Aqaba expanded to over 15,000 in a matter of a decade. To maintain quality, though, a threshold of 160,000 beds has been set, a level that may be reached by 2017.

In all sorts of other ways, too, the creation and expansion of networked protected areas on the Gulf of Aqaba has been an enlightened, forward-thinking project. Critical to success, according to Canadian coastal manager Michael Pearson and Ibrahim Shehata at the Egyptian Environmental Affairs Agency, reporting in a special issue of *Parks*, has been the fact that legislation has provided the nature conservation sector with the wherewithal, the clout, to apply conservation measures. Yet, paradoxically, effective management has largely come about due to the fact that these powers were used sparingly, in favour of a more conciliatory educational process.

Through lack of funds, management can easily run out of steam, and operations effectively come to a grinding halt; a backward (and undignified) move if ever there was one. In Southern Sinai, things have been different. Simple but effective financing means this is not a constraint, for reasons Pearson and Shehata explain: 'The running of the Protectorates has, in fact, endured through the collection of entrance fees. The Gulf of Aqaba Protectorates can now function without subsidy from central government funding.'

The achievements have been remarkable. Government objectives are being realized, coral reefs and associated marine life all along the Gulf of Aqaba coast are now fully protected. Often little more than a wish list, maintaining or re-instilling ecosystem robustness reflects strict compliance with zero-discharge policies and prohibition of coastal alterations. At the same time, Egypt's fisheries in Sinai waters are regulated, through completely closed or seasonally closed areas; these are, in effect, marine reserves, a simple but highly effective approach to fishery management. On top of that, there is consensus on management issues with resident communities, including the Bedouin, without whom the protectorates could not properly operate.

Crossing the tipping point, to when the Protectorates began to function, instead of exist – being merely a 'paper park' (all that could be claimed until 1988) – is a remarkable story. It is also testament to the vision of Pearson, Shehata and colleagues such as Omar Hassan in the Egyptian Environmental Affairs Agency. Creating a robust system that reconciles the often conflicting needs of conservation and economic expansion is challenging, in Egypt as much as anywhere else. What we're talking of, after all, is a state whose population long ago hit the 60 million mark, and with very divergent priorities to accommodate their needs. On top of that was the desire to instil principles of inter-generational equity. In this way, future generations should also benefit from the project, instead of having to pick up the pieces – a sad tale of what has happened in the case of the Aswan Dam, and in the aftermath of many other over-zealous, narrowly conceived projects failing to achieve long-lasting 'efficiency of industry and development'.

Such an ambitious venture could never be plain sailing, and few would deny that management of the Southern Sinai Protectorates has had its ups and downs. With thousands of tourists visiting an area, let's face it, some environmental damage is inevitable. Heavily dived reefs, what's more, can never be a match against pristine Red Sea reefs or reefs beyond the limits of all but the most ambitious adventurers, those prepared to travel to the ends of the earth. But that's not the only comparison possible. In the case of the Southern Sinai/Gulf of Aqaba waters, the plain truth is that reefs here are in far better shape than they would be in the face of uncontrolled, runaway tourism development: that's the alternative, in today's world, and a pathway that many governments with similar coastal assets have been lured into following.

The heart of the Southern Sinai Protectorates is the Gulf of Aqaba's west coast. Formally, it is a continuous, multiple-use protected area. Such language, though, belies what has made the region so conducive to economic development yet, without this, at the same time, causing the environment to spiral into decline. The system's foundations are three distinct units, arranged in a simple but strategic way: strict conservation areas, sandwiching ribbons of tourism and other development – which, as protected coastlines, are also tightly managed. The smooth running, almost free-wheeling, of the whole marine protected area reflects what amounts to conservation for, not against, development.

It is, of course, what parks and protected areas generally strive for. All too often, though, vision, intention and accomplishment – of any sort – are quite a different matter. Without concerted effort, on the ground conservation action easily fizzles out, or never even gets going, and corporate interests quickly step in; and, without a watchful eye, they can quickly develop a coastal area to death. For protected areas to deliver anything useful, going from aspiration to action is what counts, and to a large degree that is what has happened in Southern Sinai.

The first unit off the production line was the Ras Mohammed Marine Protected Area in 1983. As mentioned, though, it did not come into operation until five or six years later. When it did, as Pearson and Shehata described in *Parks*, this hailed the beginning of a process that would serve as a role model for Egyptian protected area management into the twenty-first century. One immediate action was to more than double the existing boundaries of Ras Mohammed to 233 square kilometres – and designate the area a national park.

The management approach, though not just in Ras Mohammed, was daring, novel and cunning. For one thing, Pearson and Shehata are eager to point out, there was 'the conscious decision to identify and implement management objectives with only a rudimentary knowledge of the nature of the resources being managed, and to adjust management as parallel monitoring programmes identified immediate resource management and conservation needs'. In the minds of most conservationists – certainly of mainstream ecologists – expecting to manage a marine system about whose features close on zilch was known was tantamount to folly verging on heresy. Put another way, it was a bit like shooting from the hip, but with few if any bullets. Yet simplicity of approach can be powerful and effective.

For on closer scrutiny, it turns out that there was much wisdom in this bold and cavalier approach to 'staking out territory' so early on. Normally, in complete contrast, parks can be declared only once an area is proved to be really special – for wildlife, as a landscape or seascape, for cultural reasons, and so on. As part of the justification process, scientists and conservationists are called on to survey the area – its environmental conditions, wildlife, threats, management constraints – at an extraordinary level of detail. In the case of marine protected areas, this entails above-water surveys and also meticulous underwater assessments.

The problem, though, is that survey work is time-consuming; doing it properly can take years, especially when there are specimens to identify and bucketfuls of data to analyse. But while the surveys are going on, the 'protected area in waiting' remains, of course, unprotected. In the meantime, tourism and other developers are quick to step in and build. In no time at all, hotels and other infrastructures can spring up, one after the other – quickly giving rise to 'coastal creep', just as poorly regulated development on land blights the landscape and results in urban sprawl.

Pearson, Hassan and the Egyptian authorities, in their wisdom, foresaw this likelihood; what unfettered economic growth in the interests of so-called '*efficiency* of industry and development' might do to the '*robustness* of ecosystems'. Early demarcation of an extensive protected area boundary in Southern Sinai, throughout which development is tightly regulated or prohibited altogether, helped circumvent this undesirable state of affairs. Had Egypt's environmental agency not got in there first, though, the outcome – and this tale – would have been very different: bad news for the coral reefs, the tourists, and, equally, close on economic suicide for the tourism developers themselves.

The authority's strategy, simply put, was to declare the protected area immediately (as large as it could get away with), and only survey it properly when the heat was off. In this way, detailed scientific investigations could begin later, and only then assess and reveal all Southern Sinai's secrets. In the meantime, though, many would have to remain hidden beneath the waves. The bonus is that, in all likelihood, most of the assets will still be there and intact once the scientists have completed the surveys – assuming that eventually happens. Undeniably, 'declare as park first, survey later' was a far smarter strategy than the alternative: beach-to-beach concrete, spreading like an epidemic, virtually devoid of green corridors and proper environmental regulation. And that is precisely what the visitor can expect further down the Red Sea coast, outside the Southern Sinai Protectorates. That is also why holidays are cheaper there – and why the value of tourism investments is also lower.

A parallel strategic decision and action, linked to declaration of the protected area (and the Protectorates within it), was the creation of a 'Setback Zone.' This is defined by a line, or 'datum', seaward of which no development may occur; in the case of the Southern Sinai Protectorates, the line chosen was the highest tidemark. What this single measure of 'restraint' did was ensure the safety of all shorelines within the whole protected area to the 500m depth contour – mainly for the Gulf of Aqaba coast but, additionally, for some 30 kilometres of marine and terrestrial areas on the Gulf of Suez north of Ras Mohammed. It also did much more. By maintaining tourism developments, interspersed with Green off-limits areas, not only do visitors get an experience they are unlikely to forget, but developers themselves are protected, too. The Green areas are, paradoxically, Red – 'no-go' – areas, barred to tourism or other development. Just as in fishery no-take areas boost fishermen's catches and provide secondary benefits, so too do off-limits areas for construction yield real pay-offs to the developers. The Setback Zone, unquestionably, has been instrumental in keeping the Southern Sinai system so robust.

Southern Sinai's success also lies in the development of simple, yet all-encompassing legislation to implement the Setback Zone and to cater for other demands of conservation and development: Law 102 of 1983, also known as the 'Protectorates Law'. This single law, built on only eleven articles and accompanying decrees, is the instrument for identifying and administering all the Protectorates. It is straightforward and effective. Law 102 was built, not to obstruct development, or simply to please environmentalists (although, of course, it does). Its purpose was something grander and more all-encompassing: to help make the Southern Sinai area flourish and prosper – but realizing that the best chance of success was to protect tourists' and developers' interests by judicious conservation.

But that's not all. Soon after the protected area became operational and started to function as it should, in the late 1980s and early 1990s, something unexpected happened: tourism developers no longer saw the 'no-go' development areas, and other conservation measures, as a stranglehold on their business interests. In fact, quite the opposite; they wholeheartedly embraced them – just as they now did all beach and coastal areas seaward of the Setback Zone, also barred from development.

A remarkable sea change in the developers' mindset had come about: areas where construction was prohibited, they now realized, had become their ally and insurance. The reason was that these 'restrictions' actually protected investors' investments – the hotels, supporting infrastructures, and the like. At the same time, maintaining the environmental quality of the reefs and surrounding areas meant that conservationists were reasonably happy, and tourists got a good deal, too.

What's more, tourism developers have begun not just to accept, but to demand, conservation, in fact almost as ardently as the environmentalists themselves. That is something else Michael Pearson has been at pains to point out. Further south, along the Red Sea coast of Egypt, for example, there have been recent moves to create a vast marine protected area, in the footsteps of Southern Sinai. Among the most vociferous individuals, happy to have a self-imposed, voluntary Setback Zone (in the absence of legislation), are, it turns out (once again), the hotel developers. In their eyes, Law 102 was sacrosanct, as if a gift from heaven.

What is so extraordinary – and a real bonus for the management of Southern Sinai – is that, besides being investors motivated by tourism business, these same individuals, in effect, had become ardent environmentalists. It would not be stretching things, either, to say that with hotel owners' own environmental standards now set so high, there was less need for environmental scientists to ensure compliance with Law 102. They could now focus their efforts on specific problems, like plagues of crown-of-thorns starfish (which digest and damage coral), or coral diseases, instead of routine monitoring.

The key ingredient of such vision and enlightened thinking, in brief, was economic growth through precaution – checks and balances; that is, strictly upheld Green conservation sectors within the large area protected, as well as the non-negotiable Setback Zone. On top of that came an unprecedented change in investor attitude towards conservation; this, they soon recognized, provided that magical 'whiz' for their businesses and, at the same time, helped maintain '*robustness* of ecosystems.'

The wisdom of restraint: Bermuda's cruise ship industry

Bermuda is a magnet for cruise ship passengers and holidaymakers, as well as for insurance firms and investors. In fact, people love Bermuda so much that there is precious little space on the island that is not accounted for; and every bit of the island, built up or otherwise, is worth a bomb. Yet here, as much as anywhere, appetite for economic expansion and growth is not easily satisfied. Consider, for example, the cruise ship industry. To cater for ever-changing and potentially expanded markets there is a desire, in some quarters of Bermudian society, to accommodate 'Post-Panamax' ships, whatever measures that might require.

Post-Panamax is the jargon for vessels that are so big they cannot transit the Panama Canal. The maximum ship dimensions allowed by the Panama Canal Authority are a length of 965 feet, a width of 106 feet, a draft of 39½ feet (in tropical fresh water) and a height of 190 feet (waterline to vessel's highest point), although exceptions are made in certain circumstances. As you can imagine, then, Post-Panamax ships are little short of steel giants of the maritime universe. In many ways they are so well-appointed and so self-contained that they are, in effect, their own destination; little short of a city, as well as top-notch tourist accommodation.

It is not that these ships are complete strangers to Bermuda, though. Several in fact already call there: for example, *Explorer of the Seas* goes to the old 'English' port of Dockyard and, similarly, *Costa Magica* calls at Hamilton. Hence, Bermuda already accommodates these beasts, but the fact is that some people are keen to see more of the same. That is why plans have been under consideration to make Post-Panamax and other mega-cruise ships more frequent visitors, and to modify Bermuda's ports, navigable waters and coastal facilities accordingly.

What the decision means, though, is something far beyond the size of the ships allowed into Bermuda, where they can safely go and where they can fit. It is also about far more than the amount of money spent in Bermuda by visitors. Quite understandably, these sorts of issues are paramount in the eyes of the Ministry of Tourism and Transport; and, of course, the potential for more lucrative pickings has hardly escaped the attention of tour operators and some other private enterprises. While many acknowledged that transport and safety issues should not be brushed aside, the prospect of big rewards is not something to be shrugged off, either. For Bermuda is, after all, one of the liveliest financial and business hubs of the world; not merely an island in a spectacular setting with a highly agreeable climate.

Besides, there is surely always room for greater '*efficiency* of industry and development' – even on an island as tightly packed, and as highly developed, as Bermuda – and, in the eyes of some, what better way to achieve this than through an expanded cruise ship industry.

The trouble is that catering for a greater volume of Post-Panamax and other large cruise ships comes, literally, at a high price. For there would be a need for modifications to Bermuda's ports, harbours, and/or channels, at least in part, to accommodate such enormous vessels. Undoubtedly, though, any engineering firms brought in for the 'structural alterations', which would be part and parcel of expansion plans, would be delighted, and laughing all the way to the bank.

Safe vessel transit would, of course, be paramount: getting extra Post-Panamax cruise ships safe and snug into Hamilton and Dockyard; and, similarly, getting big cruise ships into St George's, or anywhere else, with the vessel still in one piece (and the passengers relaxed). The down-side, though, is that the environment would certainly not remain in one piece. For navigation safety would call for invasive coastal surgery – blasting bits of islands here, coral reefs there; a sort of an ecological bypass operation, but with only one-sided benefits. Such ham-fisted incursions could easily undermine the robustness of the entire island, its security and economy, including, ironically, the tourist industry itself.

On 5 September 2003, Hurricane Fabian, the worst storm to hit Bermuda in half a century, battered the island and damaged the airport causeway. Its ferocity highlighted the power of natural events and the importance of environmental robustness in providing natural defences; just as it does in the Maldives and in other parts of the world. If they are honest, even individuals standing to gain from expansion of the cruise ship industry in Bermuda might (secretly, if not openly) admit that the environment should be an important factor in decisions about different development alternatives. Not only that, with so much at stake, every citizen on Bermuda should also have a say about what goes and comes.

What is important, here, is that environmental implications can vary among cruise ship alternatives. This applies not only to ships, ports and supporting shore facilities, but also to activities needed for navigation and safe passage (e.g. widening of channels and dredging) and passenger transport once cruise ships have arrived. Not only that, impacts can be substantial and long-lived. Following the accidental grounding of the cruise ship *Mari Boeing* off Bermuda in 1978, for example, few corals survived. On top of that, long-term monitoring of the grounding scar has shown that reef recovery is likely to take around 100 years.

The issue is not that Bermuda should simply turn away from any expansion of the cruise ship industry; that, of course, might be what out-and-out environmentalists would wish for, but in today's corporate climate, it is hardly realistic or reasonable. Neither too, though, is indifference to what new coastal infrastructures might do to local resources and 'robustness of ecosystems'; and not forgetting, of course, likely knock-on effects to the national economy. An inescapable fact is that Bermuda's natural assets are not immune to disturbances from cruise ships. Better decisions – anywhere in the world, not just in Bermuda – are made with awareness of the full range of potential risks and rewards associated with different development proposals.

Consider St George's, one port on the north-east coast of Bermuda, earmarked for expansion under recent proposals. It happens to be an area that has been degraded for 300 years. So it is hardly pristine; some extra port development, here and there, will hardly matter, then, is one possible take, especially on the part of those enamoured with '*efficiency of industry and development*' whatever the cost. But with ecosystem robustness already on the line, new port development would inevitably weaken the environment of St George's further; that, for sure, would be the scenario if it came to accommodating Post-Panamax ships in a safe manner.

But what is at stake extends to far more than decline in coral here, or possible loss of a few marine species there. Amazingly, one action given serious consideration has been the widening of Town Cut, a channel through which cruise ships must pass on entry to and departure from St George's. This is a concrete example of where widening the gap would require, quite literally, blasting of rock and coral, to create safe navigation and passage for the mammoth cruise ships entering port. Not only would such surgery be substantial – from the local collateral damage – but the effects would be irreversible. On top of that, this single and easily executed engineering action would have multiple effects, several potentially devastating. For one, the channel opened out would make the whole of St George's more vulnerable to wave surge; and, more worrying still, to the damaging effects of hurricanes – something one might imagine would still be fresh in the authorities' minds in the wake of Hurricane Fabian.

That is not all: after widening Town Cut, even with all the goodwill in the world, changes in natural patterns of sedimentation and erosion would unavoidably follow. Across the world – and Bermuda is no exception – sedimentation and siltation are perhaps the number one plague and by-product of coastal construction. Admittedly, fallout can be reduced, at least with time and money spent using special screens, 'curtains' and other equipment to contain the sediment plumes. Controlling it is easier in principle than practice, though.

A likely scenario for St George's, just like elsewhere, would be a double whammy. First, there would be erosion: sand disappearing from some places, including those where it is wanted, for example on beaches and sandbars which can provide valuable natural protection. And, just as disagreeable, precisely the opposite: sand turning up and accumulating in other places, including those where it is not wanted, for example in channels leading to St George's and in the harbour itself. Reversing this, of course, can be done through periodic dredging, but it is both inconvenient and costly. This sort of scourge, though, is not one confined to Bermuda, as any coastal civil engineer worth his salt will tell you. It is a poisoned chalice or by-product of coastal tinkering, particularly the sort accompanying short-sighted and ill-conceived development projects.

But these are just examples of the likely physical injuries resulting from the widening of Town Cut at St George's, and how this would cut into physical environmental robustness. What we must not overlook, too, are the ecological effects (which, for reasons already mentioned, often lead to physical consequences also). What we are alluding to here is smothering and other damage done to corals by sedimentation and siltation. Research tells us that, besides direct damage, this can induce coral bleaching – something, as mentioned, that we normally associate with seawater warming and global climate change. Either way, bleaching spells bad news for reef robustness; that is not to say recovery is impossible, but bleaching unquestionably erodes reef robustness and health. A pile of white coral skeleton or, worse still, rubble is hardly the same thing as a vibrant, living reef planted firmly on the seabed.

All this is not merely fanciful ecological speculation. Bermuda has already witnessed at first hand the price paid for heavy siltation, including that which accompanied habitat degradation during construction of the airport. Fine silt material spread over the whole of St George's and Castle Harbour, seriously affecting coral and permanently altering the marine environment. Incidentally, this is the main reason why reefs in Castle Harbour are unlikely to return to their pre-1940s condition.

The changes just described relate to only one port in Bermuda, and say nothing of what might lie in store for Hamilton or Dockyard; nor of the many other coastal alterations, and environmental altercations, that would come about if Bermuda decides to get into Post-Panamax cruise ships big-time. The truth is that different cruise ship scenarios (including the status quo) encompass a 'package' of different environmental risk factors.

Critical to all in Bermuda is understanding what various cruise ship options mean for the diverse services provided by its natural environment; enjoyment of its beauty and recreational opportunities; the protection ecosystems offer; and the ability of Bermudian people to move around the island. The degree to which port development options affect the coast also matters in other ways, for a physically hazardous environment is less conducive to international business and investment than a physically secure one. Also at stake is the environmental legacy left by port development and the potential expansion of the cruise ship industry for future generations of Bermudians.

Of course, holding back a lively industry unnecessarily would be in no one's interests, least of all the Ministry of Tourism and Transport and tour operators choosing Bermuda as a destination. Trade-offs and some collateral, after all, are inevitable outcomes of economic expansion, in the pursuit of '*efficiency* of industry and development'. Nor should one dismiss the fact that some positive effects, as well as negative ones, can arise from technology-driven tourism. Post-Panamax and other mega-ships, for example, carry highly advanced waste treatment facilities, and greater storage capacity, compared with many smaller and older ships. Admittedly, this may well not offset the weakening of ecosystems resulting from blasting bits of reef and rock to create a safe passage and a safe berth in Bermuda. Nevertheless, one advantage of being self-contained is that it places less burden on Bermuda's own finite resources and its environment. That in itself, of course, should not be the cliffhanger, the decision whether or not to allow more mega-ships into Bermuda. But, as enlightened planners know all too well, self-sufficiency is a factor than cannot simply be brushed aside.

Then there are plain business arguments, which cannot be ignored either. As many Bermudians with corporate interests point out, there is also the matter of changing markets and tour operator preferences. Bermuda simply has to go big, they argue, to accommodate the increasing number of Post-Panamax and other large vessels being thrust, more and more, down cruise ship destinations' throats. 'Thanks, but no thanks', they fear, would be the kiss of death for Bermuda, by excluding it from a big chunk of future business action. But as a recent (2006) independent evaluation of cruise ships and sustainability in Bermuda, by Mike Donlan of U.S. firm Industrial Economics Inc. and myself, revealed, that assumption may not be entirely watertight.

While future predictions are inherently uncertain, publicly available information raises questions about claims that the cruise industry will abandon Bermuda over the coming years, unless significant changes are made to Bermuda's ports to safely berth Post-Panamax ships. Not only that, Bermuda cruise passengers have a demonstrated willingness to travel on smaller, middle-aged ships (perhaps reflecting the substantial on-island time generally associated with Bermuda cruises relative to itineraries of similar duration to more distant island destinations).

Specific ships serving Bermuda will, unquestionably, change over time. Nevertheless, there is a recent precedent for replacement with relatively small rather than large cruise ships; the 2006 replacement of *Horizon* with *Empress of the Seas* bears testament to this. The truth is that the cruise ship industry will not necessarily abandon Bermuda if it does not become a follower of fashion. So mega-cruise ships may not, in fact, be essential for ongoing '*efficiency* of industry and development', irrespective of any concerns about the '*robustness* of ecosystems': going big clearly is not the only, nor necessarily the best solution open to Bermuda. Many other analyses in the recent cruise ship evaluation also point to this.

Not only that, none of these economic and environmental deliberations consider what must be the cruise ship industry's worse nightmare, and that of Bermuda's Ministry of the Environment, Department of Conservation Services, as well: the possibility of a ship grounding on coral reefs. That sort of accident causes physical and often long-lived impact, with devastating ecological effects to boot.

As research scientist Walter Jaap reported in 2000: 'Often the grounded vessel will have crushed the reef, excavating sediments and rubble that end up as a berm of material behind the ship's resting position. Dealing with massive amounts of rubble debris is challenging. The options include leaving it in place and stabilizing it with cements; moving it a long way from the site and dumping it in deep water; or reconfiguring it by moving it off reef and building piles where it can do no harm.' Sometimes blasting is necessary to free the grounded vessel, a practice which itself is very environmentally destructive. And in Bermuda local resources would probably be insufficient for freeing a post-Panamax ship (and possibly even a smaller cruise ship) should an accident occur.

Chemical contamination from anti-fouling paints on the underneath of cruise ships, and other vessels, represents an equally serious environmental threat. When a ship hits a coral reef, the action of the hull scraping over it leaves significant quantities of anti-fouling residues on corals. Even the new anti-fouling paints containing so-called 'booster biocides' (such as the product Irgarol 1051) are highly toxic to corals at minute, barely detectable concentrations. Such concentrations, incidentally, already occur in many harbours around the world, including

Bermuda. For example, Irgarol 1051 concentrations of up to 590 nanograms per litre have already been reported in Hamilton.

This may seem only a tiny amount – especially as one 'nanogram' amounts to only one-billionth of a gram. But it is enough to disrupt coral business and reef robustness. Given that anti-fouling paints are so potent and powerful – little short of a broad spectrum chemical shotgun, just like many chemotherapies used in medicine – it would be miraculous if there was no collateral damage. Following a recent ship-grounding in Australia, for example, it took six months to clear sand and clean the site of contaminated sediment.

Admittedly, it is not entirely clear whether a post-Panamax ship is more or less likely than a smaller cruise ship to strike a coral reef (or some other major obstruction) in Bermuda. Their highly sophisticated navigational equipment certainly facilitates safe passage. Arguably, though, this might be partly offset by the sheer size of these ships relative to the channels they are navigating. Nor should one overlook the 'windage' created by the high sides of their hulls, in comparison with smaller cruise ships. To put the scale of the problem in perspective, consider the following: it is claimed that the wetted surface of all the ships and small craft in Bermuda (more than 4,000 vessels) is equivalent to less than the area of the wetted surface of just two large cruise ships.

It should also be understood that environmental risk is not merely the likelihood of a particular event happening, for example of a post-Panamax or some other cruise ship striking a coral reef or another vessel. Risk also captures the severity of the event should it occur. In the case of a cruise ship grounding, it has to be said the likelihood is low; but the severity can be very great, should the worst happen. Not only that, we should also be clear that the risk is actually greater than zero.

In fact, a ship-grounding did actually occur, ironically only months after the evaluation of alternatives for the cruise ship industry for Bermuda's National Trust. The ship *Norwegian Crown*, coming into Hamilton, grounded and stuck on the rocks off Dockyard in June 2006. Fortunately it soon got off, though no one is sure at what cost, physically or chemically, to the robustness of Bermuda's environment. One thing for sure, though, is that plans to widen Town Cut at St George's to accommodate mega-cruise ships are now firmly postponed, at least for the time being. That is not to say, though, that proposals will not be resurrected at some later date.

Simple solutions

Often, of course, the tourist industry, or any other industry for that matter, does not simply stop in its tracks, or slow down, even when something as valuable as coral reefs and environmental robustness happen to lie in its path. In these cases, let's face it, there may be not a lot that followers of slow-tech can do to stem the tide of rising '*efficiency* of industry and development' at the expense of the '*robustness* of ecosystems'.

Yet small can be powerful, as well as beautiful. In Eritrea, for example, 1 million local people have recently planted mangroves to help green and restore degraded sections of coast. On top of this, and the main benefit, have come some unexpected by-products from a verdant coastal landscape: surplus seeds and leaves, it turned out, were successfully used as fodder, to feed sheep; though it is better still when fish is added. A mixture of marine plant and animal resources would seem most unlikely sustenance for sheep, but according to reports in Eritrea, the sheep cannot get enough of it.

It might seem like a low-tech solution for a country experiencing the beginnings of coastal development. But that is not to say it does not work or that it is inefficient. Recall an even simpler expedient that helps keep coral reefs robust: minimizing sewage dumping, controlling sedimentation, and the like. That is the premium for insurance, to help retain environmental robustness; the surprising thing is that it goes a long way to help countries like the Maldives and Marshall Islands, which depend for survival, quite literally, on healthy coral reefs.

Under the sun

It comes as no surprise, as many illustrations bear testament, that our oceans are under the weather – and under the spotlight, too. Curiously, though, marine health is not the only thing disturbed. Consider, for example, what happens when sewage is discharged into the sea. Even treated sewage is still full of nitrogen, phosphorus and other nutrients which, in high concentrations, bring about algal blooms; this depletes seawater oxygen, sometimes so severely that not even algae can survive. But as bathers know all too well, viruses, *E. coli* bacteria and other nasty pathogens from raw sewage can be a human health hazard, too.

And some algae themselves can be even more harmful. *Gambierdiscus toxicus*, for example, has a name well matched to its influence. For this is one of the organisms responsible, especially in bloom conditions, for ciguatera fish poisoning in coral reef areas. No one is completely sure why blooms occur, but sewage discharge, pollution and other human activities seem partly to blame. Annually, there are now some quarter of a million cases of ciguatera poisoning in humans worldwide. Severe illness or, in extreme cases, a very painful death is what follows. Blooms of other microscopic algae are known to cause paralytic, diarrhoeal and amnesic shellfish poisoning in humans, and other toxin-related medical conditions.

More surprising still is that marine systems, when they are under the weather, can affect human health in less obvious ways. Take, for example, the 1998 El Niño Southern Oscillation (ENSO), or other El Niños, episodic events which seem to be one signature of global climate change. We now realize that these are linked to something far more than seawater warming and coral ill-health. For they are increasingly blamed, at least partly, for droughts, floods and rains and similar catastrophic events in distant corners of the globe. Not only that, El Niños and climate change may actually be influencing diseases, such as Dengue fever and malaria, both transmitted by mosquitoes.

But this particular tale has some rather unexpected twists. For example, scientists predict not just future extensions in malaria distribution, albeit small ones, but also some areas where malaria would actually diminish. Similarly, temperature rise may kick-start or accelerate development of malarial parasites in mosquitoes; but at the same time increased water evaporation, another effect of warmer temperatures, might disrupt the mosquito's life cycle.

Weirder still, though the evidence is actually stronger, is the association between cholera – on the face of it a land-based disease, if ever there was one – and marine ecosystems. For more than forty years scientists in Bangladesh have in fact spotted a seasonal association between cholera outbreaks and coastal algal blooms. Until quite recently, though, the reservoir of the pathogenic bacterium responsible, *Vibrio cholerae*, remained a mystery. It turned out, though, that a range of marine organisms, including so-called 'blue-green algae' (actually primitive bacteria), phytoplankton and other algal species, act as reservoirs.

But the pathogen's main alliance proved to be with zooplankton; specifically, certain free-swimming (copepod) crustaceans, whose egg sacs can contain up to a million of the bacteria. During times of stress, cholera bacteria become dormant or 'quiescent'. But under favourable seawater conditions, for example sufficient nutrient levels, they revert to an infectious state. The really unexpected thing, reported Harvard-based medic and researcher Paul Epstein and his colleagues, was *V. cholerae* turning up in the bilge waters of vessels docked in Caribbean ports. The pathogen appears to have hitched a ride from Bangladesh across the Pacific.

Epstein and his colleagues suggest that rapid invasion of cholera in the Americas might well be reflecting an enhanced plankton reservoir. More surprising still is the linking of efficiency of healthcare and robustness of marine systems in a medical journal. As the authors conclude: 'Changes along coastlines are contributing to public health hazards, and are causing hypoxia in the breeding grounds of marine animals and plants. Physicians may see the remedial actions – a reduction in inputs [such as nutrients from sewage and agriculture, which help trigger algal blooms] plus protection of wetlands, and preservation of species diversity in the oceans – too remote from their clinical practice. Our contribution, and the *Lancet* series as a whole, is aimed at closing that gap in perception.'

CHAPTER 5 GONE FISHING

We plough the seas and gather

Is John Cabot turning in his grave?

High on a hill 260 feet above Bristol harbour stands Cabot Tower. By day it is a dramatic landmark, visible even from the window of my daughter's room at the university's Manor Hall. Down at the quayside sits John Cabot himself – or at least a bronze of him, gazing towards some distant horizon. Italian-born, later English, Cabot was an explorer and navigator like no other. In 1497, in search of a new route to Asia, he set out across the Atlantic aboard the *Matthew* and 'discovered' North America; although actually the Vikings and perhaps the Irish monks beat him to it, and some claim the Chinese did, too.

Every night, to commemorate the explorer, the beacon on John Cabot's tower flashes a message in Morse code: 'God speed *Matthew*'. It is not only the explorer we should remember, but also the way our seas once were. Besides celebrating the past, though, the signal is supposed to give hope for the future. Judging from the appalling state of world fisheries and the oceans today, though, we need something more than just hope. Part of the problem for fisheries, it turns out, lies where you might expect it least: in science itself. Many of the models used to predict safe levels of catch are too simple; they ignore the environment and other important things that drive fish production; they fail to capture properly what is going on or, more simply, are off key. Put another way, fisheries science and management has lacked robustness, just like the fish populations we now exploit so ruthlessly.

In his chronicles, 500 years ago, Cabot wrote of dense cod shoals off

163

Newfoundland. Catching them involved simply hanging baskets over the side of the ships. Cod abundance then was not unlike the great herds of buffalo that once roamed the American plains. By 1978, though, stocks were close to collapse from heavy fishing; just over a decade later they had virtually gone. Catch quotas were over-optimistic. Closure of the fishery, at least initially, cost the Canadian government more than $2.5 billion a year. On the other hand, this is at least partly offset by the recent bonanza in shellfish catches, which today are worth more than the cod catches were. For as cod stocks busted, lobsters and other species lower down the food chain boomed. But switching to small fry, like capelin, is a risky business, for they happen to fuel the marine food chain, and capelin are a favourite prey species for cod. Some believe that while fishing targets them, cod may never come back. In the case of capelin, it should also be added that Canada has cut back catches drastically; it even closed the fishery offshore (although there is still illegal fishing for this species).

Similar tales plague the eastern Atlantic. Few now doubt that North Sea cod has been knocked for six. Once one of the world's richest fishing grounds, sporting bluefin tuna and even whales, heavy harvesting has transformed the North Sea beyond recognition. These giants are now gone and, in just over a century, the North Sea's total fish stock has dropped from around 26 million tonnes to only 10 million tonnes. Cod face complete collapse (some would argue that collapse has already taken place), with as much as 60 per cent of the fishable stock creamed off every year. But it is not just cod that are going. Consider, for example, plaice. Studies early in the twentieth century showed that trawlers, even then, were removing around half the plaice in the North Sea every year. Few fish species could be robust against those high levels of exploitation, especially when it is part of Europe's quest for ever greater 'efficiency of industry and development'.

The litany of fishery disasters extends to virtually all corners of the ocean. According to Ransom Myers and Boris Worm at Dalhousie University in Canada, more than 90 per cent of large predatory fishes have gone from the ocean in relation to pre-industrial levels. What's

Even in 09, trawlers were wrecking an incredibly rich marine environment under the North Sea.

more, as this chapter goes on to tell, seafood species do not always spring back and recover. Worse still, though, scientists may not even be aware of what has been happening. In 1998, for example, the US National Marine Fisheries Service knew the status of only 40 per cent of more than 800 species of fish stocks exploited in its territorial waters.

And it is not just fish that are involved. We have hunted other large marine animals ruthlessly, too – sometimes to extinction. Steller's sea cow, a prime example, was a mammal and close relative of the Atlantic and Caribbean manatee, and of the dugong found in the Indian and Pacific oceans. Naturalist Georg Wilhelm Steller first recorded the creature – later named after him – in 1741, while over-wintering on Bering Island along with other survivors of the wreck of the Russian ship *St Peter*. The sea cow was truly massive; it grew up to ten metres long, it was easy to catch and good food. So great was its abundance that Steller declared that the animals could feed everyone in Russia's Kamchatka peninsula. His pronouncement was never put to the test: by 1768, Steller's sea cow was extinct, yet only twenty-seven years earlier its existence had been unknown.

Other marine mammals may not have become totally extinct. But we have certainly driven many whales to commercial extinction. Beginning in the 1700s, we hunted down one species after another, first in the Arctic and then in more distant Antarctic waters. At least all seven species of turtles, miraculously, are still with us. Before Columbus arrived in the New World in the late fifteenth century, marine biologist Jeremy Jackson points out, the population of green turtles in the Cayman Islands may have stood at 6.5 million, and possibly much more. By 1800, though, its fishery in this part of the Caribbean had crashed and turtles were almost entirely gone. The Cayman islanders then did precisely the same thing to turtles along the Moskito coast of Nicaragua, where numbers plummeted, too. The status of green turtles, globally, is 'endangered', not quite as serious as 'critically endangered' – the category of threat for hawksbills and leatherback turtles, whose risk of extinction is greater – but hardly grounds for complacency.

What went wrong?

Besides the obvious – plain need or greed – how could marine resources have disappeared so spectacularly? It is a question Daniel Pauly, Jeremy Jackson, Callum Roberts and many other ecologists have grappled with for decades. It turns out that many factors, environmental and social, have put fish stocks, turtles and other marine resources in the state they are in. Ultimately, though, it boils down to too much robustness squeezed out of them and the habitats which sustain them.

On top of that, many models used by fishery scientists were over-simplistic, making too many assumptions and ignoring many things that really mattered. You could say that the models, especially the early ones, were too fragile. Models applied to the North Sea, for example, focused too narrowly on cod, plaice and haddock. They took insufficient account of how 'target' fish interact with other species in the system. More surprising still, they seemed completely blind to what trawling does physically – besides, of course, removing cod; that is, the devastating effects of the nets dragging over the sea bottom. In other words, the '*robustness* of ecosystems' suffers enormously. Part of the problem was that the natural environment was virtually ignored. So, too, was something else equally fundamental: the behaviour of fishermen. On so many counts the models could not have been further 'off-centre'. Recognizing that there were omissions and uncertainties would have been a start. Even smarter would have been to build insurance into the models, to make both the science and management of fisheries more robust against future surprises. One simple way to do this is to create marine reserves. But, even in the wake of one fishery disaster after another, this has been remarkably slow to happen. Enlightened members of society are under no illusion about the power of fishing and what is at stake, and they are not alone. For experts now point the finger at this activity as the longest-standing and most disruptive of our influences on the oceans.

SLOW-TECH

Too few small fry

The English clergyman Gilbert White followed nature as well as the church. In his *Natural History of Selborne* (1778) he observed, repeatedly, that the village church tower contained eight pairs of swallows. Just over one [~~Two~~] century later, in 1983, ecologists John Lawton and Bob May visited Selborne and noted twelve pairs. Year after year, the swallow population must have kept on going. Despite disturbances going beyond organ music and hymn singing, the local population seems to have been remarkably robust.

Fish might seem a far cry from swallows. But in the sea, as on land, species go on replacing themselves if only we let them. It is a maxim so glaringly obvious, yet so easily overlooked. In the case of fisheries, we seem even blinder to another truth: that powerful engines, ruthlessly efficient but unselective trawls, extended vessel range and freezer facilities (allowing ships to stay out and scoop up fish 24/7) have pushed many stocks close to or beyond the edge. As well as modern trawlers, though, there are thousands of low-tech fishing craft; so overall mortality from fishing becomes substantial. Not surprisingly, fish stocks fast become non-renewable. Reproduction fails to make up for the losses – something made worse by coastal dredging, landfill and pollution – and populations falter; stocks once robust become fragile and easily crash.

Whether for fish and chips or gourmet seafood, products of shallow seas and ocean depths are an endowment like no other. Increasingly, though, 'fish for finance' rather than 'fish for food' is the name of the fishing industry's game. But then that is perhaps not so surprising in a world where '*efficiency* of industry and development' increasingly matters more than the '*robustness* of ecosystems'. The average annual squid catch in the Falkland Islands, for example, was recently worth a staggering £250 million. As one commentator points out, 'the islands have been transformed from a feudal backwater into an enterprise culture with a debt-free government and rumours of up to ten individual millionaires'. This happens to be a fairly sustainable fishery. All too easily, though, stocks 'here today' become 'gone tomorrow'.

An undeniable fact is that fishing has knocked too much reproductive oomph out of marine stocks. The trouble is that trawls are double-edged, and both edges cut deeply. One problem is linked to the fact that smaller females produce fewer offspring than bigger ones. So removing the oldest and largest (and most valuable) individuals – something fishing does effectively – decreases the average body size, which leads to an overall decline in reproduction: too few mature individuals remain to replenish the population. On top of that, the relentless capture of large individuals by fishing has acted as an evolutionary pressure; the effect has been reduced age of maturity and average size of individual fish. North Sea plaice, for example, now mature at half the size they did only fifty years ago. All this has a knock-on effect, cutting egg production even more; it is an example of positive feedback – the process that makes things either better and better, or worse and worse.

Added to the problem of capturing the largest and oldest fish is the take of too many juveniles, which are often resident in and grow up in coastal shallows or 'nursery' areas. Here small fish are easy takings, particularly to low-tech, shallow-draft craft. Going for fish young threatens the resource less than fishing the adult population too heavily, so it receives less attention; yet it still reduces a fishery's potential yield. Less fishing for smaller fish would actually produce higher landings – even, curiously, when the resource is abundant.

Whether over-take of small or big fish, populations of many marine species have declined, locally and often globally, to critical levels. Few fish stocks are robust against current fishing intensities. Part of the problem is that once at low densities, fish populations become more vulnerable to unseasonal (low or high) sea temperatures and other unnatural environmental conditions, as well as to oil spills and physical disturbances. It is the rare events that can be so crippling to a fishery, and to any other system, as explained in the Introduction, in accordance with 'robust yet fragile' principles.

Yet, one might wonder, has robustness in fisheries really diminished? It is one thing that populations fall, but quite another if they spring back easily. A stark revelation came in 2000 from Jeffrey Hutchings at Dalhousie University, who examined the fate of twenty-five commercial stocks fifteen years after their decline. Only 12 per cent, including herring and sardines, made full recovery; there was no population recovery in 40 per cent of the stocks; and little recovery in most others. The clear message here is that stocks are not robust to the harm we inflict upon them from heavy fishing.

We plough the seas and gather

Taking too many fish, whether for Paris restaurants or the local market, is not the only damage done by fishing. Intensive trawling in the North Sea 'ploughs', quite literally, vast areas of sea bed three or four times a year. Each pass of a trawl during a fishing trip can remove or dislodge 5–20 per cent of other organisms – urchins, molluscs, sponges, etc. In no time at all, the seabed becomes as sterile as a ploughed field. All that persist are organisms forming simplified, low-diversity communities resilient to trawling.

It is a condition that may seem normal enough, but only because we are unaware of how different the seabed once was. In the 1800s, for example, steam trawlers in the North Sea dragged up from the sea bottom vast amounts of decaying vegetation that had become inundated when seas began to rise after the last Ice Age. Not only that, the nets brought up the bones of land mammals, long since extinct, too. Yet, based on what the nets disgorged on trawler decks 100 years later, not even the most lateral of thinkers would ever have guessed that, until quite recently, ancient plants and animals sat on the seabed.

Transformation of the landscape is more visible, whether through forest clear-felling, conversion to farming or for towns and cities. Writing and art have chronicled such modifications for at least 1,000 years. Change has happened. The sea still looks the same, but this masks changes going on below the surface. What is surprising is that seabed damage from trawling and other fishing gears is controversial. Part of the problem lies in finding pristine areas, or 'reference sites', for comparison. The truth is that they too are badly damaged by trawling, obscuring the true extent of modifications to the bottom. Some scientists rightly point out that fishing actually benefits some fishery species. Beam trawling for flatfish, for example, can smooth out the seabed and create prey communities favourable to the target species. Shrimp populations, too, can benefit from disturbed states maintained by relentless trawling of the muddy and sandy areas they inhabit.

Something else irrefutable, though, is that there are limits to the 'robustness of ecosystems', and the fisheries they sustain, against the physical harm caused by fishing. Dragging several tonnes of steel gear over the seabed can easily outstrip the capacity of all but the hardiest of seafood species to regenerate themselves. The net effect, as Callum Roberts and Julie Hawkins explain, is destruction and ruin – something hardly surprising: 'The passage of trawls across the seabed destroys and transforms ecosystems, often converting them from rich, structurally complex, biologically-created habitats dominated by invertebrates into low diversity, much simplified habitats dominated by physical disturbance.' More amazing still is that the effects of fishing are swept aside as unavoidable 'collateral'; it is a state of affairs similar to that occurring in war, where civilian casualties become casually dismissed as unavoidable sacrifices.

Worse still, in the case of fishing, is that collateral damage from the gear extends beyond target fish, and the seabed, to a broad spectrum of marine species, euphemistically called by-catch. Inadvertently, these get caught along with the fish. In 2005 alone, the UN Environment Programme reports, 250,000 turtles became tangled in fishing gear – despite turtle exclusion devices offering some protection. That same year, more than quarter of a million seabirds, including 100,000 albatrosses, met their end by longline fishing. The problem is that populations of several by-catch species are already precarious: added mortality from fishing only jeopardizes them further.

Despite the down-side of trawling and other destructive fishing, it is hardly likely to stop. Besides, its operations are 'efficient', in terms of capturing large quantities of fish at a very low cost – just as in agriculture land is put under the plough and transformed for our use. As many examples argue, though, much hangs on what we mean by 'cost': what we include, and what is conveniently overlooked. At least on land, though, extensive areas are protected from agriculture in national parks. Without similar protection and insurance built in to the oceans, the ocean larder could become very bare indeed.

The problem is that not only are shallow seas under the plough. Nowadays trawling at depths of 1,500 metres is routine, while experimental fishing reaches even greater depths. An inescapable fact is that areas once thought to be too rough for fishing are no longer impenetrable: modern trawls can make light work of moving heavy rocks – up to three metres wide and weighing sixteen tonnes.

Yet to blame only industrial fisheries for causing so much harm would be to miss something else important going on. Even traditional fisheries, often using little more than a hook and line or traps, can impact biodiversity, as well as the target fish species. Take the kelp forests off California, formerly home to abundant massive black sea bass and sheepshead wrasse. Once a magnet to spear fishermen, these luxuriant pastures are now virtually empty of these fish, and others, too. According to Paul Dayton of the Scripps Institute of Oceanography in San Diego who documented their disappearance, these kelp forests today are nothing but 'ghost habitats': the kelp remains, but, as he and others lament, 'the canopy is filled with only memories of the large animals that once flashed and shimmered among the fronds'.

How much is too much?

When the new millennium dawned, the world fish catch was around 80–85 million tonnes, according to Reg Watson and Daniel Pauly of the Fisheries Centre at the University of Columbia in Canada (excluding, incidentally, aquaculture, which produced a further thirty-five 35 million tonnes). It was a time when catches had already plateaued, after decades of steady growth, but then they started to falter. A starker revelation is that some three-quarters of ocean fisheries are fished at or beyond their sustainable yields. The statistics suggest that we really have been catching too much.

Nearly fifty years earlier, in 1957, British biologists Ray Beverton and Sidney Holt published a seminal work, *On The Dynamics of Exploited Fish Populations*, which became, along with later printings, the most widely cited fisheries book ever published. The book is full of equations, production models and theoretical ways of getting the most out of the ocean. To most people, it would hardly be bedtime reading or a gripping tale. But to fishery scientists and population biologists it was, and certainly the 1960s and the next two decades were heady times; global catches were increasing and there was a widespread belief that expansion of fishing and fisheries science could help feed the growing population. Beverton and Holt's catch equation seemed to have almost universal applicability, and their approach was the core of modern catch forecasting, and much more besides.

The trouble, though, is that the book's disciples strove for a precision and certainty that was rarely warranted. Valuable as they were, many of the models – even their underlying concepts – carried huge assumptions and overlooked all sorts of things that go on beneath the waves. They also required levels of information that were unattainable, even for well-studied fisheries.

Take total allowable catch quotas – a management tool used in places as far apart as New Zealand and the European Union. They are supposed to deliver sustainable fisheries, be good for business and at the same time conserve stocks by keeping populations above predetermined levels. Besides their needing more information than is often possible, there are other problems. For one, they apply to particular species, like cod and haddock, but in reality fishing scoops up other fish, as by-catch – usually dead upon arrival on deck, or almost certainly by the time they are thrown back into the sea. Removal of these fish from the system must be having an effect on the fishery. Then there is the physical damage from fishing, considered earlier, yet this too is completely ignored in catch quotas.

On top of these shortcomings comes an even greater problem. For catch quotas to do their job, the size of fish stocks, catch quotas and fleet size should be well harmonized. Although this is the intention, of course, precisely the opposite can happen. In an illuminating study of Nova Scotian haddock, in the late 1980s, mathematical ecologist Jacquie McGlade demonstrated why.

The problem, McGlade discovered, relates to the delay – normally two years – between collection of stock assessment data and enactment of a total allowable catch. A quota translates into vessel licensing, which is what regulates fishing levels. Even in normal times, it turned out, year-to-year oscillations in haddock abundance and catch are pretty wild. The time lag introduced, between determining haddock quotas and implementing them, unexpectedly made the oscillations even wilder; and fisheries management, embarrassingly, had caused this to happen. For the fishermen, trying to decide how many vessels to commission or lay off, from one season to the next, must have been like tracking a bee with a laser beam. The ups and downs in catches may not have been quite so chaotic, in the mathematical sense, but the effect on the fishery certainly was. On top of that, for coastal communities in south-west Nova Scotia, there is little alternative employment besides fishing.

Catch quotas are not the only problem. What we see, time and time again, is fishery scientists mathematically analysing stocks with the same determination as the fishing vessels exploiting them. Yet, Callum Roberts remarks, yield predictions made by fishery managers carry a 'cachet of precision that masks their inherent uncertainty'. The bottom line is that, without insurance against uncertainty, most are insufficiently robust to the known and unknown things that drive a fishery.

Of course, it is possible that the models have been right all along, and that fishery problems simply reflect unwillingness of managers to implement them; after all, draconian cuts to an industry can make politicians unpopular. European total allowable catches, for example, are often 15–30 per cent higher than scientific advisers recommend. But this is by no means the whole story.

By not incorporating safety factors, fishery scientists are losing credibility. On top of the examples already mentioned, the news abounds with stock collapses. Fisheries are complex systems, and things can go wrong all too easily. Engineers, in contrast, have long recognized the need to confront uncertainty directly by building robustness, through insurance, into management. As US ecologist Larry Crowder once remarked: 'If engineers adopted the same approach, for example by building bridges strong enough for just the average flow of traffic, they would soon share the reputation that fishery managers enjoy.'

While modern management measures bring conservation benefits, they do so only up to a point. Many, though, are limited and the loopholes are almost as easy to exploit as the fish stocks themselves. Mesh size restrictions, for example, aim to protect young fish from capture and safeguard the stocks. Like their counterparts on land, fishermen are hunters, and are both skilful and crafty. By towing nets faster, for instance, the mesh can close up, increasing the total fish caught and the numbers of small fish retained.

Even with all the good will in the world, designing an ideal aperture size for a net is impossible. Set the mesh size too big, and the small fish species escape. Like flies, many small fish like anchovy have a short lifespan, reproduce at a young age and produce many offspring; if the nets do not get them, natural predators or 'old' age will. So setting the mesh size smaller is a good strategy for these sorts of fish. But groupers, halibut and other long-lived fish are slow-growing; they do not breed at an early age and produce (relatively) few surviving offspring. For them, heavy fishing and smallmeshed nets can have disastrous effects on their numbers, and populations easily become depleted. Mesh size, then, is an intricate balancing act between production and protection. To make matters worse, fisheries have species with a mix of reproductive strategies, especially in tropical seas; there are long-livers, short-livers, and many in between.

Another solution of modern fishery management is to cut down fishing pressure to desired, more moderate levels. Managers attempt this by limiting the number of vessels in a fishery, and by vessel retirement schemes. The problem, though, is that an existing vessel can be upgraded to increase the fishing power, or be operated round the clock by different crews. Neither does control, in itself, limit vessels heading for over-fished areas and species, or vital breeding areas – the life and soul of the stocks.

Perhaps the greatest delusion of fisheries science was maximum sustainable yield – the best catches possible, with the level of fishing set to achieve this, but leaving sufficient fish in the sea for the future. But what many hoped would conserve wild stocks, or at least ensure wise use of them, actually put many at risk. It was also something that damaged the credibility of fishery science for several decades to come. In hindsight, it is not difficult to see why. If you think about it, the very concept is shaky, even though the intention is clear and commendable. The truth is that 'maximum' and 'sustainable' trade with each other; they cannot easily coexist. High sustainability means catches cannot be maximal, but if they are, exploitation cannot be sustainable. So maximum sustainable yield, or MSY, is close to being an oxymoron, a contradiction in terms – an impossibility, rather like 'bureaucratic efficiency'; or, as some (perhaps) jest, 'military intelligence'.

Most fishery scientists today turn their noses up at the MSY approach to marine harvesting (though many of the newer approaches carry many of its assumptions and uncertainties.) It suffers from several flaws, sometimes fatal for a fishery. For one, MSY considers just fish, or other seafood species exploited; sea temperature and other environmental features also influence catch levels, yet are ignored.

Another problem of maximum sustainable yield surrounds overall fishing effort. Being difficult to determine directly, effort is usually estimated instead – by dividing total catch by catch per effort (e.g. catch per vessel, or hour). The problem, though, is that effort is easily *under*-estimated, because catch per effort – most often determined using trawler information – tends to be *over*-estimated. It is not difficult to see why. As a fishery matures, vessels in the fleet, not surprisingly, tend to home in on the best areas. Put another way, the inclination will be for skippers to move away from heavily exploited areas, where catch per effort will now have fallen. Hence the catch per effort information fed into the models is not typical, not representative of the fishery: it is over-optimistic, because it is based upon where skippers decide to fish. (To some extent, independent estimates from a research vessel get over this, but they are often highly controversial with the fishing industry, who claim, usually wrongly, that they are unrepresentative.) Either way, under-estimating fishing effort and over-estimating catch per effort – a proxy for stock abundance – easily leads to over-optimistic forecasts and over-harvesting.

Equally or more serious is that maximum sustainable yield considers only the species caught intentionally, for market or the restaurant. Yet fishing cannot avoid targeting others, too. If the trawl takes large numbers of the prey (food) on which the exploited fish depends, the actual yield will be lower than the estimated MSY. Similarly, if trawling captures large quantities of key predators of the target species, this reduces predation pressure, resulting in greater quantities of target fish species than predicted. Finally, what if too much fishing has led to catch levels falling below the MSY? 'Backing off', i.e. reducing fishing, would surely result in the return of the bumper harvests experienced in former good times. The problem is that this comes with no guarantee; natural systems are complex and human changes to them are generally not easily reversible. Worse still, a fishery can be part of a catastrophic 'phase shift', something leading to a persistent and often undesirable altered state. This is probably what Canadian cod, through over-fishing, got caught up in, and why it has not recovered.

As another bleak reminder of what over-simplistic science can do, consider the fate of the once-famous anchovy fishery off Peru. Anchovy are prey not only to humans but also to other takers, including guano birds. In years gone by, the guano birds' nitrogen-rich excrement was mined for fertilizer. Besides boosting production in the fields, it generated colossal economic revenue. But it was ephemeral; none of it lasted. Throughout the 1970s and over the next decade anchovy stocks were heavily exploited. Inclement environmental conditions made things worse. 'El Niños', periodic anomalous weather events, were the main problem, as they led to seawater warming and reduced ocean productivity.

Combined with unrealistic maximum sustainable yields, high levels of fishing and natural mortality led to a catastrophic failure of the anchovy fishery. At the same time the bird population, with its food reduced, fell to one-tenth of its former size. The guano industry also collapsed, although this was apparently based on mining accumulated deposits rather than taking guano produced year by year. Either way, piles of fertilizer are now little more than a past memory. Although anchovy did spring back, the UN's Food and Agriculture Organization has expressed concern over potential over-fishing, recommending that stock are maintained through the 'continued application of robust effort control and surveillance measures'.

What Charles Darwin's friend felt about the sea

Science is only one bit of the jigsaw in fisheries management. An even more fundamental problem, it turns out, lies in legacies of our perceptions about the ocean carried over from the past. Understanding the limits to exploitation, we now realize, is as much a matter of mental models as mathematical ones. Even back in the fourteenth century we see evidence, surprisingly perhaps, that fishermen pleaded with their sovereign to control use of the then newfangled beam trawl. The future of the stocks was clearly bothering them. Such worries were, as Callum Roberts reminds us, 'brushed aside then, as they have been many times since'.

But just how limitless really are our seas? Completely inexhaustible was the view of many, including the distinguished and influential naturalist Thomas Huxley, Charles Darwin's close friend and ally, back in the 1800s; what a contrast to the take of medieval fishermen. It is hardly surprising, then, that 'freedom of the seas', and with it freedom to exploit, was the belief that prevailed for so long. Even today, it is easy to view the sea in the same way: a vast blue hole lined with everlasting supplies of fish, which produce unlimited offspring. Fishing, Huxley and like minded colleagues believed, could only ever remove a tiny fraction of what the ocean holds. Besides, if catches dwindled in one place there was always somewhere else to drop the net. So strong was this conviction in the UK that a Royal Commission, established in 1866, removed all restrictions on fishing. That was what it did, though it wasn't what it was actually set up for.

It is hard to believe that 'freedom of the seas' had no connection with commercial interests. Arguably, the two were a formidable force, which played a part in the plundering of fish stocks, in local and more distant waters. Beginning in the nineteenth century, tropical fisheries of distant colonial states represented a new and lucrative source of revenue. Whatever the motives, there is little doubt that colonial presence on many small island states had an impact that would change them for ever. (As I point out later, though, it would be unfair to blame the colonizers for all every decline in tropical marine resources.)

Because many fish produce young that can drift long distances on ocean currents, as part of the plankton, scientists assumed fish and other marine species to be more widespread – and hence immune to complete extinction, compared to animals on land which could be driven to extinction; exploit one area heavily, and it will eventually be colonized by fish from another. This comforting belief, though, like that of Thomas Huxley, does not hold up. In one recent study of more than 3,000 species of reef-dwelling fish, lobsters, snails and corals, over half of all lobsters and a quarter of fish and snails had small ranges. This places them at far graver risk of extinction than we could have ever supposed – from fishing, habitat damage and other disturbances. Something else easily overlooked – though not by fishermen – is that some fish, like the Caribbean Nassau grouper, aggregate to spawn at certain times of the year; this behaviour makes them even more vulnerable. Hit populations of restricted range species, or spawning aggregations, hard and there is no guarantee they will spring back.

Worse still was something Annalie Morris and her colleagues at York University discovered. In their investigation into more than 100 grouper species, most of the species considered 'vulnerable' to extinction were unexpectedly wide-ranging; being broadly distributed across the oceans, it seemed, brought no guarantee of safety. Greatest conservation attention has normally gone to restricted range species. We clearly need a rethink.

The seas are so vast that the optimism expressed by Huxley, and many others since, about what the oceans hold in store is perhaps understandable. An indisputable fact, though, is that renewable ocean resources are exhaustible; they can easily pass what Malcolm Gladwell calls the 'tipping point', then become fragile; the litany of fishery collapses across the globe is testament to this. But there is another twist to the tale. It is one thing not to realize that ocean resources are finite and limited; but quite another to accept that over-harvesting can happen, then fail to see or accept it when it has.

Shifting baselines

Daniel Pauly is a fisheries biologist at the University of British Columbia. In a 1995 article he told a simple tale, but the shock-waves reverberated far and wide. Ecologists started to change how they go about determining change – even how they think about it. Pauly's story was an anecdote about a colleague's grandfather in the Kattegat waters of Scandinavia. The man remembered, in his youth, being annoyed by predatory bluefin tuna attacking the mackerel in his nets. Today bluefin tuna are virtually unknown there. Nowadays, young fishermen in the Kattegat would find it hard to believe that bluefin tuna had ever roamed their waters.

Thomas Huxley genuinely felt that we lack the means to make a serious dint in the ocean's vast resources. Pauly's story, and many confirmations of the same phenomenon since – the 'shifting baseline syndrome' – demonstrates the very opposite, that the extent of past environmental changes by humanity goes by unnoticed: the appearance of environment as 'natural' is simply the perception of each generation.

Anecdotal records of the past abound with snippets of how abundant marine resources once were. William Dampier, for example, might have been a pirate, but he was also a well-seasoned traveller, navigator, diplomat, sea captain and author. In parts of his 1697 book *A New Voyage Around the World*, he talks of the large, then undisturbed, seal populations off Chile: 'Here there are always thousands, I might say millions of them'. He talked of the sea being covered with them up to a mile offshore. So great too, were the numbers of turtles and manatees, especially (but not only) in the Caribbean, that Dampier and his shipmates were not averse to dining on these large animals. There were certainly plenty to choose from: 200 years earlier, at the time of Columbus's voyage in 1492, turtles there probably numbered over 30 million. In fact the ships in the Caribbean normally carried several Moskito Indians, particularly skilled in clubbing turtles, manatees and large fish. Or, consider how abundant cod stocks once were off Newfoundland back in the days of John Cabot. You would never guess it though, from today's catch statistics.

All too easily, fishery science and ecology disqualifies and dismisses historical information as being 'anecdotal', unreliable. As Pauly himself laments, there is an inability to incorporate past observations about marine resources into current thinking. Yet, as he points out, both astronomy and oceanography value insights thousands of years old. In answer to those claiming history as unscientific, Pauly explains, evolutionary biology is historical. And it is not entirely tongue-in-cheek that he goes on to remark: 'Just as no historian could have witnessed the collapse of Rome, no evolutionary biologist has witnessed speciation directly.'

It is now abundantly clear that fisheries science and decisions would be far better if placed in correct historical context. The fact is that scientific records and ecological surveys generally extend back only decades at most. Yet, as many examples demonstrate, important changes occurred before then.

Just why this matters, for fisheries management and conservation, is something Mexican green travel guide turned ecologist Andrea Sáenz-Arroyo and colleagues have made obvious. They examined changes in Gulf grouper in the Gulf of California. Using 'proper' catch statistics, there is no evidence of stock decline, but these records extend back only twenty years or so. By delving more than fifty years into the past, by questioning older fishermen and gleaning catch information from 'non-scientific' sources, Sáenz-Arroyo paints a very different picture. Gulf grouper were surprisingly abundant, even in living memory. Their population in the Gulf of California today, using information spanning a longer time period, *has* fallen dramatically. Gulf grouper have fallen to only a small percentage of the numbers present back in the 1940s. Its decline is certainly more than ninety percent.

So scarce is this prized fish in the region today that it faces complete disappearance. The extent and rate of its decline, based on the period between the 1940s and 1970s, qualifies the species to be listed as 'critically endangered'. Yet the fish is actually classified as 'vulnerable' – still threatened, but with far lesser risk of extinction. The reason is that this listing is based upon 'scientific' data, which is only recent, masking the Gulf grouper's longer-term decline and its true status.

Believing that the population of Gulf grouper in the Gulf of Mexico is stable, whereas in reality it has plummeted, means that management is viewing the fishery and taking poor decisions: by using information that is (presumably) accurate, but which extends over a time period that is too brief. Quite clearly, the information system itself, the conservation status of Gulf grouper based upon it, and fisheries management measures then put in place are insufficiently robust.

The information gathered by Sáenz-Arroyo and colleagues is, undeniably, low-tech, and in some ways old-fashioned and 'unscientific', too. But that does not automatically lessen its value for fishery management.

What about the hunters as well as the hunted?

Getting the science right is one thing – knowing, most fundamentally, how big or small fish populations are. That is hard enough, but it is not all that matters. Back in the 1980s, British/Canadian mathematical ecologist Jacqueline McGlade was one of a handful of scientists to realize that modelling fisheries without the human dimension was a sure recipe for disaster. So she and colleague Peter Allen looked at how fishermen actually go about 'hunting'. After all, behaviour underlies all human endeavours, she argued, including the processes of resource discovery, exploitation and even innovation. In economics, it is the same. Economists were slow to realize that it is more than just the flow of dollars between national and international markets that matters; people should be part of the equation. As marine ecologists Julie Hawkins and Callum Roberts also lament: 'In their mathematical models, fish have become particles within homogeneous seas that are fished randomly by unthinking fishers.' The reality of course is different, for fishermen's behaviour, as much as anything else, can determine what happens to a fishery.

According to McGlade and Allen, fishermen are either Stochasts or Cartesians. Stochasts are those who do not act merely on information that exists about previous returns on fishing effort; they have some other knowledge, or intuition, that is less influenced by the norm, by the average view. Simply put, they are optimists – the risk-takers. It is a mindset and game plan that is totally different to that of Cartesians – the solid cornerstones of the fishing fraternity. They prefer the certainties of low but safe returns rather than, as Allen and McGlade say, 'the "promise" of some "Eldorado"'. In the mid 1980s, these researchers showed that the successful long-term functioning and survival of a fishery actually requires both kinds of behaviour, so in this sense fisheries are no different from an individual, a firm, a society or a nation.

Not realizing, though, that some fishermen might reap as if there is no tomorrow is missing something important. The truth is that seas are *not* fished randomly by unthinking fishermen. But the answer lies not in suppressing the Stochasts, but protecting certain areas from any fishing at all. This, as I will explain, is what helps ensure a vibrant fishery in many other ways too.

Stocks here today, still here tomorrow

Take a trip to Falmouth on England's south coast and you might witness something rare – the only oyster fishery in Europe, if not in the world, to operate under sail power and pulling simple dredges: it is a relic from a bygone era. For their daily catch, the fishermen rely on everything except modern technology as they work the oyster beds, marked by sticks or 'withies': the wind, the tides, their skill and their local knowledge. This oyster fishery spans three centuries, and the oldest boats in the fleet go back to 1860. Motorized vessels, as well as heavier and more destructive fishing gears – which require greater towing power – have always been banned.

In operation this fishery may look inefficient, but it is quite another matter if you count damage to the seabed as a loss and a cost, and long lifespan of a fishery plus steady catches as a benefit. Unlike most of the world's fisheries, this one has remained intact and viable. It has kept going through the use of closed seasons, restricted types of fishing gear, and restricted types and numbers of craft: time-tested life insurance. There is also a lower limit to the size of oysters that may be caught, measured using a simple brass hoop – 2⅝ inches; like my father, this fishery refuses to go metric. As fishing craft, Falmouth working boats may appear, and actually are, old-fashioned. When it comes to retaining robustness of the oyster beds, and a sustainable fishery, though, its ways are hardly behind the times.

On the other side of the Atlantic, in Chesapeake Bay, the oyster fishery could not be more different. So full of oyster beds was Chesapeake when European ships first landed on the coast of Virginia more than four centuries ago that they were, quite literally, a navigation hazard. But not only are oysters a prized delicacy: left alone in the natural environment they filter and purify seawater – part of the ocean's free service, except we may not recognize this until it is too late. Back in the 1800s, Chesapeake oysters would have done the job about every three days. Intensive dredging changed all that. Today, with the oyster reefs all but gone, filtering takes hundreds of days because so few oysters remain. On top of that, harmful algal blooms have increasingly plagued the bay. Jeremy Jackson and colleagues recently showed that, contrary to popular belief, pollution from upstream cities and agriculture was not the main cause, for it preceded the algal blooms. Things only got bad once the oysters had become scarce. Looking at Chesapeake today, it would be easy – but misleading – to imagine an oyster-less state to be normal. Yet, as already indicated, over the generations the environment and its resources can easily slide, unnoticed, into a new unwelcome state.

Besides its good health, there is something else special about Falmouth's oyster fishery. This stems from its seasonal operation: dredging is allowed only from October to March. During the summer months the 'Falmouth working boats' switch from being packhorse to racer, as they compete in waters around the Fal and at many regattas in Cornwall. With their fine gaff rig and long bowsprits, they might look old-timers, but they can go like the wind. The closed fishing season, not surprisingly, eases pressure on the oyster stocks. But that is not all. Time spent racing makes the fishermen really hone their sailing skills, as they pit their wits against each other to reach the marker buoys first. Indirectly, this helps them to exploit oysters around Falmouth as efficiently as possible, using only the 'inefficient' ways permitted. You could call the switch from fishing to racing multi-tasking. This is yet another subtle way in which robustness can help things keep going.

Tales from the unexpected

Three thousand miles south-west of Falmouth, give or take, lies St Lucia; somewhere very different, yet also special. On its west coast, two massive rock pinnacles, Gros Piton and the smaller Petit Piton, rise over 2,000 feet from the Caribbean's turquoise waters. To the north is Marigot Bay, once a location for *Dr Doolittle* – the 1960s film whose make-believe animals included the giant pink tropical sea snail. Closer to the pitons, and near the town of Soufrière, is the luxury Anse Chastanet Hotel. It is a spot that has turned out to be a sanctuary for more than residents and guests. How that happened, though, was almost completely by accident.

The Anse Chastanet reserve is probably the world's smallest marine protected area. In 1992 the hotel closed off a tiny sea area – just 150 by 175 metres – as a safe haven for its bathers and snorkellers. But the protection zone did other things, too: it kept fishermen out. By 1995, the size and weight of snappers and other commercially important fish doubled in the Anse Chastanet reserve, compared with similar adjacent fished reefs. Not only that, highly mobile species, like the Spanish grunt, benefited from protection. In agreeing to a reduced fishing area, fishermen took a gamble, but it was one which paid off. Because of the 'spill-over' effect, explained later, some of the best hook and line fishing occurs right beside the reserve, though not actually in it – where fishing is banned.

This simple reserve is only small in size, yet it demonstrates the remarkable power of what full protection might do for fisheries on a larger scale: low-tech management indeed, yet from it comes greater reliability of harvests. Put another way, marine reserves are sanctuaries, 'retreats of robustness', where fish are free from fishing. In areas like the North Sea, reserves could protect the seabed from the ravaging effects of trawl nets. What is so surprising is that such a simple expedient remains so controversial, despite successes in St Lucia and many other places.

The reserve at Anse Chastanet might be one of the smallest, but it was not the first one created. No-take reserves are much more old-fashioned; they may not be as ancient as fishing itself, though taboo areas go back perhaps 1,000 years or more in some societies. Not only that, making off-limits to fishing is only what an inhospitable environment does naturally. What happened in the North Sea provides a poignant illustration of this. During the First and Second World Wars fishing more or less stopped. Vulnerability to gunfire, bombs, mines and submarines was a deterrent to trawling; this eased pressure on the stocks by indirectly creating 'protected' areas – for fish, if not trawlers.

Tales from our ancestors

Centuries before Western scientists even realized the need to conserve fish stocks, the people of Vanuatu, Palau and particularly the Asia-Pacific region had already developed many of the conservation methods used by fishery managers today. The late Canadian scientist Bob

Johannes, initially an oceanographer, was someone who devoted much of his life to understanding their ways. His approach, though, was radically different from that of fishery scientists before him. After spending a memorable evening with Bob in San Francisco in 1989, following a conference on marine reserves, I began to understand why. In several villages in Palau where Bob worked, I later read, people had commented that while fisheries researchers had visited before, he 'was the first one who ever asked us about our knowledge; the others only told us about theirs'.

Traditional conservation was something well developed in coral reefs, lagoons and other areas where territorial boundaries of resources could be identified easily. It turns out that islanders had the very management tools we might suppose were invented by modern fisheries science: closed seasons, closed areas and size limits for catches. What's more, coastal communities had rights to exclude trespassers from their fishing grounds. Limited access, as a conservation tool, probably evolved over centuries, or longer. Over time it became part of customary marine law – rules and codes enshrined in, and an integral part of society. After all, UN conventions and other legally binding environmental measures never existed then.

Why marine conservation was and still remains so critical on tropical islands and atolls is another insight Johannes and others gleaned. On coral reefs, highest biological productivity (and by far the greatest fishery catches) comes from a narrow strip of shallow water, coinciding with the relatively small extent of the reef. Just as water depths drop off beyond the edge, so too does fish abundance. Any fisherman or diver worth his salt knows this. Early in the century many Pacific islands were colonized by Europeans, for whom the fisheries, as mentioned, were a lucrative asset. One result of the increased demand for fish, not surprisingly, was over-exploitation. In reef areas that were once coastal food factories, fish production all too quickly tailed off; the stocks were insufficiently robust against the additional pressure. Part of the problem lay in colonial familiarity with wide continental shelves back home in temperate waters, and more extensive, productive fishing grounds compared with reefs.

Also, recall, the newcomers advocated 'freedom of the seas'; 'the oceans shall provide', the colonizers supposed, correctly – but only up to a point.

But just how good was old-fashioned controlled access as a means of conserving seafood stocks? This has been a matter of increasing debate. Josh Cinner of James Cook University in Australia and colleagues went to Papua New Guinea to look for hard evidence. Among the villages visited were Muluk and Ahus, where closures, or *tambu*, still operate under traditional management. This involves closing part of a reef to fishing during certain periods, or restricting damaging activities within the *tambu*. The investigation revealed increased size and weight of fish in the enclosure. In Muluk, Cinner discovered, there was a bonus: traditional management cuts down damage to corals from fishing and gleaning of other reef produce. Not only that, periodic closure is valuable for 'taming' the fish, so that they can be speared more easily and efficiently when the *tambu* reopens. In Ahus, closures had a valuable social function by providing a 'bank' of fish, drawn on for feasts and special celebrations; it was a way of maintaining links with the community's cultural heritage.

Or consider the Hikmani people, in Oman off the Arabian Sea coast. Through long-standing, self-imposed restraint, as marine conservationist Rod Salm once reported, fishing normally takes place only in deep waters. Like other reef fishermen, the Hikmani realized it would require much less effort, and that they would get better catches, if they fished the shallow-water reefs – an area far richer and closer to home. But the Hikmani also know that continual fishing over these limited patches can (and probably did) easily deplete the stocks. So instead, they normally fish offshore. Only when life gets really tough, when stormy weather makes access to deeper water difficult or impossible, do they fish the shallows. In this way the productive inshore waters remain as sustaining 'cold storage areas'; it helps the reef fishery remain robust.

We have evidence that partial closure to fishing, through seasonal or other restrictions, was the way traditional maritime societies conserved their stocks. Yet in Hawaii, for example, areas where fishing is totally banned may be seen today, and we are talking here of long-standing management. Not only that, a recent (2006) study in Hawaii demonstrates, unequivocally, the greater power of complete rather than temporary closure as an essential means of regenerating and safeguarding fish populations.

As this chapter goes on to explain, this is precisely what modern fishery management needs more of today: at least some areas where no fishing or harmful extractive activities may occur. If it sounds a plain, old-fashioned remedy, that would not be wrong.

On the other hand, several studies have revealed something which, on first reckoning, deals the notion of the 'noble savage' – voluntary, self-imposed conservation by our ancestors – a blow. They provide evidence that traditional societies in a number of regions plundered resources on an unprecedented scale long before colonials arrived on the scene. The marine resources they encountered, therefore, were not untouched virgin stock after all. Some sceptics even argue that a conservation ethic did not actually exist among tropical island communities.

What is undeniable is that colonial presence made matters worse, through additional demands placed on fish stocks and erosion of traditional ways of conservation. Not only that, although pre-colonial over-harvesting happened, it was by no means universal. Early records demonstrate, for example, that abundant and rich seal populations inhabited the Aleutians – and many other areas, too – centuries before Queen Victoria sat on the throne. It should be added, though, that the people of the Aleutians over-harvested sea otters near settlements, causing loss of kelp forests. Quite likely, though, as Bob Johannes and others argue, at least some communities developed an ethic, albeit the hard way – becoming acutely aware of the need for conservation through food shortage and hunger.

The truth is that remnants of traditional management – in places like Papua New Guinea, Japan, Fiji, the Marshall Islands and Oman – still survive today, providing some testament to an ethic developed long ago. Despite some fisheries scientists questioning their value, no-take reserves are making a comeback, for one simple reason: there is a payback.

Designer reserves

Marine reserves work simply by increasing the age, size and numbers of fish. Within their boundaries, fish find sanctuary, producing many times more offspring than in nearby fished areas. This helps populations recover from heavy exploitation. Consider, for example, Sumilon Island in the Philippines. It was here, in the early 1970s, that university biologists struggled to create one of the world's first (modern) reserves. After just eight years of protection, there was rapid build-up of fish predators from around six to seventeen individuals per 1,000 square metres. But the Sumilon reserve was bedevilled by a roller-coaster ride of protection, fishing violation, and protection again, causing a headache to managers if not a nightmare for resident fish. Biologists Angel Alcala and Garry Russ showed that after fishing in the reserve resumed, despite the larger area now available, the total yield was actually 54 per cent less; catch per unit of fishing effort fell also.

Reserves, when respected, help fisheries through the 'spillover' effect. Once numbers of fish, or other seafood species, build up sufficiently in areas of protection, animals move to less crowded areas outside the reserve boundary. Here, of course, fishing is allowed. On Apo Island, the site of another reserve in the Philippines, fish numbers built up rapidly over eleven years; outside the reserve numbers also increased, but very slowly, with nothing much happening for six years. On the face of it, this was how long it took for conditions to become sufficiently crowded in the reserve before leakage, or spillover, occurred. But net increase, 'stockpiling', beyond the border only happens once the rate of spillover exceeds removal, suggesting the reserve was probably supplying the fishery all along – just unnoticed.

What really demonstrates the practical value of reserves, though, is 'fishing the line' – fishermen operating close to the boundary. Once a reserve is created, you soon see this tactic in action: whether in the Tabarca reserve in Spain, Belize's Hol Chan reserve, or New Zealand's Leigh marine reserve. Here, surprisingly, it is not buoys that indicate the reserve limit, remarked reserve co-founder Bill Ballantine, but the floats of lobster pots.

Something fishermen are quick to cast doubt on is the time it takes for reserves to work. Normally, it turns out, benefits come within five years, building up for ten or twenty years thereafter. In heavily exploited species, population build-up is seen within a year or two. In fact models suggest that the more heavy past fishing, the more rapid the build-up, provided stock levels were not depleted to critically low levels. Of course, there are costs – setting up the reserve, inevitable reduction of fishing area and potential redirection of fishing elsewhere – but the pay-offs more than compensate.

Reserves might work for fish that do not roam far, but many fishery scientists have been unconvinced that migratory species benefit. Highly mobile fish, such as bluefin tuna, will spend more time outside a reserve than in the much smaller area inside. Critics argue that most commercial fish – not just tuna – are just too mobile to benefit, and that loss of fishing grounds could easily outweigh any benefits. Yet mobile species stand to benefit in many ways. One reason is that many migratory fish congregate, in hundreds or thousands, in certain places at certain times. Here they are easily caught. The Nassau grouper, for example, has virtually gone from large areas of the Caribbean, simply because of over-zealous fishing of spawning aggregations. Another benefit of reserves for migratory species is that, as juveniles, fish may aggregate in nursery areas, where they often remain for months or years. Hence, both the young and old stand little chance in the face of eager fishermen. Strategically placed reserves in nursery and spawning areas can provide valuable protection.

An undeniable fact is that fish in protected areas survive longer and produce more young. 'Fishers have nothing to fear from marine reserves,' Callum Roberts once remarked; 'they should worry about a future without them.' No-take areas could even help to save the North Sea's dwindling cod stocks. It is something that might help save the totoaba in the Gulf of California. Back in the 1940s, this fish underwent remarkable annual migrations. Individuals that once grew to over two metres long and weighed 140 kilos would now be lucky to reach ten kilos. Today the totoaba is endangered and on the brink of extinction. Besides over-fishing and loss of critical spawning and nursery area, young fish end up as by-catch in the shrimp trawls.

Reserves are remarkable in all sorts of ways. For example, they do not have to be large to work. The Anse Chastanet Reserve in St Lucia is tiny in relation to the open sea, just over two hectares. It occupies an area smaller than four football pitches – quite literally a drop in the ocean – yet it has benefited coral fish and bathers, too. But bigger can be better. Highly mobile fish, for example, gain greater protection from large reserves, and large reserves also give greater protection against catastrophic disturbances, which may be localized. Paradoxically, though, once a reserve gets too big, the likelihood of a fish ever getting from an area of protection to an area of fishing diminishes. It is a difficult juggling act. When it comes to exporting eggs, juveniles and adults to adjacent fishing areas, several small reserves are better than one large one. Make them too small, though, and they become so leaky the reserves themselves can never build up stock.

As research and common sense dictate, robustness is never possible against everything. Size of reserve is no different; trade-offs are unavoidable. The difficulty is that as fishing and human use of the sea escalate, so too does the minimum reserve size needed to be effective. What's tantalizing, though, is that as we use the oceans more and more, we increasingly appreciate and value what is left, so the size of reserve that is socially acceptable actually gets less: a Catch 22 if ever there was one. The goal, globally, to fully protect 20 per cent of the oceans by 2020 seems far from what may happen. For at present only 0.6 per cent of the world ocean is (nominally) protected. Paradoxically, in countries like the USA, most marine parks encourage fishing.

Meeting of minds

Marine reserves are a simple, old-fashioned extension of protection to species and habitats once provided naturally by conditions that discourage fishing – the deep sea, a rough sea, a mined sea or a rocky seabed. It is not that protected areas should replace modern management, though, for it too has some conservation value. In some ways reserves are similar to conventional tools, for example through reducing fishing effort and increasing the age of fish at first capture. The added value, as Callum Roberts explains, arises because reserves extend protection from one or just a few species to many species (including fast- and slow-growers), and from temporary protection to total protection. On top of that, information levels needed are far lower than for modern management.

What is undeniable, though, is that without more time-tested fully protected reserves, the litany of fishery disaster will go on. As Roberts remarked recently, 'We can get more out of the sea by leaving some of it alone.' You could call it a robust way of getting more from less – the goal of every efficiency seeker.

CHAPTER 6 AQUA VITAE

The mainspring for everything

Connect up and be damned

Built in the 1960s, the High Dam at Aswan was a landmark engineering achievement. It was all the more remarkable since the British and US governments suddenly pulled the plug on their financial loan ($270 million), four years before construction began, for reasons not fully understood. Standing 111 metres tall, the dam certainly lives up to its name. The massive rock and clay structure contains 43 million cubic metres of material – apparently eighteen times the amount of material used in the Great Pyramid of Cheops. The dam was designed by a Russian, whose government, as things turned out, footed a sizeable chunk of the bill.

Spectacular and imposing as it is, the Aswan Dam was, of course, not built simply for show. With up to 11,000 cubic metres of water passing through it every second, capacity for power generation and water supply was, on the face of it, second to none. The designers and engineers must have known, of course, that some undesirable knock-on effects would be unavoidable from a venture as colossal as this one; the '*robustness* of ecosystems', after all, could hardly escape totally unscathed. Nevertheless, any unfortunate by-products delivered by the dam, in their eyes, would not matter compared with all that stood to be gained.

Hydroelectricity came on line in 1967, from twelve huge generators, together producing a hydro-electric output of 2.1 gigawatts. Once at peak flow, it delivered around half of Egypt's entire electricity production. For many villages, what's more, it meant electricity for the very first time. Besides obvious utility value, the new-found power was a huge boost to the nation's economy – in the order of $500 million annually. It was as if, all of a sudden, engineers had given the nation a new lease of life.

Equally important was the dam's ability to control fresh water: to combat both floods and droughts. For thousands of years the Nile had burst its banks every spring, wreaking damage and devastation, even in regions far downstream. Exceptional floods occurred in 1964 and 1973. But with the dam's capacity to hold back the waters and divert them to where they were needed, it averted catastrophe. Quite plainly, without the dam, the droughts of 1972–3 and 1983–4 would have taken a very serious toll.

In any low-water year, in fact, there was widespread drought and famine, whereas in a high-water year the whole crop might be entirely wiped out. For Egyptian agriculture, then, the dam seemed a gift like no other. By controlling the height and flow of the Nile, the Aswan Dam was, in effect, a giant safety and rescue operation, but not just on land. If you happened to be in shipping, or simply travelling up and down the Nile, the dam was a bonus, too, as it made navigation far easier and safer: for the first time ever, a minimum river depth was more or less guaranteed.

On closer inspection, controlling the Nile's water was made possible from a by-product of the Aswan Dam, in fact one spawned from it: Lake Nasser. In a mere twinkling of the engineers' eyes, the 550km long body of water became one of the world's biggest man-made reservoirs – so large that nearly one-quarter of it spills over to Sudan in the south. In one sense, Lake Nasser became the dam's sentinel and control centre – rather like the pituitary gland, the endocrine organ masterminding many functions in vertebrates, including ourselves. By tapping into Lake Nasser's waters, new farms sprang up in once barren desert lands. Not only that, brand new aquatic habitat led to a completely new fishery; a welcome bonus, though not exactly flourishing due to the distance from markets of any significance.

But there were even greater inconveniences, it soon became clear, than merely offloading the catch: unwelcome visitors, especially if you happened to be a fisherman, or simply a hapless bather. Like the fishermen, crocodiles were also attracted by extra fish in and around Lake Nasser. Crocodiles were not new to the area – they have always been residents of the Nile. The trouble was, with a new food resource available, they soon began to multiply. Local people got so scared that they asked the government to do something about the problem. Besides, they protested, it was responsible for the dam and its unwelcome visitors in the first place. But even crocodiles were minor in comparison with other side-effects to follow – from both the construction and the operation of the dam.

A sad and inescapable fact is that many giant hydro-electric schemes, initiated on the basis of narrow projections of performance, for greater '*efficiency* of industry and development', have yielded only limited benefits (at best). This usually amounts to short-term 'measurable income', as increasingly admitted by governments and agencies that initially lent support. As a source and symbol of power, as mentioned, the dam seemed unrivalled. But as the laws of physics tell us, there is seldom, if ever, a free lunch; sooner or later there will be a price to pay. Subject a vast arterial system, like the Nile, to invasive surgery and that there is trouble ahead should come as no surprise. You could say it is inevitable.

In the case of the Aswan Dam, unmistakable signs of collateral damage were evident early on, when Lake Nasser filled. While what came down was a gift from on high in some respects, village people of both Egypt and Sudan – the Nubians – saw it otherwise. For 90,000 of them were displaced and had to be relocated to avoid becoming flooded. The hefty deluge that turned the Nile into Lake Nasser took its toll on cultural assets, too. At Wadi Haifa, for example, a famous ancient Egyptian temple, cut into the cliffs, had to be removed and found another home; countless other assets, no doubt, never made it to the safety of dry land and may be gone forever. Not only that, the cost of the various relocations ran into billions of dollars.

It was starting to look as if plugging into electricity, and the ability to control water, was going to be a very costly venture indeed. Not only that, output from the mighty Aswan Dam, it turned out, was either unsustainable or it failed to keep abreast of Egypt's needs. By 1998, according to one estimate, the dam produced only 15 per cent of national electricity consumption. Given that it produced around half of the country's total electricity in its heyday, the figures did not look very encouraging.

Failing to perform is one thing, but worse was to come in terms of the side-effects, the actual impacts of the dam's operations on the '*robustness* of ecosystems' – after, that is, resettlement of the Nubians and rehousing the cultural assets. What happened, for example, to fisheries? The increase in crocodile numbers was something not bargained for, but the real problem, it turned out, lay beyond the horizon, in the eastern Mediterranean. Like crops on land, fishery stocks require nutrients, to enrich the waters and create sufficient plankton for food chains, which culminate in harvested seafood species. The eastern basin of the Mediterranean is naturally nutrient-poor – low in fertility. That was its normal situation, in times when enrichment with vital phosphate and silicate came about from the Nile's unimpeded outflow. But with reduced water flow and nutrients – now trapped behind the dam – the Eastern Mediterranean shrimp and sardine fisheries, to put it simply, crashed. Some assessments showed that catches decreased by approximately half following the construction of the dam. Even allowing for other possible influences, not least heavy fishing, the general consensus is that reduced nutrient throughput down the Nile into the sea had a very deleterious effect on marine fisheries.

Greater robustness of the land – against floods and droughts – might be one thing the Aswan Dam has brought about. When it came to the nearby ocean and fisheries, though, it was starting to look as if the project's operations were creating an increasingly fragile system instead.

But that's not all. Agriculture cannot be productive from water alone – essential though it is (and it could be distributed to where it was needed most, once irrigation came on-stream). The other vital requirement, for agriculture and fisheries alike, is nutrients. During predam times, they arrived on land at least once a year – when the Nile flooded its banks, and silt-laden waters fertilized croplands. But now, without periodic inundation with silt and nutrients (they were ending up, instead, in Lake Nasser), the deficit had to be made up in another way. Farmers in the lower valley soon had to buy, and add, thousands of tonnes (more than a million, according to at least one report) of artificial fertilizer each year. They had no alternative but to replace the elixir of life that once washed over the river banks – and, what's more, was free on delivery. Having to go high-tech, many began to realize, was slow, hard work, and it was costly, too.

Perhaps the Aswan Dam, contrary to initial expectations, was not making agriculture in and around the Nile more robust after all. The impact experienced by farmers on land seemed to be mirroring the changing conditions in the Mediterranean, reflected by fishermen's falling catches. In both cases, decline in nutrient levels is where the problem lay. Added to that, Lake Nasser began to evaporate (as well as silt up), leading to an increase in the salt content of its waters. For irrigated agriculture, it is an input that could not be worse: it ruins soil quality, and it stunts or kills crops grown on it. Adding more water only brings the salt up to the surface – into direct contact with crop roots, adding to the problem further. Put another way, the '*robustness* of ecosystems' was on the line, and the benefits to the '*efficiency* of industry and development' were not looking quite so promising, either.

Looked at simply, much of what sprang from the Aswan Dam – but was not bargained for – was the price to pay for not considering sufficiently the benefits: Of what? To whom? And for how long? Ignorance is one possible area for blame, but even in the 1960s, the decade of construction, much of the impact to come could have been (and probably was) foreseen. Take fisheries, as an example. For decades, oceanographers have known that, once starved of nutrients, coasts and seas soon become unproductive, as, consequently, do the fisheries; coral reefs, it happens, are an exception to the rule, but they do not occur in the Mediterranean. So retention of nutrients by the dam and Lake Nasser, and the calamitous effects on seafood stocks that followed, should hardly have been a surprise. One could say it would have been little short of a miracle if the '*robustness* of ecosystems' had held up.

Perhaps construction of the dam still went ahead because it was simply assumed – though clearly by wishful thinking – that the benefits of electricity production, flood control, irrigation and the like would *far* outweigh any unwanted side-effects of construction and operation. To this day it remains an issue under hot debate, but, in the eyes of many, the Aswan Dam was a hasty, ill-conceived construction project.

One could even say that the venture provides modernity with a showcase, or blueprint, of how not to do things in the future. The focus on '*efficiency* of industry and development' was simply too strong and narrow. Conversely, what the Aswan Dam was likely to do to the '*robustness* of ecosystems' was a matter that seemed to have escaped the attention of all those at the drawing board. Perhaps the strongest irony, though, was that the services of the Aswan Dam to development and industry – in particular agriculture and hydro-electricity – did not seem particularly efficient either.

In all truth, though, some of the side-effects were most probably unexpected. One was the dam's knock-on effect on the long-standing red-brick construction industry in and around the Nile delta. For rather subtle reasons, the industry took a severe hammering. As a source of material, brick-makers were dependent on the delta mud, formerly provided as the Nile's silty waters made their way downstream. Once the Aswan Dam slowed the flow, however, mud could no longer be relied upon, or drawn on, as the raw ingredient for their work. The point eventually came when erosion of the river banks was no longer compensated by replenishment from sediment; in a word, the natural cycle got put out of kilter. For the brick-makers, the Aswan Dam, indirectly but unequivocally, meant reduced or lost livelihood and greater hardship.

Worse was to come. Starved of sediment, sandbars near the shore also began to disappear, increasing erosion and exposing the delta and coastline to storms and damage from the sea. This has been serious not only for Egypt, but also for its Mediterranean neighbours, for there has been significant shoreline erosion along virtually all its eastern shores. And the impact is now accentuated by sea-level rise and increased severity of storms brought on by global climate change.

Perhaps far-fetched, but some forecasts make for even gloomier reading, due to the Aswan Dam's creation of higher salinities – arising from reduced freshwater inflow into the Mediterranean. This mother of all regime changes affects, according to some, the Mediterranean's outflow current, which can be traced far into the Atlantic. Some even speculate that the dam's effect on this outflow accelerates processes that will lead to the next ice age.

Egyptian implementers of the Aswan Dam, undoubtedly, still stick to their guns, believing the project was worthwhile. Looked at one way, it certainly bought the nation extra time, staving off drought and providing (some) positive benefits from irrigation as well as electricity. Another undeniable fact, though, was that the project compromised the robustness not only of agriculture, but also of adjacent marine systems, both physically and biologically. What's more, impacts extended far beyond Egypt's territorial waters; the dam had transnational repercussions.

Put another way, the Nile's 'non-essential' services, its invisible productivity, were believed to expendable and traded for on-tap services, whose benefits are now proving to be ephemeral.

Other free-flow fantasies

The disagreeable by-products that flowed from the Aswan Dam were bad enough. Consider, though, what happened as a result of a development project for irrigation in and around the Aral Sea. Lying between Kazakhstan and Uzbekistan, this inland sea has been shrinking and drying up, quite literally, over the past fifty years. Even the steady, natural inflow of submarine groundwater (6 billion cubic metres annually) – a far larger quantity than previously supposed – was insufficient to slow the Aral Sea's disappearance.

By the 1980s the drop in water level was almost one metre each year, resulting from the then Soviet Union's intervention in diverting – for irrigation, as with the Aswan Dam – the Amu Darya and the Syr Darya rivers, waterways that normally feed the Aral Sea. It was all part of the Soviet plan to green the desert, in order to grow rice, melons, cereal and cotton. In all fairness, too, by the mid 1980s Uzbekistan had become a major global exporter of cotton, or 'white gold'. But there were some very dark consequences. It was not just a case of some diminution of the '*robustness* of ecosystems', either. With the insufficient lubrication that the project brought about, the environment well and truly buckled under the strain.

Besides the Aral Sea drying out, and fishing boats left high and dry, the salinity of its waters rose more than four-fold. Not surprisingly, this was bad news for the Aral Sea's ecosystems; most, if not all, of the sea's twenty or so species of freshwater fish, for example, disappeared. Furthermore, the winds picked up the dried salt deposits – over which water had once stood – and blew the residue inland. There, of course, it did untold damage to crops. If that were not enough, the Aral Sea became highly polluted from a mixed bag of activities before and after the break-up of the Soviet Union. Fallout from various industrial projects was partly to blame. On top of that, weapons testing and fertilizer run-off impinged on environmental robustness and human health. Chronic bronchitis, for instance, has risen by 3,000 per cent in the area over the past fifteen years. Virtually all women of reproductive age on the Aral Sea's southern shore, according to local doctors, have anaemia, and more than 80 per cent of their babies are born with the condition.

This sorry state of affairs came about because it was assumed that a lucrative cotton industry was more important than fish production, nature's own waterworks and other contributors to the '*robustness* of ecosystems'. As with the Aswan Dam, there were undeniable benefits, 'white gold' being a case in point. But this seems scant compensation for the predictable and catastrophic misery the Soviet plan brought to 3.5 million people inhabiting the shores of the Aral Sea. To add insult to injury, Grigory Voropaev, the architect of the ill-conceived scheme, is alleged to have said: 'Let the Aral die beautifully.' He apparently uttered this sentiment echoing the belief of the planners that the Aral Sea was 'a mistake of nature' and that it was their duty to rectify it. As 'Soviet' was synonymous with 'communist' back then, one can hardly blame free-for-all 'capitalism', either. On any count, though, the bypass operation affecting the Aral Sea was a misguided one. Any contributions to '*efficiency of industry and development*' turned out to be meagre in comparison with the project's devastating side-effects. We are talking here of the direct negative social and economic impact, as well as the phenomenal collateral damage wrought on the environment caused by undercutting the '*robustness* of ecosystems'.

Amazing to many was that, in the face of such environmental assault, all was not completely lost, as restoration under way to revitalize the northern Aral Sea bears testament. Since work to separate the two halves of the dam was completed in August 2005, for example, the water level of the northern part has risen and, at the same time, its salinity has decreased. In no time at all, in fact, the depth rose from thirty to thirty-eight metres – forty-two metres being reckoned to be the magical level needed to get things back on ecological track; in other words, to help rejuvenate the '*robustness* of ecosystems'. There are even reports of a return of economically viable stocks of fish; so much so, in fact, that the fishing industry began exporting catches to the Ukraine.

Installing desalination plants to produce freshwater 'artificially' should help, too, as would switching to alternative cotton species that require less water. More encouraging still, Aral Sea restoration is, apparently, beginning to recreate long-absent rain clouds and changes to microclimate; so natural climate regulation, one important signature of robust ecosystems, might come about once again.

'The rebirth of the northern Aral Sea is a good showcase project,' reported Viktor Danilov-Danilyan, an expert in water problems at the Russian Academy of Sciences. 'It shows that if we fret about the environment and invest money, it is possible to get reassuring results.

The loss of such a unique natural resource as the Aral would be a global tragedy. And it cannot be allowed to happen.'

Whether we conduct a post-mortem on the Aswan Dam, the Aral Sea, or any other bypass operation, decrease in the '*robustness* of ecosystems' is a side-effect from big dams and water redistribution that is not to be taken lightly. Despite the benefits, large-scale projects of this sort may not be the answer for the '*efficiency* of industry and development' in the long run: the downstream costs may simply be too great. Yet there seems to be no stopping them.

One recent report, for example, revealed that by the turn of the millennium 45,000 large dams were in place, to generate one fifth of all power, and to irrigate one third of all crops, as well as to control floods and store water. But these construction projects, several of them massive, like the mighty Aswan Dam – have also been hugely invasive. It perhaps comes as no surprise that they have compromised the ecology of half of the world's rivers and displaced more than 40 million people from their homes and lands. It is hard to imagine a higher price to pay for the '*efficiency* of industry and development'. It would seem logical, then, that the UN and other development agencies are now not quite so quick to lend a helping hand, or a fistful of dollars, to initiate large-scale surgical procedures.

On the other hand, assistance still seems to pour in. Consider, for example, Turkey's recent and highly ambitious Southeast Anatolia Development Project. This is one of the world's largest engineering projects, and has funding from banks and international financial circles. That is the irony, given the devastating side-effects that have sprung from the Aswan Dam and other similar ventures. Set for completion in around 2013, the new project involves, among other things, at least fifteen dams (twenty-two according to some sources) in the Tigris and Euphrates. All in all, the project area covers some 70,000 square kilometres. In other words, the scale of the venture is phenomenal.

Widespread sustainable development, especially from the spreading of water and wealth, is one expected benefit. At an estimated cost of some 32 *billion* dollars, hopefully it will inject something into the '*efficiency* of industry and development' for Turkey. One thing for sure is that diverting water from the Tigris and Euphrates is likely to have serious repercussions for the Gulf – potentially undermining the '*robustness* of ecosystems' in the entire region. What's more, all the good done by recent projects to reinstate the marshlands around these waterways, drained at the command of former Iraqi leader Saddam Hussein, could very quickly become undone. Given the problems or dubious benefits that trickled down from the Aswan Dam, one shudders to imagine the unprecedented collateral damage that must surely follow in the wake of the Southeast Anatolia Development Project.

A more down-to-earth problem, of course, though also one largely responsible for the decline in environmental health in the first place, is the sheer quantity of water the world now consumes. But this is not just to quench humanity's immediate needs. For the volume needed to lubricate and facilitate the '*efficiency* of industry and development' almost defies belief – aside, that is, from what steel plants and other industrial plants must guzzle to keep production going.

The fact is that modern agriculture itself is incredibly thirsty. The volume of water typically needed to produce just 1 kilogram of three different types of industrial agricultural produce is in the order of: 500 litres for potatoes, 3,500 litres for chicken and a staggering 100,000 litres for beef. Given enough water, wheat can be grown even in arid countries, like Saudi Arabia – though, as already mentioned, at a huge environmental cost to the country itself and to its neighbours. Looked at this way, mass-produced food does not always come cheap, at least not if you take into account the direct costs and knock-on effects of redistributing such large quantities of water.

Water consumption is now so great, and the demands we are putting on our natural systems to generate it are now so huge, that some believe water is fast becoming the resource over which conflicts and skirmishes could turn into outright wars. Equally, though, many of modernity's efforts to bridge the gap with dams and large-scale irrigation have been little short of disastrous – that is, if you worry about the '*robustness* of ecosystems' being put on the line; and the negative knock-on effects this can have on the '*efficiency* of industry and development'. The good news, though, is there are alternative solutions and, on many counts, better solutions.

Water from oil and from sunshine: desalination

Tapping into the sea as a source of water, using desalination, has an obvious attraction, especially in arid quarters of the world. In the Gulf States, as a case in point, 80 per cent or more of residents now rely on desalination for satisfying their daily freshwater needs. Most plants work by pumping seawater through a very fine membrane, which allows water molecules to pass through, but not salt. The other main approach to desalination utilizes what are effectively giant distillation plants, from which comes more then 80 per cent of the world's 'artificially' generated water. One plant in the United Arab Emirates, possibly still the largest anywhere, produces a staggering 300 million cubic metres of water every year. Often these sorts of plants produce electricity, as well as freshwater, to help economize on fuel use. No one, after all, wants to waste it unnecessarily – not even in the Middle East, where there is (still) plenty of fossil fuel around beneath the nation's feet or under the sea.

Fuel bills aside, there is, of course, no such thing as a free lunch. Desalination plants, which are on the go day and night, generate brine as part of the seawater conversion process. Once discharged, briny effluents create chemical and ecological disturbances, affecting marine species at the receiving end. In the case of distillation plants, the brines are hot, too, which adds to the injuries to local flora and fauna. On top of that, various chemical agents added to desalination plants also come out at the other end. One such additive is sulphuric acid, to control scale formation; then there are compounds containing chlorine, to discourage encrustation by bio-fouling organisms. An inconvenient fact is that, when seawater passes by, these species happen to clog up pipes (as well as the underside of ships).

A long discharge pipe from a desalination plant can go a long way to help reduce the ecological effects of unwelcome by-products in coastal shallows: it works by 'dilution and distribution'. Yet there is no denying that effluents do create some environmental damage. This, incidentally, can be greater during commissioning, re-commissioning or start-up (following periods of shut-down for maintenance) than during normal daily operations.

Then there is the non-trivial matter of powering the life-sustaining, and (to a lesser extent) life-threatening, beasts in the first place. The majority happen to run on oil. In other words, producing desalinated freshwater this way is dependent on an exhaustible energy resource; and this adds, naturally, to our greenhouse problems. In the years ahead, nuclear-powered desalination might become economical on a large scale, and could be a viable means of production, assuming, of course, that safety standards meet approval from an increasingly sceptical public.

Better still, if the technology can be cracked, would be solar-electric plants. For this would avoid both the environmental down-sides of using oil. The problem, though, is that most solar-electric desalination plants – and direct solar-powered ones, effectively solar stills – are only small-scale plants. Quite plainly, that is something very different from the commercial systems needed for serious-scale water production.

Critics – techno-phobes, some might label them – point to the high costs of desalination. It is, after all, a high-tech process whose set-up and running costs can be crippling, especially for developing countries. Then, they add, there can be the impracticability and financial drain of moving vast quantities of desalinated seawater throughout the interiors of large countries. Besides, desalination's by-products, as mentioned, are nowhere near as green as the sea. Some out-and-out environmentalists even claim desalination effluents to be 'a major cause of marine pollution' when dumped back into the oceans at high temperatures'. As one assessment put it, 'Desalinated water may be a solution for some water-stress regions, but not for places that are poor, deep in the interior of a continent, or at high elevation. Unfortunately, that includes some of the places with biggest water problems.'

On the other hand, capital and running costs continue to fall, so these sorts of sentiments may become less of a worry as technological know-how advances. Some would argue that, certainly in some situations, desalination options (on balance) may be more cost-effective, at least for affluent countries; so dismissing technology, altogether, is not the best way forward. Enlightened thinking, after all, boils down to balance, compromise and good judgement. In the case of desalination, on balance, it can actually be a good deal less invasive to the '*robustness* of ecosystems' than several alternatives. We are referring, of course, to mammoth dams and irrigation networks emanating from them, of the sort already described.

For any country going down the desalination route, though, there is an entirely different matter to be on guard against. As theory tells us, there is no such thing as universal robustness. Systems can be immune against disturbances that are common or designed for; yet the unexpected, events appearing out of the blue, can be completely crippling. Seen in this light, desalination plants are no different from any other non-living or living system.

As the following tale reveals, any village, town or country contemplating the desalination channel must always be mindful of unlikely events – however improbable their occurrence might seem at the time. What happened during the 'first' Gulf war is a case in point. In 1990–1, when Iraq invaded and occupied Kuwait, 8 or more million barrels (about 280 million gallons) entered the waters of the Gulf as a result of a deliberate act of political and environmental terrorism, of a sort never before experienced by the world. Not surprisingly, the pollution threatened the '*robustness* of ecosystems'. As a result of this, as an aside, neighbouring countries filed enormous damage and compensation claims amounting to tens of billions of dollars (which have now been settled).

But the unprecedented oil spill did more than disrupt fishing and natural ecological services. In any country, assured '*efficiency* of industry and development' depends on an uninterrupted supply of uncontaminated freshwater. In this regard, the Gulf States are no different from anywhere else. Concern arose, of course, that the gallons of oil sloshing around in the Gulf's waters might easily foul up the workings of the desalination plants – and, on top of that, contaminate what came out the other end. And that is precisely what happened, but, ironically, only in Kuwait during the months that country was in Iraq's hands. In response, the (temporary) occupier had to shut down, albeit temporarily, at least one of its 'host's' desalination plants.

The tale just described is a salutary and cautionary one. Yet that is not to say that modernity should simply shun technology altogether; rather that it needs more enlightenment, sense and sensibility in its use, and in its planning of present and future needs. Nor, by the same token, should we always close our eyes to lower- and slower-tech solutions to water production – of the sort hard-nosed Luddites, for one, would stand up for, were they still around.

Low-tech through and through

Getting *aqua vitae* directly out of the sea is perhaps the most unlikely means of freshwater production imaginable. Yet in days of old, how Bahrain for one obtained freshwater was even more novel, perhaps, than desalination. What we are referring to is freshwater springs exuding, quite, literally, on to the seabed; in fact, the name Bahrain in Arabic means 'two seas'. Bahraini legend and folklore has it that freshwater springs that bubble up offshore from beneath the sea were caused by falling stars that knocked holes in the ground.

Whatever its origin, this highly improbable though fortunate circumstance was something that had not escaped the attention of local communities. The only harvesting technology necessary for the 'clear gold,' what's more, was a goatskin bag, or something like it, for use as a receptacle. In fact, undersea freshwater deposits have attracted settlers to the shores of Bahrain and other regions of the Gulf since ancient times. Despite increasing desalination, according to some sources, the springs are still used by some coastal communities.

Tapping *only* undersea freshwater in today's world would amount, quite literally, to a drop in the ocean, especially as Bahrain is a modern state as much as any other, an earnest seeker of '*efficiency* of industry and development'. On the other hand, desalination is still very costly, and freshwater aquifers shared by member states of the Arabian Peninsula have dropped to well below a sustainable level, driven that way by unsustainable agriculture. Perhaps, then, Bahrain's offshore water deposits should be nurtured like there is no tomorrow. The problem, though, is that these undersea water deposits are connected to the Arabian acquifer. Once again we see collateral damage from heavy-fisted development and modernization.

Being an enterprise demanding virtually zero technology, harvesting freshwater from the seabed is an approach quite unlike any other. At least it would have been had the wisdom of restraint, and 'waste not, want not' been heeded more widely by agricutural development. For both help prevent modernity from weakening its life-support and business-support systems, as it strives for ever-greater '*efficiency* of industry and development'.

Consider the harsh reality for a country that, in some ways, could not be more different from Bahrain: the Maldives, a string of small islands and a remote holiday paradise in the central Indian Ocean. Yet desperate shortage of (natural) freshwater is feature common to both. Like Bahrain, the capital, Malé, and some other developed Maldivian islands have opted for desalination. Even before the remote destination became a tourism hot-spot, though, heavy use of groundwater pushed its aquifers down to alarmingly low levels. One simple remedy, it turned out – although far from a complete solution – was simply to conserve what water did drop down from on high. It does not mean desalination is redundant, but it certainly helps.

The truth is that the Maldives is blessed with surprisingly high quantities of rainfall, in fact around 190 centimetres annually (more or less, depending on the geographical location of the atolls). The trouble is that in the case of Malé, much of what fell, if it was not consumed, simply disappeared. For on this island, the cause of much wastage proved to be high-tech roads. When the rains came, instead of the water seeping into the ground and recharging the aquifer, it simply ran off the roads and into the sea, lost for ever. Yet the fix, and something that significantly helped keep the aquifer level up to the mark, was something equally obvious: the use of old-fashioned cobbles on the roads. Thereafter a good deal of the rainwater, surplus to immediate requirements, went down, instead of to the blue out yonder.

Floating on the stock market

Even in more rainy latitudes, water resources remain our most treasured asset. It is, after all, the raw ingredient of commerce and industry, not just agriculture and households. Aqua vitae is, as many examples (and plain common sense) testify, the mainspring for everything, our fluid powerhouse. One would think, then, that everything possible would be done to ensure the continued wise use and safe keeping of water; not treating it just as any old commodity, there for the trading. As economist Will Hutton wryly remarked in the *Observer* recently, water companies are not, or at least should not be, casino chips. But you would think they were, judging from how the government and the corporate world sometimes treat and mistreat water.

Even quite recently (summer 2006), it turned out, the then German owner of England's Thames Water, RWE, decided that becoming a world power in water had just not worked out. The water supply of 20 million Londoners, as a consequence, was to be sold to the highest bidder. This turned out to be a private company, Terra Firma, Hutton explains, whose 'swashbuckling owner', Guy Hands, was allegedly offering £8 billion, which would leave RWE a handsome profit of £3.2 billion.

But in the eyes of Hands, it was never to be a long-term investment. His plan was to float Thames Water, quite literally, on the stock market, taking the gamble that investors would pay top whack for this utility company. The problem – though not for Hands of course – is that once in the hands of a private company, instead of a public corporation, Thames's financial affairs would no longer be open to quite the same level of scrutiny.

An inescapable fact, in ownership matters, is that profit and the right of the owner to invest, or not, counts more than Londoners' rights to flush the toilet more than once a day and water their lawns. As testament, Hutton reminds us, consider what happens to water in England and Wales: a staggering 3.6 billion litres are lost, instead of used, each day. What sort of a way this is to uphold the '*efficiency* of industry and development' is a question any enlightened water rate payer worth his salt will be quick to ask.

The reality, and bitter irony, is that in the case of the London waterworks it had been left to leak for decades, mainly because of Thames Water's inefficiency and unwillingness to put sufficient resources in to keep water flowing out. And when providing more than a quick fix did become unavoidable, it required hugely expensive and disruptive work over the summer and autumn of 2006 to make water production robust.

Yet, as Hutton explains, watering the nation need not be like this. Much better than bog standard public or private corporations, and actually now put in place by Welsh Water, is something different and novel: the right to profit, even hugely, but also accepting public obligation as part of the deal. The deal cuts both ways, though: there is no side-stepping and shirking responsibilities. For the company is publicly held to account for non-delivery, by shareholder and stakeholder alike.

What Welsh Water has created is mutual ownership, in the hands of its citizen consumers. Under this arrangement, remarks Hutton, 'Welsh Water is in the water business for keeps; no private equity house is going to be able to buy it as a financial gamble.' What's more, through enlightened management – combining latest business practice with sense and sensibility – its operations apparently have had the best performance record in Europe. You could call it a robust water supply through robust business operations.

CHAPTER 7 ROBUSTNESS COUNTS

Indispensable whiz for all systems

Inefficiency, or what really matters?

Modernity's obsession with immediacy now borders on a religious conviction. It supposes, as many examples demonstrate, that a here-and-now attitude – with barely an ounce of slack kept in the system – is the best way of ensuring '*efficiency* of industry and development' in particular, and performance in general. Anything less, at least when viewed through corporate goggles, would be tantamount to gross inefficiency.

Such a daring manifesto, though, is far from risk-free. For it has led to the environment, and our world, becoming far less immune to future assaults and blows: things here today can easily be gone tomorrow. Time and time again, it amounts to pulling the '*robustness* of ecosystems' from beneath our feet; that indispensable provider and insulator. The problem is not just corporate fallout, as mentioned, but the sheer number of people, including residents of non-industrialized nations, eager for a slice of the cake or a piece of the action. This is also responsible, inevitably, for the relentless squeeze on finite resources.

Either way, it is evident that the environment is not the only thing bearing the brunt of heavy-handed development. Modernity's insistence on quick fixes and 'superficial efficiency', in particular, has also created completely unrelated problems. Strangely enough, this can be bad for business, too, for it can lead to '*inefficiency* of industry and development': precisely the opposite of what was intended, and much else besides. That has to be one of the greatest ironies of our times; and further proof that modernity's efficiency quest, in one instance after another, seems little more than an efficiency delusion.

What is needed, believers in slow-tech will be quick to point out, is greater robustness throughout – both in nature and in the things we do and create – as an antidote to a world that is becoming ever more overwound. Only this can help prevent us careering headlong and headstrong, further and deeper into an efficiency trap.

Adopting enlightened principles of robustness from an earlier age – tailored, of course, to meet today's needs – would go a long way towards preventing modernity from bumping along, from one year to the next, trying in vain to overcome one crisis after another. It is the same whether we're talking about healthcare, the military world or travel. More often than not, problems with modernity's approach to these endeavours boil down to corner-cutting and squeezing things too far, until eventually the system reaches the tipping point and can go no further – at least, not in a useful direction.

As part of our efficiency drive, we cut down on materials and drive out time, even though slow actions often turn out to be anything but wasting time. For time, in all honesty, is 'of the essence'. But that's not all. Advancement through technology, something modern Luddites should not automatically malign, is all well and good up to a point. Yet, as many examples reveal, going high-tech can create as many problems as it solves.

Health and efficiency

Healthcare systems, paradoxically, are fast becoming as overwound as Japanese business guru Kamei Shuji (recall what happened to him; as we saw in Chapter 2, he had a very untimely end). Consider, as another case in point, the 'queuing' system for surgery in the UK. As happens in many other aspects of this country's National Health Service, adopting the principle of efficiency at all costs is proving to be a dangerous precedent. With too much robustness squeezed out, it is a strategy that carries a cost, especially if you happen to be a patient on the receiving end.

Surgery in British hospitals is of two sorts: elective and emergency. Elective surgery includes hip replacements, hernia repairs, tonsillectomies and the like – procedures not requiring urgent action; here, it is not a matter of imminent life or death. In contrast, there is emergency surgery, operations which if delayed really would be life-threatening or result in severe disabilities. With a severed vein or artery after a road traffic accident, the last thing one would want is to hear is that no free slots are available at the hospital until next week.

In 2006, elective surgery and emergency surgery in the UK were done together, but serious plans got under way to separate the two: the process of differentiation is continuing. Hospital advisers believed that, by doing this, they could streamline the system and make it more cost-effective. In elective surgery, for example, surgeons could plan the day's list and draw upon resources far more efficiently. But as health care analyst Seán Boyle at the London School of Economics remarked, separating elective and emergency surgery can carry serious costs as well as benefits. One of these would be a decline in robustness of this part of the healthcare system; diminishing the ability of surgeons to perform operations, perhaps just when it mattered most.

In the pursuit of greater efficiency, Boyle explains, it is easy to turn a blind eye to what is actually valuable in the existing, 'inefficient' system, by focusing solely on what is wrong with it. The truth, though, is that the present system does something mutually beneficial to elective and emergency surgery; physical and human resources can be shared. Inevitably, there is some unused and unproductive slack in the system. Far from dispensable and inefficient, though, this robustness is precisely what can make it possible for surgeons to get through all emergency operations on one especially busy day, or extra elective ones the next. Without the shared resources – which help create something in reserve – the system would lack buoyancy; with too much robustness driven away, it could easily fail just when it mattered most.

One specific problem here is training junior surgeons. If the independent sector treatment centres (ISTCs) cream off all the straightforward, relatively easy operations (they specifically exclude elective operations on high-risk individuals, the obese, heart disease, etc.), district general hospitals are left with the complex ones that are not suitable for trainee surgeons to work on. ISTCs have so far been entirely staffed by consultant grade surgeons. Juniors in National Health Service hospitals are therefore suffering loss of training experience, and in some areas this 'streamlining' may force the eventual closure of smaller district general hospitals.

No system, as wide-ranging examples remind us, can be robust against everything that can happen and go wrong. In the case of surgery, though, trimming things down by separating emergency and elective procedures may prove to be a risky business, at least if you are a patient.

An even scarier symptom of modernity's over-zealous drive for efficiency is a growing problem that can actually make you worse off than when you entered hospital in the first place. A disquieting fact is that preventable hospital-acquired infections in the USA have been killing around 90,000 patients and making some 2 million sick every year. Similar problems are plaguing the UK and other countries, too. Even more extraordinary is that hospital management itself – heavy staff workloads and overcrowding – is part of the problem. In this instance our hospitals are, quite literally, killing us.

Yet it is not just bacteria, protein prions – the agent responsible for so-called mad cow disease (BSE) – and other disease organisms we want to keep out of harm's way. Antibiotics might be a quick and efficient remedy for throat and other bacterial infections. But, as the case of avoparcin, used too liberally for agriculture, reminds us, they carry all sorts of costs and trade-offs, including serious implications for our own health. So robust are some new streptococcal and other bacterial strains, particularly in hospitals, that they continue to flourish even after assault by vancomycin, an antibiotic of last resort. And aside from growing resistance, there are difficulties in producing the drug on an industrial scale. While robustness of bacteria grows, that of patients and treatment does precisely the opposite.

The hospital-acquired infection, methicillin-resistant *Staphylococcus aureus* (MRSA) is one strain of bug posing an increasingly serious threat to public health. This strain of 'staph', in particular, seems very robust against many antibiotics. For the infected person, quite plainly, robustness hangs in the balance of being one step ahead with bacterial control. Hence, as reports of the strain's resistance continue to increase, and therapeutic options decrease, infection control methods are ever more important.

Yet the simple expedient of staff hand-washing (plus more discriminate use of antibiotics – for people and livestock) comes at little cost. As a healthcare strategy, it adds robustness and can work wonders. All it takes is time; an approach which, unlike modernity's corner-cutting for cost-saving and superficial efficiency, instils the treatment strategy with greater effectiveness and robustness. Hence, making time – rather than always fighting to save it – is, ironically, often what's needed; that is, if real efficiency is what you care about. In the case of MRSA, hand-washing helps reduce transmission opportunities between patients, though it is not specifically directed at infected patients themselves.

Another approach to dealing with MRSA also requires time, in the form of screening, to identify the source of infection, then preventing its spread through isolation. Part of the problem here, as British epidemiology researcher Julie Robotham and her colleagues point out, is knowing who are the main carriers of MRSA in the first place. Infection resides not just in hospitals, but also in the wider community. Without such knowledge, derived from time-consuming monitoring, treatment strategies can be little more than groping in the dark; an expensive and inefficient approach if ever there was one.

The take-home message from Robotham's painstaking research is that on-entry screening alone provides an incomplete picture of MRSA prevalence; it is a good reflection of infection in the community, but not generally in hospitals. On-entry screening alone, then, is unlikely to be effective for the control of MRSA, and against other infections driven by transmission between in-patients. The scary thing is that these include pending epidemics, for example VRSA – vancomycin-resistant *Staphylococcus aureus*. What is also needed, Robotham revealed, is random screening. For this is a good reflection of MRSA prevalence in hospitals. This means that outbreaks can be controlled, by isolation wards, while the number of patients is still low – allowing the epidemic to be controlled before it becomes endemic. But that depends, of course, on always ensuring that some beds are kept available. In Thatcherite eyes, that might look like inefficient use of resources – wasteful slack – but actually it is the opposite.

Compared to the simple, time-tested remedy of hand-washing, as a means of combating infection, screening is obviously far more sophisticated: it takes longer and requires more resources, especially as patient isolation should be an integral part of the strategy. Nevertheless, far from unnecessary and inefficient, something we could easily do without, it adds indispensable robustness to healthcare. The fact is that assault on bacteria, through antibiotics alone, may be little more than an ongoing arms race; as a new antibiotic comes on-stream to fight a new strain of disease organism, resistance to it sooner or later develops – so a better antibiotic is needed, and so on. Just as screening in MRSA demonstrates, complementary approaches – requiring, above all, time – are also needed to ensure robust responses against hospital infections and other epidemics that may be lurking.

MRSA is bad enough, but the prevalence of this superbug, and the mortality caused by it, have now been eclipsed by another, *Clostridium difficile*, which has become the leading cause of hospital-acquired infections in developed nations. According to the UK's Office for National Statistics, the number of death certificates that mentioned *C. difficile* in England and Wales increased from 1,214 in 2001 to 3,807 in 2005. Between 2004 and 2005 the number of deaths involving *C. difficile* increased by a staggering 69 per cent.

Part of the problem, it turns out, is that the organism can thrive when patients are dosed with wide-spectrum antibiotics; this, unfortunately, wipes out the gut's own naturally protective bacteria. Again, the simple expedient of only taking antibiotics when absolutely necessary, plus more scrupulous hand-washing, can go a long way towards undercutting *C. difficile*'s robustness while increasing the robustness of *Homo sapiens* against nasty infections from this bug. These might be obvious, low-tech measures, yet they may have a lot more going for them than many of the quicker, higher-tech fixes modernity seems so fond of.

It is easy, of course, to pick holes. To put things in perspective, few would deny that modern medicine's achievements, over the past half-century, have been remarkable. We can opt for keyhole surgery, with its tiny incisions and quicker recovery time. Through micro-dissection and other cutting-edge technologies, surgeons now separate conjoined twins with greater success; they excise bigger and more difficult brain tumours; and we see multiple transplants involving combinations of heart, lung, liver and kidney. The list goes on: corrected vision using laser beams; test-tube babies through assisted conception; use of artificial joints to replace worn-out or damaged ones; even face transplants following horrendous burns and injuries. ('Slow-techies' might chip in here, though, to say that the biggest impact on public health was something far less complicated: nineteenth-century 'sanitation' reforms.)

Often the level of sophistication and technology, and the know-how of the surgeons, required to carry out such procedures almost defies belief. No one in their right mind would wish to return to the days when surgeons – at least in England – were little more than butchers. If you were lucky you may have got ether as an anaesthetic; if you were wounded and required repairing while fighting for King and Country at sea, rum may have been your only option and companion.

Long before the days of high-tech medicine, as we know it today, medicine and surgery in some corners of the world had, curiously, reached a remarkable level of complexity, dexterity and robustness. Consider, as one illustration, the Incas. Aside from the environment – a matter on which, as mentioned, they were experts – they knew about medicine (together with engineering and mathematics); and advanced medicine at that, including brain surgery.

For the Incas had a knowledge of anatomy that would surely astonish surgeons of today: they were, quite literally, cutting-edge surgeons of their time. What we're talking of here, though, extends far beyond the infamous craniectomies – that delicate, and indelicate, procedure of sucking the brain out through the occipital bone, part of the process of obtaining the most prized war trophy, an opponent's dried and shrunken skull. Using the numbing effects of coca leaves – cocaine being one of its pharmacologically active constituents – the Incas also undertook life-saving operations with, one assumes, similar dexterity. Whether coca was actually the anaesthetic used, though, still seems not entirely clear. Quite possibly, instead, the patient got extremely drunk and plucked up courage to face the scalpel, and the surgeon, that way. If the knock-out potion was not robust, the patient's constitution certainly needed to be.

Furthermore, the administering of herbal antiseptics, handed down over the ages, apparently kept infection rates low. Given the problems the modern world faces with increasing bacterial resistance to antibiotics, it is an approach that modern medicine is beginning to treat with less disdain than it once did.

In terms of quality assurance and robustness, it seems, the Incas delivered a surprisingly creditable medical service; the statistics speak for themselves, for 70 per cent of patients, allegedly, could expect healing and recovery from common brain operations. What a contrast to the outcome of surgery in Europe – even three centuries later – where the outcome of skull puncture was, at least according to one source, 100 per cent mortality; in less technical parlance, it was certain death.

The Inca surgeon's arsenal of instruments included knives of volcanic crystal to cut bone, suturing needles and wool tourniquets. So advanced and widely practised was brain surgery in the fifteenth century that the Incas established what was, effectively, a centre of medical excellence. Perhaps concentration of expertise, together with centralization of their records, is not such a modern contrivance after all. You could say it helped the Incas achieve the right economies of scale and helped instil robustness into their medical actions.

As testament to the admiration, and trust, in medicine practised by their ancestors, two Peruvian surgeons in 1944 tried their hand at rekindling what was, in effect, a lost art. The patient chosen was a twenty-two-year-old woman who had been taking a walk when a tree fell on her head. According to final-year medical student Jamie Wilson, at the University of Leeds, she provided a 'suitable subject'. Besides a depressed cranial fracture, it turned out, the woman also suffered epilepsy and, not surprisingly, impairment in communication. Given that the surgeons were sticking to pre-Colombian procedures, what they were about to undertake was going to be the mother of medical challenges. What they did, of course, took medical ethics far beyond the normal boundaries; in today's world it would have provided lawyers with litigation and lawsuits lasting for years.

Quite amazingly, as Wilson reports, with just an obsidian silex chisel to open the skull, a tourniquet made from llama wool, a special Incan needle for stitching, and a few sulphur crystals in the place of antibiotics, all initially went to plan. Apart from ice chips, to reduce post-operative swelling, the surgeons used no twentieth-century interventions at all. Despite or because of the Inca-style surgery, the patient was apparently perfectly well after the procedure and enjoying good recovery.

Seven days later, though, she unexpectedly died – not, ironically, from the surgery itself, but from broncho-pulmonary infection. Mistaking it for ice cream, nurses later realized, the woman had sucked the ice chips from her head pack during the night. She must have ingested, inadvertently, bacteria from the wound along with her 'on the rocks' thirst quencher. It was as if, remarked Wilson, 'the Incan gods bore a grudge against this hijacking of their culture'.

Most of modernity (and humanity) would retort, quite understandably, that subjecting yourself to this sort of medical experience would be crazy, and little short of a nightmare – with or without coca, to 'rearrange' brain cells. Back in the fifteenth and sixteenth century, though, the Incas had to endure far worse things than being a patient. There were even greater challenges to their constitutional robustness. According to a Minnesota State University website, 'If someone stole, murdered, or had sex with a Sapa (Emperor's) wife or a Sun Virgin, they were thrown off a cliff, hands cut off or eyes cut out, or hung up to starve to death.' Perhaps cruelty, combined with slow-tech creativity, is what helped build up the Inca empire and make it so robust, at least up to a point.

Besides death from sexual misadventure, though, civil war and smallpox also took their toll on the Inca population. Yet never in their wildest dreams could the Inca have imagined what finally would bring their civilization tumbling down. There was probably no one single factor, but gunpowder was certainly instrumental: Inca warriors were simply no match for the guns of the Spanish conquistadors, who also had horses, yet numbered less than 200 men. Within thirty minutes in 1533 up to 3,000 Incas were killed, and it was not long before the Incas' entire army – some 40,000 strong – was defeated.

Against the formidable physical arsenal, never before encountered – and, on top of that, totally stressed out by the capture of their leader – the Incas, all of a sudden, had become frail. That combination of physical and psychological events proved, quite literally, to be deadly. Hence, the 'robust yet fragile' paradox applies to human civilizations as well as to environmental systems, and engineering systems.

In the case of the Incas, it was a sure case (directly or indirectly) of being outsmarted by modern technology. Nevertheless, over the period when they flourished, the Inca civilization was founded upon robust, slow-tech systems. In many ways these were forward-looking, effective and surprisingly advanced. Not only that, their ways continue to inspire and provide salutary lessons to the modern world. As the Incas and many other examples demonstrate, the 'old' ways are not necessarily such a bad thing, especially if they come without ditching robustness of the environment, or daily operations, as part of the deal.

Similar principles apply, even though it is an eye-opener to some, when it comes to modern healthcare. Few can deny what modern science has done for medicine and healthcare. But consider something equally sobering and poignant: an anecdote from a senior healthcare researcher. She recounted the tale of a consultant geriatrician who, as a trainee, was interested to hear from ward staff how they were able to identify those most likely to die, and those most likely to survive the night in hospital.

Thinking ward staff had access to some clinical innovation of which he was unaware, he found that the solution turned out to be something remarkably simple: going to sleep lying down in bed can lead to the 'pearly gates'; sleep sitting up, the ward staff explained, and the elderly were more likely to make it through the night and greet another dawn. Ward staff may not get the same lengthy, elaborate and technical training as their doctor or consultant colleagues. Yet, as this tale demonstrates, old-fashioned principles combined with uncomplicated, hands-on experience handed down from one generation to another still has its place today – even when it comes to the hospital bedside.

In less critical situations, too, simple low-tech fixes can prove to be remarkably effective and robust. It turns out that a drink of water and, if available, a banana eaten before intense sport can go a long way towards helping avoid muscle injuries. Robustness can arise, then, in quite unexpected and simple ways, when it comes to keeping fit and even staying alive.

By the same token, just because something happens to be modern, high-tech, and, on the face of things, efficient, we should not be bamboozled into believing it is always worth having, and that it is completely flawless. In this regard, Western medicine and medications are no different from anything else. Few, of course, would reasonably deny that remedies like aspirin and paracetamol are little short of wonder drugs; the advanced treatments, already mentioned, are pretty amazing, too.

Unfortunately, though, it is not always like that. In his recent book, *Avoiding Pharmageddon*, Paul Clayton reports an even scarier revelation – beginning, in fact, in his opening paragraph: 'Pharmaceutical medicine is failing. It's ruinously expensive – and drug side-effects are now a leading cause of death.' Unfortunately, one cannot simply brush this aside as merely journalistic spin, for Clayton himself is a Fellow of the Royal Society of Medicine, a doctor of pharmacology and a former senior scientific adviser to the UK government's Committee on the Safety of

Medicines. Of course, that in itself does not prove Clayton is right. Yet if his assertions are only half true, major sections of medicine may not be quite so efficient and robust as modernity would have us believe.

Consider, in a similar vein, the broad-spectrum, 'shotgun' approach frequently used to combat cancer. The intended target of invasive chemotherapy, for example against certain aggressive leukaemias, is malignant (i.e. rapidly dividing) cells; this, after all, is what cancer treatment is all about. The problem, though, is that healthy, non-malignant cells can easily be in the line of fire, too. Sometimes this compromises a patient's overall robustness – so much so that the benefits of the treatment can start to become questionable. It is not difficult to understand why.

The human body is an incredibly evolved biological system: the parts all work together to form the whole, rather like our 'global ecosystem', and it is normally incredibly resilient. Infect it with, say, a virus and it will, in all likelihood, fight off the invasion and correct itself. This is partly because the body has so many identical cells that when some break down, there are others to take their places. But if we take too much out of our body too quickly (from drinking or smoking, for example, or by wearing it out with insufficient sleep and too much work), for immediate gain or gratification, those spare cells are, effectively, destroyed or fail to work properly. Either way, our bodies are weakened and are no longer as robust as they should be. Then, if the weakened human body is submitted to further assaults or insults, it is far less able to withstand them and won't be able to bounce back so easily.

Although this sort of description is highly simplistic, as a way of thinking about robustness and our immune system it may not be so wide of the mark. It also helps us understand what aggressive medical therapies, or 'assaults', can do to the overall system. A disagreeable fact is that restoring robustness at one level (halting rapid cell division), for example through chemical infusions, does not guarantee positive impact at other levels; nor for the system overall (the patient's health).

Military walk-overs and walk-unders

When it comes to the military one might suppose that high-tech must always rule supreme. Robustness, through doubling up and other forms of overkill, might have been all well and good for the armies of Ancient Greece or Imperial Rome. Let's be honest, though: given the limited technology of the day, there was not a huge amount of choice. But for today's fighting forces, adopting what was, effectively, little more than brute force would be tantamount to suicide, surely; or would it?

Not necessarily, is the short answer. The so-called 'first' Gulf War in Kuwait in 1990, following the unlawful invasion and occupation by Iraq, was over quite quickly; high-tech certainly played a major part. But the 2003 conflict in Iraq, involving the invasion by the USA, the UK and other allies, dragged on and on. Not only that, even by 2008 hostilities and other atrocities were continuing, unabated. Some say Iraq was responding to the unlawful diversion of Iraqi oil by and to a neighbouring country, and that the US-led military incursion was unlawful too – a matter on which the courts may yet decide.

The main objective of the 2003 assault, as is well known, was to topple Saddam Hussein's regime. In the eyes of Prime Minister Tony Blair and President George Bush, it was – unquestionably – 'mission accomplished'; another inescapable fact, though, is that it came at a price which is still being paid, including the deaths of many thousands of innocent Iraqis.

When the US forces did finally track down Saddam Hussein, it was only after seven months and with a 25-million-dollar bounty on his head. Not only that, it took 600 soldiers, including cavalry, artillery, aviation, engineer and special operations forces. And that was just on 13 December 2003, the day of capture. The irony was that Saddam's spider-hole, camouflaged with dirt and a carpet, was simple yet incredibly robust. It also provided safety if not comfort – at least for a while.

George Bush's second dearest wish (many assume) was the capture of Osama bin Laden. With a price tag on his head since 1998, Osama is used to life on the hoof. His last known hideout – several years ago

– was a secret labyrinth of caves and boltholes in Afghanistan (pounded by American B-52 bombers). From there, best intelligence estimates are that he left on foot, by donkey, or a bus into Pakistan. More certain is that Al-Qaida used donkeys to send messages: texting, normally efficient communication, was too dangerous given all the eavesdropping by Big Brother, i.e. the USA. In uncertain times, in particular, this sort of slow-technology can be highly robust and remarkably effective. The fact is, at the time of writing, Osama has been at large for eight or nine long years.

It comes as a bitter irony that high-power military hardware alone does not always ensure a quick 'walk-over'. As the military historian Frederick Kagan reminds us: 'Above all, the US must avoid the search for "efficiency" in military affairs. Redundancy is inherently a virtue in war. America's leaders should intentionally design systems with overlapping capabilities, spread across the services, and should intentionally support weapons that do not directly contribute to the overarching vision of war that they are pursuing.'

But unlike spider-holes or donkeys, modern high-tech military operations imbued with robustness through deliberate redundancy – that is duplication or 'overkill' – do not come cheap. Yet, on Kagan's reckoning, it is almost certainly a price worth paying. It might seem, then, that hurling money at the military machine with the same unbridled passion as hurling missiles should provide the wherewithal to achieve this. But reality tells us otherwise; things are never that straightforward, especially when it comes to military matters.

In Britain, at least, heavy funding seems to have resulted not in deliberate redundancy, as part of a pre-planned strategy for greater robustness, but more in bloatedness and outright inefficiency, instead – at least according to Lewis Page's analysis in *Waste and Blundering in the Armed Forces*.

The truth, according to Page, is that the Ministry of Defence wastes much of what it gets. Take the money provided for the fighting people's support. Much of this, it turns out, is simply frittered away. More important than good equipment and good value for money, he asserts, is supporting thousands of medium-cats to plump-cats – senior staff who have no military tasks to perform at all; and, what's more, even greater numbers of civil servants and contractors are on a good number, too, courtesy of the Ministry of Defence.

In the case of the 2003 conflict in Iraq, with the toppling of Saddam Hussein's regime as the main objective, many British personnel lacked proper equipment and food; some, allegedly, even had to provide their own boots. What sort of military efficiency is that, one might wonder? It is hardly the way to instil an elite fighting force with robustness (or confidence), either.

The real irony, Lewis Page points out, is that relatively untrustworthy pieces of equipment, such as personal computers, are angels of robustness side-by-side with their military equals. And to add salt to the wound, what funds do trickle down to the relatively few who are engaged in combat are, paradoxically, wasted further. An inescapable fact, Page reminds us, is that much of the £30 billion of taxpayers' money spent on UK defence each year is simply blown away, not put to effective military use by making it more robust.

Yet the spending of just an extra £10,000 annually on each front-line infantryman would pay dividends. That would really boost the robustness and efficiency of operations. It would be sufficient, Page explains, for boots that really do the job, an excellent new rifle and other equipment – not as one-off items, but every year; and the overall cost would be peanuts: a mere £250 million, equivalent to less than 1 per cent of the current budget. Low-tech maybe, but it does not mean they cannot instil the military with greater robustness: in fact, quite the contrary. It doesn't take rocket science, or military intelligence, to see that something in the military think-tank – if not the missiles themselves – is way off the mark.

These, in a 'bomb-shell', are some of the crazy things going on, and not going on, in the UK's fighting forces. But what about the state of military might in the world's biggest super-power; how robust is that? With a defence budget close on twice that of the rest of the world in 2004, the USA's armed forces should be able to 'conquer this whole planet and another one like it' – provided, Page adds, 'that the other planet lacks a USA of its own, and that money was the only factor in military power' – which of course it is not.

When it comes to high-tech, an undeniable fact is that the US military is second to none; it is brilliant, it gets gold stars, especially when, as Lewis Page points out, it comes to high-tech prevention. In the event of Britain going to war with, say, a Eurofighter or Type 45 Brit-Euro destroyer, against the USA's wishes, Big Brother would soon put a stop to that. Eurofighters are no match for F-22 Raptors, or long-range missile exchanges. And, according to Page, any realistic number of Type 45s would be blown to smithereens in just minutes – and that's with everything working to spec. One serious constraint, he adds wryly, is that Type 45s run on Microsoft Windows; hence, 'Bill Gates will probably be able to shut the ships down remotely, assuming they haven't already crashed on their own.'

It was the USA who invented, developed, launched and pays for the current GPS (global positioning system), principally for military purposes. For the non-military, for those without access to the codes for high-precision position fixing, accuracy was little better than around 100–150 metres. The USA retains the option to limit access to the high-accuracy GPS signal if required. Ironically, though, non-military users in the past sometimes managed to get greater accuracy than the US forces themselves. Eventually, as things turned out, the USA unlocked the restrictions altogether, with high accuracy available to all, though it retains the option of turning off the system completely in some regions. The paradoxical thing here, Page points out, is that that would severely restrict US military work in the region, too, so it would not be so much of a threat, or robust strategy, after all.

Nevertheless, yachtsmen, for example (including many hard-core traditionalists), owe the USA a great deal for free position-fixing on the ocean, whether near land or on the high seas – especially if has been cloudy for days, making sun or star sights impossible (assuming, of course, that a modern-day yacht actually carried a sextant). An even better service will come when GPS is complemented by the new European Galileo satellites, which will also mean less reliance on US hardware, as it will be independent of GPS.

The ups and downs of satellite systems aside, the brutal reality is that the US military arsenal can strike formidable, high-tech deadly blows. As testament to this, recall the recent Gulf Wars or, for example, what happened in Vietnam in 1972 after a decade of war: statistics reveal that, for every American lost, US fighting forces left between ten and twenty bodies behind them.

But statistics seldom reveal everything; it was, as it happened, far from plain sailing for either side. In the case of the USA, as Lewis Page points out, its military is (generally) great with high-tech stuff. But it is not so great at doing low-tech, like rifles – at least not when it comes to targeting the opposition. Recall, for example, the infamous 'friendly fire' – that euphemistic term for shooting, inadvertently, members of your own side or your allies. Self-inflicted shootings, it turns out, can sometimes be an even greater threat than being killed by the enemy. It is hard to imagine a less robust military action.

In the case of the Vietnam War, there was something else to be reckoned with. Despite the heavy toll on the Vietcong, in the end the US military operation went hard aground. What it had not counted on was the resilience of the opposition, and the power of simple, old-fashioned, low-tech principles. This, not being outsmarted technologically, is what made the going get really tough for the US military, and what was partly instrumental in the US government calling it a day.

One reason that communist forces won the Vietnam War was that the Vietcong built, lived in and fought from underground holes. These low-tech hideouts were extraordinarily robust, as MSNBC's Kari Huus and *Newsweek*'s Ron Moreau explain; they 'were built by night over many years, one scoop of dirt at a time, dirt that was carried off and secretly dumped into the rice paddies'. The vast Cu Chi tunnel network, built just outside Saigon, was a prime example; it bears testament to the will of the Vietcong, flexibility in approach and the power of the old-fashioned way – robustness counts, on all counts. You could say this is what helped prevent an easy military walk-over by a vastly superior fighting force.

With 130 miles of passageways, the Cu Chi tunnel complex allowed the Vietcong to become invisible. Safe and sound inside, they could move weapons silently. Also, unknown to American soldiers, snipers and booby traps lurked below. To American soldiers, Huus and Moreau add, 'the tunnels stood for all that was horrific about fighting in Vietnam'.

Some GIs, the 'tunnel rats', specialized in raiding the tunnels; but apparently they were more of a rare breed than the rats that must have also shared the underground quarters. Tunnel entrances were designed with extraordinary foresight and cunning that almost defies imagination. In the dark, for example, a soldier would grope and feel his way along the wall, only to fall into a pit of *pungi* stakes – sharpened lengths of bamboo, smeared with dung: low-tech indeed but, as Huus and Moreau point out, a simple means of ensuring infection, if not death.

You could say the tunnels were the epitome of robustness. They provided an ideal facility for defence and offence or, put another way, flexibility of operations and multi-tasking; and, what's more, without the enemy even knowing what was going on beneath its feet – until, of course, it was too late. There are tales, for example, of what the last guerrilla fighter did when entering a tunnel: that person could, effectively, 'mine' the entrance with explosives, so that any American trying to follow would be blown up. Not only that, the explosion would seal the entrance, allowing the Vietcong to vanish into safety through another passageway.

The tales are almost as endless as the tunnels themselves. As Huus and Moreau go on to explain, so well concealed were the entrances that sometimes even the fighters themselves needed an experienced guide. For five years, Duong Thanh Phong, a Saigon-based photographer, recorded the war from inside the tunnels. At least once, 'he was mortified to find himself above ground, unable to find his way back to the entrance'.

On top of that, there was little forest cover, for most had been blown away by US bombers and helicopters; Agent Orange, that deadly concoction containing dioxin, helped see to that. Between 1961 and 1971, more than 80 million gallons were sprayed over 10 per cent of South Vietnam, defoliating and contaminating millions of hectares of productive cropland and forest. In case this was insufficient, bulldozers and other mechanical aids helped complete the job, generating a wasteland and 'free-fire zone'. Yet, despite all the assaults and insults, many tunnels were so robust that they survived the destruction; some have been reconstructed and are a surviving legacy, and major tourist trap, today. The amazing thing is that the tunnel builders had burrowed so deep that the lowest were immune even to B-52 bombs.

Another inescapable fact is that the Vietcong's low-tech spider-holes outsmarted and defeated an enemy with infinitely more military might. One cannot pretend, though, that it was an easy ride, for the going often did get really tough. Even when there were no deliberate blackouts, malaria was rife and oxygen thin on or under the ground. Not only that, because the Americans poisoned drinking wells above the ground, the Vietcong's solution was painstaking yet simple: to build water wells undergound. This is, of course, precisely where cooking had to be done, too. But, as Huus and Moreau add, that was not enough. So as not to draw the attention of American troops, elaborate venting systems to release smoke were necessary as an additional survival strategy.

The lesson from these tales of Gulf conflicts and underground tunnels in Vietnam is, of course, not abandoning high-tech military might; not ditching B-52 bombers altogether in favour of low-tech or no-tech operations – just as it would be crazy for any modern mariner to shun GPS. Nevertheless, these examples illustrate that simple approaches, which recognized the value of robustness and its supremacy over misguided, over-enthusiastic 'efficiency', have a place in military activities, even today. So perhaps even tunnels are not so backward-looking, and, paradoxically, they can be a vital part of an elite and enlightened fighting force after all.

The sky is the limit

In or out of combat, robustness counts, ultimately, above all else. For (superficial) efficiency alone, that is without adequate robustness, can mean dicing with death, especially when it comes to penetrating seriously high altitudes. The space shuttle Atlantis, for example, is one of the most complex machines ever created, and Mission STS-115 – the world's largest orbiting laboratory – probably the most ambitious human venture ever attempted; at least it was at the time of writing. One might reasonably have called it Mission Hold-Your-Breath, especially after some of the earlier space disasters. But it turned out to be Mission Successful.

Three hundred and fifty kilometres above earth, flight commander Brent Jett gently connected Atlantis to the international space station. Three strenuous spacewalks later, the crew unpacked and installed giant solar panels which, together, will generate a quarter of the international space station's power. Not only that, the astronauts completed their work without suffering the bends – a potentially fatal condition, well known to divers, and caused by the dangerous and painful release of tissue nitrogen into the bloodstream if pressure drops too suddenly. Any significant loss of pressure in the shuttle, of course, is likely to have very serious engineering consequences, too.

Much of what it takes to build, launch and keep spacecraft like Atlantis airborne hangs on computer super chips and many other different parts. The price to pay for extremes of performance efficiency is heavy reliance on these, and potential disaster if anything goes wrong. For any chance of success, spacecraft must be above all fast and light. But things also have to be strong and safe; robustness is paramount. The trouble is that safety back-up systems, like everything else on board, act as cargo and add to the weight or bulk.

A tantalizing fact, though, is that without sufficient back-up and other forms of robustness, disaster can suddenly strike; too much excess baggage, though, and the machine might not even get from A to B – for example, to deliver solar panels. That's the rub, and it seems to be an intractable dilemma.

Yet, as three separate space disasters (and hindsight) demonstrate, something vital missing, just where and when it matters most, can carry a high price. What turns out to be lacking at the time of an accident, of course, is not seen, or even understood, earlier, at the design and engineering stage. This revelation is perhaps surprising – especially given that space missions use state-of-art technology, which is very thoroughly researched before engineers deploy it: the risk and financial cost of a failure is too much of a concern to use unproven technology. Yet it still can and does, sometimes, fail. Not only that, once a space mission is accomplished – or ends prematurely – what turns out to be essential or expendable may not even be something material.

The truth is that robustness against every possible event is unachievable. Equally, though, trading robustness for superficial saving, for extremes of efficiency, is highly risky: the challenge lies in getting the balance right. For a chilling reminder of what is at stake, look no further than one of the early space disasters. Although built to be fast and to last, the Challenger space shuttle blew up in 1986 just because of a dodgy seal or 'O' ring in one of the solid rocket boosters. It was the NASA Failure Review Board – one distinguished member being Nobel physicist Richard Feynman – who discovered that. Whether down to unfortunate engineering, or a disaster waiting to happen, adequate robustness just was not there.

Worse still, the 1999 Mars climate orbiter ended in pieces simply through failure to spot a mix-up of metric and imperial units. Being wise after the event (again), of course, is easy. Considered another way, though, flight insurance is something extending far beyond physical and electronic engineering; there is also the human factor. In the case of Mars, the time spent on safety checks was clearly insufficient, for even something blindingly obvious was overlooked. Extra time double-checking every single calculation and minute detail, as we now know, would have made the technical safety systems more robust and, quite likely, have paid off.

Other space shuttle missions have failed spectacularly, too: Columbia, for example, broke up on re-entry in 2003 due to foam damage to heat-proofing tiles on take-off. It is easy to blame sloppy engineering, human error, or (cynics might unreasonably claim) NASA's thrift – but that hardly seems likely. Undeniably, corner-cutting can work and improve efficiency; it is necessary, to some degree, to get the machine off the ground in the first place. The price, though, as mentioned, can be high. Superior, thicker or extra tiles might have helped, but then at what cost to other parts of the spacecraft? It might never have taken off in the first place.

Or take the later Discovery shuttle orbiter, launched on 26 July 2005. On take-off a piece of insulating foam peeled off, calling into question the robustness of this space mission, too. Fortunately, it and the crew landed unscathed . . . though it was not plain sailing. Then there is the space shuttle Atlantis, already mentioned; its achievements, by any reckoning, were truly awe-inspiring. Despite encountering a piece of debris, which left a tiny hole, the shuttle ran like clockwork, without endangering the crew or the space craft; and that was after a twelve-day journey of nearly 8 million kilometres in space. Atlantis landed in one piece – and with all its pieces – on 21 September 2006.

The truth is that there is seldom (if ever), to use the words and title of Robert Kanigel's book, 'the one best way' to achieve success; it is the same whether we are talking of space missions, yacht races or anything else. The person Kanigel was writing about was Frederick Taylor, the first time and motion expert, an American whose life spanned the nineteenth and twentieth centuries. He believed something different: that there *is* only one approach to efficiency, at least in engineering and business. And that is to strip every bit of spare capacity, or redundancy, out of the production system; in other words, to minimize robustness.

In Taylor's eyes, and the eyes of his many disciples, becoming lean and mean is the only pathway to productivity and perfection. It is a legacy, what's more, that lives on – rejuvenated in Britain by Prime Minister Margaret Thatcher, and neo-liberalism, in the latter part of the 1990s. It is also a view that seems deeply engrained in our psyche, even to this day.

The point of these tales about space missions is not to point the finger, but to reveal an inescapable fact: there is no perfect solution – trade-offs are inevitable. This is, after all, precisely what the 'robust yet fragile' paradox tells us about how all systems behave – whether we're talking of human, biological or engineered ones.

What's also clear, though, is that cutting back on what might seem expendable – time as well as the physical – can prove to be a perilous action; the odds of an accident might be low, but the consequences if one does occur can be calamitous. Whatever accidents boil down to, the right level of redundancy or 'overkill' provides both insurance and performance. In the case of spacecraft engineering, multiple redundancy is critical to reliability; single point failures, as it happens, are always avoided. Any designer worth his salt has to respect the power of duplication and back-up.

All down to a magic mark

Besides the military, aviation and healthcare, one finds a string of other fine examples that demonstrate how robustness helps make the things we do and create be more effective and long-lasting. What is so surprising is that this can often come about using low-tech principles and in inexpensive ways. It is an approach which would resonate strongly with the sentiments of my father, and of modern-day traditionalists, too, for that matter.

One case in point was a novel and ingenious breakthrough that happened in nineteenth-century Britain and proved to be an invaluable boost to trans-shipment of goods across the high seas. What's more, this single, simple, yet remarkably cunning device not only added to the robustness and efficiency of operations, but it proved to be, quite literally, a life-saver, too.

Anyone who has set foot on a ship, better still a small yacht, might recall the hymn, 'For those in peril on the sea' – especially if they've been exposed to the church as well as the elements. The fact is, being on the high seas can strike fear into your veins just as powerfully as driving on a busy highway, when everyone is in a hurry. Even in an age of stabilizers, satellite positioning and air–sea rescue, a full gale (or worse) works wonders at focusing the mind about what really counts.

Back in the nineteenth century, going to sea was an even riskier business, especially when it came to transporting merchant freight. Many ships were rotten, fit for nothing except scrap metal. On top of that, though, owners who were unscrupulous had an uncontrollable desire to load them almost to the gunwales. In their eyes, the lives of the crew were more expendable than the goods they carried – especially as they were over-insured as well as overloaded: speed of returns, at least of profits, was what mattered most. It was hardly surprising, then, that what the crew signed on to became known as 'coffin ships'.

It was Bristol-born Englishman Samuel Plimsoll, later MP for landlocked Derby, who, rather ironically, did more than anyone about the seamen's plight and the rottenness of so many owners. Having already campaigned on behalf of miners and exposed the cruelties of cattle-shipping, you could say he was a human (and animal) rights activist before he became the seaman's best friend; perhaps he was the world's first maritime safety officer, too.

Plimsoll wanted nothing short of government legislation to protect seamen against their terrible predicament. To add power to the cause, in 1873 he published *Our Seamen*, an account revealing the true scale of Britain's abysmal safety record at sea. It turned out that 1,000 sailors each year were being drowned on ships around the British Isles; not only that, in the same year half the ships that went down in European waters were owned by Englishmen. As part of his campaign, Plimsoll gave a copy of his book to every member of the House of Commons. The trouble was that ship-owners had powerful supporters there. They argued, not surprisingly, that the government should not pass legislation which restricted the freedom of employers to run their companies. It echoed the same convenient 'logic' the slave traders had used, and got away with, · for so many years, for transporting human cargoes across the oceans.

For Plimsoll, the going was uphill nearly all the way, with three Plimsoll bills actually rejected by 1871. The upshot of his tireless campaigning, though, was an action and legacy that still bear his name today – brought about in 1876 by an amended Merchant Shipping Act, to enforce the loading line. But it took the support of many, including Queen Victoria, the theosophist Annie Besant (who helped India achieve independence), and John Burnes, boss of Cunard – one of the shipping lines that did, unusually, take care of the crew.

The Plimsoll line is simply a line – actually several different ones – marked on a cargo-bearing ship's sides, which disappears below the waterline if the ship becomes overloaded. The simplicity of the mark, though, belies its effectiveness as a maritime safety measure. Of course, knowing precisely where on the hull to position the mark requires considerable skill; it calls for calculations by naval architects about mass, volume, hull characteristics, water density, and likely weather conditions, too. But it is hardly cutting-edge science and technology: more, in fact, old-fashioned mechanics, combined with enlightened thinking, master-minded by Plimsoll all those years ago. It could be little else back then, since we're talking of the mid to late 1800s, when high-tech was barely in its infancy, and certainly not yet in full swing.

Essentially, the higher the line, the deeper a ship can be loaded. Not all waters, of course, have equal density or buoyancy. Ships float higher in salt water than in fresh, and higher in cold water than in warm – because of the greater uplift provided by denser water. These simple principles of oceanography, combined with the conditions that might be expected in different aquatic environments, are what govern the level of the six markings on the hull: Tropical Fresh Water and Fresh Water uppermost, followed in descending order, by Tropical Salt Water, Salt Water (summer and winter) and Winter in North Atlantic. The Plimsoll line is a maritime safety measure which is robust against different weather and sea (including freshwater) conditions.

But of course the system can only be robust in respect of the vessels to which the enforcement regulations apply. As Nicolette Jones explains in her recent book *The Plimsoll Sensation: The Great Campaign to Save*

Lives at Sea, the Plimsoll line actually contains a glaring omission; you could call it a bitter-sweet irony. Although Plimsoll left his mark on ships of virtually of every nation, there is, even today, no Winter North Atlantic level of loading for ships longer than 330 feet. That is what seems, on the face of it, so surprising, especially given that this is where you are likely to encounter some of the roughest weather north of the equator.

Actually, though, there is probably a simple explanation, at least according to Geoffrey Moorhouse, author of *The Boat and the Town*, a book based on a year he spent as a deep-sea fisherman. His explanation is: the quest, unrestrained, for profits at all costs, especially for container ships and supertankers. All of these, of course, happen to be longer than the 'magical minimum' length. This enabled their owners to escape the restrictions and safety measure 'enjoyed' by smaller vessels. As Moorhouse put it, 'In some ways, nothing has changed in 150 years'.

Slipping between the legislative cracks aside, it is hard to imagine a simpler, low-tech, low-cost measure, yet one that is so robust (against different conditions and the guile of unscrupulous owners) than what Samuel Plimsoll devised; he might justly be branded the Magic Marker. Not only that, a circle divided by a horizontal line (extending slightly either side) – Plimsoll's signature and legacy – is also the motif used for London's underground rail system. What better evidence that Plimsoll's enlightened thinking has been transported far and wide?

Aga sagas

Seen with expanded vision – one that recognizes the value of robustness – even the old-fashioned Aga cooker becomes not quite the inefficient, cast-iron dinosaur so beloved of my family. In our home, three 'cookers' stand side by side in the kitchen: an oil-fired heat-storage Aga, a magnetic induction hob, and a combination microwave-electric oven. The last two came from our previous home and, at least when we bought them, were very much at the top end of a low-tech/high-tech scale. Like our family's vintage Bentley, Agas are completely different. They have massive amounts of spare capacity, or redundancy – if not in parts, then in strength of materials. In a word, they are robust.

Domestic appliances, particularly cookers, are excellent examples of the interplay between efficiency and robustness. What's more, they make us step back and reconsider the very meaning of the two concepts – particularly efficiency.

Our Aga is on constantly, except during summer months. Invented and patented in 1922 by Dalén, this large and heavily engineered cooker is by conventional reckoning relatively inefficient – the joke being, as already mentioned, that it's not unlike burning ten-pound notes one after the other; or perhaps fifty-pound notes, given the current price of fuel – especially oil. But in fact the Aga was designed solely to maximize efficiency and conserve energy and fuel. Introduced into the marketplace in 1929, it offered an attractive, economical and efficient alternative to the highly temperamental traditional kitchen ranges that had been around since the late eighteenth century.

Ideas about efficiency have evolved over the years. Yet, as Agas demonstrate so wonderfully, it now seems that some early concepts and applications of efficiency were surprisingly advanced. Coal, oil and gas Agas contain vermiculite, a natural insulation material, whereas electric Agas differ slightly in having ceramic insulation. Whatever the insulation, though, it helps to maintain an internal temperature of several hundred degrees centigrade and minimize heat leakage.

The Aga's body is made from cast iron, which accumulates and retains heat well. A thermostat controls the Aga's core temperature automatically. Surprisingly, the heat source for an Aga is comparatively small: the gas version, for example, runs from a small burner of similar rating to a conventional gas hotplate burner.

But just how efficient is the Aga? Although an hour or more might pass before the temperature starts to creep up, the Aga adopts a principle of temperature control completely different from simply turning a knob. Through judicious choice of hotplates, ovens and shelf positions, the cook can take advantage of a remarkable range of temperatures.

A further point, not linked directly to efficiency or robustness, concerns food quality. People often remark on the wonderful taste of food cooked using an Aga. Is there any scientific basis to this claim? The manufacturers suggest that it is 'the radiant heat from the cast iron ovens which gives the Aga its legendary cooking excellence'. This is the type of heat transferred when energy is emitted from a heated mass such as cast iron. Electromagnetic in nature, radiant heat can travel through empty space (as opposed to convected heat, which depends on the movement of molecules). Heat reaching the (upper) hot roasting oven seals the surface of the food, apparently allowing it to maintain its natural succulence and flavour. And because temperature fluctuations are less with radiant than with convected heat, the cook does not need to remove food from the oven at precisely the right moment. In this sense Agas are more forgiving. Finally, I for one claim that toast done on the Aga's hotplate is superior to that prepared in an electric toaster: only the outside of the bread is toasted, while the inside retains some moisture without becoming overly crisp.

Besides cooking food, the Aga heats domestic water and – in some cases – radiators. If clothing is hoisted above it on a rack, it dries that too, making electricity-gobbling tumble-dryers redundant. And through the Aga's high thermal inertia, one gets a distinctive gentle background heat that not only keeps the kitchen warm, but also permeates through the house – central heating is required only during the coldest of times, so there is a saving on energy. On top of that, air circulation, induced by the combustion process, also keeps the house well ventilated and helps prevent dampness. Less obviously, as an aunt reminded me recently, the lid over an Aga's hotplate doubles up as an iron; that is what she uses and, in a small way, it saves on electricity.

By contrast, the magnetic induction hob is a fast, highly responsive cooker. It boils water almost instantly; its ceramic plates remain cool – at least initially – even when boiling water in a pan; temperature control is as precise and immediate as the volume control of a hi-fi system; and unlike the Aga's hot plates, which gradually lose heat and efficiency when the lids are up during prolonged cooking, the magnetic hob never loses power – unless there is a power cut. (In Agas the last of these is less of a problem if cooking is confined to the oven.)

As a cooker, the induction hob is extraordinary. In terms of robustness and simplicity, the Aga probably wins, and will probably still be in our kitchen long after the induction hob's electronic chips have ceased to function and replacements might well become unavailable. On the other hand, the hob requires no routine maintenance and servicing, in contrast to the Aga. And our combination microwave-electric oven? That ensures that we can still grill food during those heat spells in summer, when the Aga is put to rest!

Even in a high-tech age, Agas are still very much in demand in the UK, where their virtues are regularly extolled by celebrity television chefs; and it is not only members of the UK's Saga Club, and others over fifty, whose kitchens they grace. Agas are also exported to the rest of Europe and to many other countries, including America, Australia, Canada, New Zealand, South Africa and Japan – and, curiously, their use is not confined to land.

On holiday in the early 1960s, for example, it was extraordinary to see an Aga-type cooker (Rayburn) in a most unexpected setting: a 24-metre French 'tunnyman' or *thonnier*, named *Pas de Loup*. Like the cooker in its bowels, this sailing vessel itself was heavy and old-fashioned – a traditional gaff-rigged ketch, skippered by Mike Willoughby, ex-submarine commander and, later, skipper of the British sail-training ship the *Winston Churchill*. *Pas de Loup* was shortly off to the Caribbean for charter, and the Willoughbys were paying us a visit in Anglesey. Only a truly massive vessel like theirs could bear the extra weight of an Aga-type cooker (half a ton). Undoubtedly, it was a great source of warmth and comfort while the boat was still in cold north Atlantic waters, but you can bet it was put out before arrival in Antigua – unless, of course, they were intending to run a sauna as a sideline.

Nostalgia is no doubt one reason why the Aga became a well-established symbol of English country life, and an occasional feature in boats too.

Yet, for the many reasons mentioned, there is more to its popularity than that. An undeniable down-side is that Agas do consume their fair share of gas, oil or wood – something that cannot be brushed aside in an increasingly greenhouse world.

On the other hand, Aga hardware can be converted to switch from burning one fuel to another; some even run on electricity which, of course, ultimately derives from coal, oil and gas or more greenhouse friendly fuels. Given the soaring price of oil, and its searing effects on the planet, we are looking into running ours on waste vegetable oil or 'green electricity'. The potential is there, then, for Agas to operate on whichever fuel happens to be not only the most cost-efficient, but also the most environmentally benign – although, of course, there are capital costs involved to make this possible. Flexibility, in terms of ability to function in different ways, also happens to be one hallmark of robustness. So perhaps Gustaf Dalén's concepts of efficiency and performance, and their manifestation through his Aga – perhaps the epitome of robustness – weren't so far off the mark after all.

On any count, Agas are slow-tech. But as Carl Honoré reminds us in his book *In Praise of Slow*, slowness has some remarkable applications, including settings where one might expect it to act as nothing but a hindrance.

Change and innovation

If you suppose that robustness amounts simply to over-engineering, unrefined doubling up – or even self-adjustment – that would be an understandable viewpoint. Agas, our old Bentley and natural ecosystems (through their myriad of species) are prime cases in point. Here, basically, we are talking of robustness as back-up or insurance; and these same examples point to the wisdom of not ditching robustness, for example in the face of modernity's demands for ever-greater '*efficiency* of industry and development'.

But this portrayal, accurate in part, would be downplaying the real whiz of robustness. For adaptation through *change* is another, equally important side of robustness, especially in organisms and ecosystems. Yet, strangely enough, it is an approach also finding a place in systems we ourselves create.

On the face of it, change sounds nothing at all to do with robustness, for normally we think of robustness as precisely the opposite: resistance to alteration. Yet, curiously, change can be one signature of robustness. That is what is so fascinating, and at the same time so tantalizing, about robustness; it has multiple meanings, the eighteen or so different ones posted by scientists working on robustness and complexity at the Santa Fe Institute bearing testament. At one level, this breadth of meaning is enough to make you tear your hair out in frustration. On the other hand, it is probably why robustness is such a powerful means of capturing (and, better still, instilling or retaining) the extraordinarily rich behaviour systems are capable of displaying, including multi-tasking.

Striking the right balance between rigidity, flexibility and changeability – all hallmarks of robustness – is something evolution and top designers are good at, for it helps ensure survival, in nature, machines and organizations.

The ability to change, or evolve, then, is a side of robustness that seems even more astonishing, even magical, than self-regulation. Robustness, normally seen as *in*sensitivity to external and internal disturbances, as many examples remind us, would seem completely at odds with changeability or evolvability.

Consider, first, the situation in living systems. Through mistakes in copying genetic material – so-called mutations – an organism's DNA or RNA, its hard-wiring, undergoes structural change. Biologists consider many mutations to be neutral, that is, they produce no major (harmful or beneficial) effects on functioning of 'the system'. Seen in this light, the overall system is immune or robust, by definition, to these mutations. Surely, then, neutral mutations, which go hand-in-hand with robustness, cannot possibly provide the seeds of change and evolutionary innovation? It seems counter-intuitive, yet robustness can actually promote capacity to change.

Andreas Wagner has recently devoted an entire book (*Robustness and Evolvability in Living Systems*) to revealing and explaining this apparent paradox. Evidence from his and his colleagues suggests that robustness (through neutral mutations), perhaps surprisingly, *can* promote novelty and change, i.e. evolvability. Many mutations, Wagner concedes, do not change the system's primary function. But they can alter other system features; for several generations these mutations may simply remain neutral, but lie dormant and masked. Following some new environmental conditions, or a (different) genetic change, though, neutral mutations can suddenly spring to action; they can, in fact, become 'non-neutral', and active. Hence, this now provides a source of innovation, through effects on the organism's survival and reproduction – in other words, its fitness. Put slightly differently, a change may become an adaptation only long after it has happened.

Simultaneous robustness and evolvability helps explain a remark once made by medical geneticist Marcus Pembrey, that genetic systems seem fine-tuned, or poised, efficiently balanced in a state between high stability (resistance to change) and responsiveness or evolvability.

Obviously only living systems have genetic material, so robustness to genetic changes can surely apply only to organisms? Yet, as Andreas Wagner also points out, robustness involving evolvability can be instilled, surprisingly, in engineered systems, too. Genetic algorithms, one illustration of this, are essentially software utilizing principles of variation and selection to produce an 'evolutionarily tuned' product. That can be almost anything ranging from a programme to a picture, to determining electronic circuits that perform two or more computational tasks. However you look at it, even when it comes to the most advanced technical systems, it boils down to learning from nature. On the other hand, not even nature has absolute robustness; engineered systems and other human creations perhaps even less so.

CONCLUSION

Towards a new efficiency: a civilized approach

Time for a better balancing act

Having reviewed the different ways in which principles of robustness can be applied, this book demonstrates that short-term corporate interests and development are decaying the '*robustness* of ecosystems' – the legs on which a society can stand or fall. No one can deny that we must catch fish, or till the land, to feed ourselves. But if hauling several tonnes of steel equipment over the seabed is so devastating, perhaps the time has come to question the wisdom of hunting in such a 'medieval', ruthless way; then perhaps switch to more benign ways of getting seafood to our mouths and on to restaurant tables.

More astonishing still is the fact that many are so dismissive of the environmental damage caused by fishing; just as in the food industry, where agrochemical interests increasingly call for excessive/harmful use of antibiotics and other disagreeable by-products. Put more starkly, heavy-handed industries echo some of the features of military conflicts and skirmishes. Here civilian deaths, conveniently and euphemistically, are also brushed aside as unavoidable collateral.

One take-home message from *Slow-Tech* is that the very process of development, without careful attention, easily transforms resources into non-renewable assets, of dwindling value. Sooner or later that undermines a society's power base and stronghold. Unless safeguards are deliberately introduced, development turns out to be a rather perilous venture. It is particularly so in a world driven by the need for ever greater '*efficiency* of industry and development'. Seen in this light, unfettered growth can be tantamount to ecological suicide. For destruction of environmental resources, as several examples in the book reveal, can be enough to push a civilization over the tipping point. It is not something that only past societies had to worry about, either.

The price of getting somewhere, being successful, seems to be environmental deterioration – sometimes only a decade or two after reaching peak population and peak power. That is the real paradox, and perhaps why politicians are so dismissive (though, in fact worried) that environmental decline might foreshadow social decline or collapse. Or perhaps it is just an inconvenient truth. Either way, the simultaneous vulnerability and power of ecosystem robustness is what hard evidence, overwhelmingly, is pointing towards. Like it or not, life and prosperity remain firmly grounded in a healthy environment and natural resources.

A related fact to which much of modernity seems blind is that high technology sometimes creates as many problems as it solves, or more. Use of water for agriculture produced from highly invasive irrigation schemes is one case in point. Here, quite plainly, the antennae of decision-makers are insufficiently tuned in to bothering about the 'robustness of ecosystems'. That is what happens in a society driven by the relentless pursuit of (superficial) efficiency; but without time to stop and consider: 'Efficiency for whom?', 'Efficiency at what cost?' and 'Efficiency over what time?'

Consider, as another poignant reminder of the dangers we face from pursuing unbridled 'efficiency of industry and development', the cruise ship industry, for example in Bermuda. As we have seen, one development option given serious consideration recently has been the widening of the Town Cut at St George's, to safely accommodate more massive cruise ships. In the eyes of certain ministries and tour operators, this stood to create more visitors, and more spending, in Bermuda. Expanded port facilities, they understandably felt, should lead to greater efficiency of cruise ship operations and, hence, greater business opportunities.

Yet this single, highly invasive action of 'opening up' St George's would have created calamitous knock-on effects. Most seriously, the blasting of bits of coral reef and island would result in the undercutting of Bermuda's (free) natural defence system. Squeezing out robustness from a short-sighted development plan would not only cause ecological injuries, but would also render the whole area highly susceptible to hurricane damage. Because it was still fresh in people's minds, most people still vividly recalled what followed in the wake of Hurricane Fabian on 5 September 2003. The worst storm to hit Bermuda in half a century, it wrought havoc on the island and had a devastating effect on the airport causeway. For a number of reasons, the project has gone on to the back burner. Perhaps the cruise ship *Norwegian Crown*, which grounded and stuck on the rocks off Dockyard en route to Hamilton in June 2006, albeit temporarily, also forced the authorities to rethink: to realize that over-zealous expansion of the cruise ship industry carries costs as well as benefits.

Inefficient operations, quite plainly, are little use to anyone. But when modernity's quest for unrivalled '*efficiency* of industry and development' eclipses the '*robustness* of ecosystems', surely things are getting out of kilter: it is bad news not only for nature, but often for industry and development, too, if your sweep of the horizon penetrates beyond the short-term. Dig into the environment too much, and it easily backfires on us.

What happened to New Orleans, with too much natural salt marsh eaten away to pave the way for development, also bears testament to the vulnerability and power of the 'inessential'. Naturally, intact marshes along its shores would not have made the city completely stormproof and impenetrable. But they would have done a pretty good job, which the engineered floodwalls or levees were clearly unable to do on that ill-fated day in 2005. Like the marshes they, too, had insufficient spare capacity; they lacked robustness, just when it mattered most.

In so much of what modernity now does, touches and creates, robustness ends up playing second fiddle to efficiency, despite the cascading collateral damage and debris piling up before our eyes. Consider, as a more recent, bleak reminder, the unprecedented rainstorms in Britain beginning on

25 June 2007. As much rain fell in the downpour that day as normally descends in the entire month. Worse still, people drowned, and the total price tag of dealing with the aftermath, and costs for what was lost, ran into hundreds of millions of pounds; insurance companies alone put the figure at around £1.5 billion.

Some believe this strike, and others like it (for example the deluges in 2008), to be simply one of the more gloomy and fiery indictments of nature; you could say the rougher edges of its calling card, something unavoidable and uncontrollable. An increasing number, though, consider climatic extremes and episodic events to be part and parcel of global warming. They are what we may now have to expect as commonplace in the coming years, due, in no small way, to our drive for greater '*efficiency* of development and industry'. Worse still, such events could actually be on the increase.

Whatever the root causes, when it comes to the devastating effects, it is clear that de-greening of the land has much to answer for. No one denies that damage after a major storm is completely unpreventable (on land or sea). One thing for sure, though, is that trees and other natural vegetation work wonders at slowing the flow. In complete contrast to concrete, nature's verdant cloak acts as a giant sponge and buffer, as well as a self-regulating dam. Greenery helps dampen and ameliorate nature's nasty shocks – providing the defrocking has not gone too far – just as intact wetlands once did around New Orleans. Linked to this, deliberately choosing not to build on river flood plains – a slow-tech expedient (not an untried experiment), if ever there was one – also limits damage and works wonders.

The problem is that hasty development, often fuelled by unquenchable corporate thirst, drives away too much robustness from ecosystems. It is not only bad for conservation and the biological environment, though. By creating a hazardous physical environment, and a risky built environment, many of our actions undercut business and well-being, too. It is not stretching things too far, either, to say that ecosystem services and robustness provide (primary and less direct) business services. But that is not all. Often branded 'unproductive baggage', whenever possible we also banish robustness from the workplace and, in fact, from most human endeavours.

What is wrong with 'efficiency'?

Efficiency as we know it – 'superficial efficiency' – has so much more wrong with it than it has going for it. You could say it is too directly under the spell of a here-and-now mindset; in other words, shortsightedness. It is a mentality spawned by nineteenth-century and first 'business efficiency expert', Frederick W. Taylor. Corner-cutting, the essence of Taylorism, is all well and good, but only assuming that repercussions down the line, environmental (and social) collateral, are seen not to matter a jot.

It is a mindset that makes sense if efficiency at all costs is all that counts. The problem, though, is that it means driving out all robustness – what many view, mistakenly, as 'dispensable surplus'; that is part of the deal, though obviously not an intended one. With an efficency-driven mentality, loved by so much of modernity, the quest for immediacy does make complete sense.

Cynics would argue that the world increasingly operates like a Formula One racing car. It is fine, of course, if the only goal happens to be crossing the finishing line first, and if a car's engine does not have to last more than two race weekends before being replaced. Put another way, there is only the bare minimum of reserve, to ensure unrivalled performance over a brief period; it amounts to deliberate built-in obsolescence. Back in the 1920s and 1930s, in contrast, racing Bentleys adopted very different principles; their designer and manufacturers valued robustness through and through. Some would argue that we should take greater heed of these same principles today. For mechanics like Billy Rockell, who built these much feared yet highly respected high-speed 'green monsters', and the men who raced them, winning still mattered enormously. So, too, though, did the car lasting more than two race weekends. In fact Bentleys won Le Mans five times by

1930, often beating leaner and lighter cars, and with Team Car No. 1 winning twice.

The racing strategy of W.O. Bentley, founder of Bentley Motors, was remarkably cunning. Besides entering a race only if there was a very good chance of winning, Bentley advocated winning by the smallest possible margin, so as not to over-stretch his cars (and not to reveal to competitors, unnecessarily, their true performance). The real point here, though, is that in their eyes of Bentley and his mechanics, robustness was paramount. That is why so many vintage Bentleys – like our family's 1930 Speed Six – saw in the new millennium, still in fine working (and potentially racing) fettle.

Purveyors of '*efficiency* of industry and development' today seem to adopt principles that are little different from those driving Formula One racing cars. Simply put, both focus on a very narrow and short-term objective; that is the name of the game. Never mind the aftermath; forget any unfortunate by-products and knock-on effects – like the erosion of '*robustness* of ecosystems'. In modernity's eyes, and in a throw-away society, someone else can always pick up the bits and deal with the mess later.

Another problem of efficiency at all costs comes from blindly following the 80/20 principle, a maxim so beloved in the corporate sector. An indisputable observation is that around 80 per cent of results flow from only 20 per cent of the causes or effort; no one can deny that. For business, the main take-home message is that few products are responsible for most of sales value and profits. Quite plainly, there is little sense in wasting effort on what is unimportant and unproductive. It genuinely can help avoid unnecessary expenditure in effort, and hence inefficiency; so it is not something we should automatically and summarily dismiss.

Followed too literally, though, the 80/20 principle can set a risky precedent. Worse still, it can spell disaster. Therein lies the problem, and a serious weakness. Recall, as just one case in point, the state of fisheries, to see just why. By far the greatest fish harvests come from coastal areas; a narrow strip that makes up only a tiny fraction of the oceans' total area, and which acts as a coastal food factory. The 80/20 principle tells that coasts are where fishing action should be. But look what relentless fishing in these shallow, productive waters has done to the stocks. Exploitation here has removed too much stock; not only that, though, for these rich coastal waters often coincide with major breeding grounds. So hammering cod and other fish stocks around coasts has affected reproduction, leaving insufficient fish available for capture (and reproduction) in future years. In other words, following the 80/20 principle too blindly easily 'kills the turtle that lays the golden egg'.

The problem, then, is that in our ruthless pursuit of highly productive 'hotspots' – around which, undeniably, there is much to gain – we can easily sacrifice something even more valuable. In the case of fisheries, hitting the fishing areas hard can also mean hitting breeding populations hard. It is little wonder, then, that there are unlikely to be any commercial fish stocks in our seas by 2048, if present trends continue.

So there is a wider message resonating from the 80/20 principle. When it comes to nature's assets, our focus on the disproportionately productive areas should be not just for use; there should, paradoxically, be some non-use, too. Otherwise valuable resources will continue to disappear, just as has happened in the case of our fisheries. That is the ugly truth, if a blind eye is turned to the '*robustness* of ecosystems'. That is what the future holds if present levels of harvesting and exploitation continue.

There is another important footnote to the 80/20 principle, too, though it is often written in small print. The best-performing (fishery or financial) stocks this year, or the most valuable species in an ecosystem over the last decade, are no guarantee of similar performance later. Clinging to the belief that what holds now, or what held in the past, is an assured recipe for future success can be a dangerous path to tread. One observation after another leads us to conclude that the world and its resources do not remain constant for long. But these are not the only problem with too literal translation of the 80/20 principle: for knowing where the best-performing 20 per cent actually resides, from one year to the next, can be difficult.

In the case of fisheries, problems go even deeper, for the industry now lacks robustness in other ways. Reduced fleet size with fewer trawlers, but high per-boat catch rates from wide-mouthed nets that spare few fish, might suggest efficiency of operations. What is overlooked is the long-lasting impact to the seabed from trawl-nets, precisely where ground-fish eat, live and breed; the industry seems not to realize that these areas – in other words '*robustness* of ecosystems' – actually matter. The cost of damage to these 'inessential' areas does not reach company balance sheets; nor is it reflected in national GDP figures. With robustness and health of vital fish breeding habitats eroded along with the stocks, it is no wonder fish are at the end of the line. And not even the slickest mathematical models or catch quotas seem able to save them – especially as, all too often, they lack robustness and are way off the mark.

Yet the simple expedient of instilling robustness back into fisheries by adopting 'no-take' reserves – first established centuries ago – can lead to miracles. It works by protecting fish breeding and feeding habitats; areas which, in anyone's eyes, are far from inessential. No-take reserves in St Lucia have actually doubled the catch in a matter of years. In Florida they quadrupled in just two years. And, in both cases, that is outside the protected area, in waters where fishermen *can* and *do* go fishing. In the case of trawl fisheries, reserves can protect the seabed from the ravaging effects of the nets, too. Besides their effectiveness, what is so appealing about marine reserves is that they require virtually no technology. Only by taking stock wisely, whether from ecosystems or business systems, can we come close to getting 'as good as it gets'.

Beyond insurance

The '*robustness* of ecosystems', in other words a strong environment, is what allows it to absorb run-of-the-mill shocks and surprises, yet still keep working. Directly, or indirectly, this provides industry and development (as well as the environment, of course) with extraordinary oomph: innumerable benefits, of the sort described in *Slow-Tech*. It is the same, whether we're talking big scale – societies and civilizations –

or small scale, communities on a coral island. In both cases, coral reefs and other natural ecosystems act as 'growth-promoters'; they are what keeps them alive and helps drive them forward.

One might imagine, then, that modernity would cherish and cling to environmental robustness. Yet time and time again we see behaviour pointing to the contrary: unbridled passion for ever-greater '*efficiency of industry and development*', which easily corrodes the '*robustness* of ecosystems'.

Corporate interests can also suffer *directly* from the same short-term actions that create so much wider collateral, for example in the environment. That is perhaps an even greater irony. In the case of the motor industry, curiously, the rules for Formula One racing may change. If so, cars would have to last beyond two race weekends; otherwise a race team would receive a hefty penalty. Even modern motor-racing, then, is beginning to realize that performance can (or even should) extend beyond simply crossing the line first. Quite plainly, in any venture there is 'wisdom of overkill', in other words robustness through over-provision, to help things keep going (that little bit longer).

Put another way, the magical whiz of robustness extends to all sorts of systems, ones that have nothing at all to do with the environment. It is the same, as later parts of the book reveal, whether we are talking of health care systems, military systems, engineered systems (including Aga cookers), or transport systems.

Robustness is equally critical when it comes to business health and even personal health and well-being. Recall, for example, how burnout took Japanese business high-flier Kamei Shuji to an early grave – his efficiency was short-lived. Fairy tales echo precisely the same message, even if the outcome is not so grave. For example, the story of how Tortoise beat much faster Rabbit in a race has been part of the Yoruba folk-tales from south-western Nigeria for centuries. And it was also part of Aesop's fables. For all systems – real or imaginary – having something in reserve, and other means of avoiding catastrophic failures, empowers both the present and the future; and in such an uncertain world, who knows what that holds.

Without robustness, through spare capacity or other means of compensation for unexpected problems, business efficiency – and any other kind of efficiency for that matter – simply evaporates, or is unachievable in the first place. As business guru Peter Drucker reminds us, we need a sensible aim before we can sensibly think about efficiency. Clearly one aim should be to specify and instil adequate robustness. In a nutshell robustness is what helps things keep going, even when the going gets tough. It actually does much more, though not always in obvious ways.

We might be tempted to suppose efficiency and robustness to be separate qualities, even opposites, like the two halves of an hourglass filled and emptied by moving sand. Yet, as many examples demonstrate, this view is simplistic or just plain wrong. Robustness is in fact an essential part of what efficiency should actually measure. You could say robustness is part of 'doing the right thing'. As Peter Drucker reminds us, this should come first – only then letting efficiency 'do the thing right'.

Performance comes from many things. But efficiency without sufficient robustness – superficial efficiency – is like the river Nile undernourished by the Aswan Dam, and what happened to the Aral Sea. Any benefits can be short-lived at best, calamitous if things really go wrong.

Modernity needs a fresh and radically different way of assessing performance. Our best bet, *Slow-Tech* holds, lies in robustness. For only maintaining or re-instilling this will help prevent us from ruining the environment and becoming stuck in an efficiency trap, enthralled by high-tech solutions, whatever the costs. It is not that we should simply turn the clocks back, or ditch silicon for iron and rope. Rather, by striking a better balance, both nature and the things we create would be less highly strung.

The surprising thing is that low-tech remedies – including the simple expedient of adding time – still have a place, even in the rushed, modern world. So, too, do old-fashioned, no-nonsense measures like creating 'no-take' fishing reserves to boost dwindling fish stocks; or, greater recognition that environmental damage is not 'free', and should be compensated for, a notion that ought to resonate strongly in a world high in corporate savvy. It is the same when it comes to the land: hand tools for growers and gardeners can be, surprisingly, cost-effective as well as green, that is if you take on board the wider collateral arising from many alternative high-tech approaches, including several agro-chemicals. Even the military cannot avoid the fact that low-tech tunnels, as used for example in the Vietnam War, can be a formidable and robust strategy, even, paradoxically, in an era of computer-assisted warfare.

Part of the solution is more enlightened thinking, and not always getting rid of the 'inessential'. That is what is needed as an antidote to a world increasingly enamoured with transience, impermanence and shortsightedness, the main preoccupation of modernity it seems. Among other things, it accelerates society along unsustainable pathways – something that, ultimately, is bad for business as well as for the environment.

In a similar vein, with our fixation on the here-and-now, we often react to problems by seeking an instant solution – whether we're talking simply of a hasty (and, in hindsight, ill-advised) e-mail reply, or a more concrete action. Yet, as many examples in the book reveal, the 'quick fix' or knee-jerk reaction can be very perilous indeed. A less hasty response often leads to a more robust outcome, for nature and in virtually everything we do or create.

As a really chilling reminder, just imagine the release, through accident or terrorism, of the smallpox virus – an organism now confined to just two laboratories. Mass vaccination would likely follow, if called for by medical wisdom or public demand. Yet the vaccine itself is hazardous, sometimes fatal, to asthma and eczema sufferers; immune systems are not all equally robust. It's the same or worse for HIV carriers, especially as most don't know their status. Without a more thoughtful vision of efficiency, one which pays greater heed to robustness, a reactionary assault on smallpox could be little more than a game of chance.

EPILOGUE

During the 'Sindbad Voyage', *Sohar* became more than a sailing ship, home and research laboratory. From this slow-moving platform began an investigation which pushed me into questioning the wisdom of driving out slack, in our relentless pursuit of efficiency. Like the long journey to China, *Slow-Tech*'s chapters have taken many twists and turns.

Simply put, the book exposes the hazards of squeezing things too far, and offers a time-tested alternative as an antidote. Driven to remove all spare capacity, the modern world now jumps to the crack of the corporate whip; immediacy and performance, for so-called efficiency, is the name of the game and what it all boils down to. Coming first, just like the fastest Formula One cars, is what drives us. This seems to be all that counts, whatever the knock-on effects, on the environment, or anywhere else.

To this end, we need to retain and instill more robustness – to moderate and calm efficiency's supremacy. Time-tested and old-fashioned maybe, but only at one level. As cutting-edge research tells us, robustness is a magical ingredient for performance. So it is the hallmark of enlightened thinking, not merely antiquated muddle-headedness. What we need is for robustness to be an integral part of efficiency (and other indicators of success and performance). That is our best bet for transforming 'superficial efficiency' into 'real efficiency': something more substantial and long-lasting – to ensure that the environment, and everything else, purrs along smoothly instead of failing catastrophically, once the heat is on. That is the book's core message to an increasingly overwound world; it is the same whether we're talking farms and fisheries or other natural ecosystems – the major thrust of *Slow-Tech* – or when it comes to engineered systems and business systems, and even ourselves; that is something the book also touches on.

Back in July 2004 my own robustness was beginning to falter. It was not simply the matter of trying to get *Slow-Tech* off the ground; there was something more immediate and pressing to deal with, for the storm just went on and on.

Tied up in Denmark's Limfjord, at least boat and crew were safe, despite a two-inch coating of sand everywhere. Our boat had over-wintered in Denmark after a family cruise in Sweden with my wife, Sylvia, and son, Joseph. It calmed a little, but soon another front would arrive. All we asked for was a clear three-day spell for the return passage to Whitby, Captain Cook's home port in England. Better, though, to be in harbour preferring to be at sea than at sea wishing we were still tied up. The weather, thankfully, did improve slightly and, after a bumpy ride, we returned to base.

Sara Ann, the boat we owned for many years, was a replica of a traditional craft – a Falmouth working boat – designed for oyster dredging: a workhorse. In stature she was not unlike the Arab dhow *Sohar*, which took us safely albeit slowly to China; or our family's old gaff pilot cutter, *Mermaid*. Both contrasted markedly with my earlier yacht, and the really slick one before. Back in 1972, *Domino* rolled our family hastily along the Milk Run to Antigua, then home to Anglesey.

Those journeys are now over. So too is *Slow-Tech*'s voyage of discovery into the state of different systems – seen through the binocular vision of efficiency with and without consideration of robustness. To this end, one might now consider what 'performance' means where robustness and back-up really matter: in sailing boats which, quite literally, face the rough as well as the smooth like no other. What new understanding might one also gain from this in other spheres of life?

Sara-Ann's predictable and ponderous motion, both at anchor and at sea, portrays a solid workhorse rather than pedigree thoroughbred. Her Cornish design and ancestry have persisted through three centuries. As a piece of working machinery, these boats are immensely robust. This was achieved the old-fashioned way: from strength in design and construction, just as in Falmouth quay punts and Bristol Channel pilot cutters, through massive over-engineering and redundancy.

Few of these old workhorses would have carried insurance, as we know it today. Risk management took a different form – at least in vessels owned by more scrupulous owners: robustness to ensure capacity to combat even the worst winter gales. Of course in some cases, owners carried neither legal insurance, nor insurance in the form of a sturdy, well-maintained vessel; safety, after all, is what Samuel Plimsoll strove for, and achieved, through his Plimsoll Line. In the case of oyster dredgers, some argue that the vessels themselves, and the fishery they still exploit around the Falmouth estuary, are inefficient; obsolete dinosaurs, reminiscent of Aga cookers or our old Bentley. Unlike most others, though, both the fishery and the boats have truly stood the test of time. One way or another, both are extraordinarily robust.

Even in today's ultra-tech world, old-fashioned principles should not be jettisoned, out of hand – even, perhaps surprisingly, when it comes to crossing the line first. Consider, as a case in point, ocean racing. British yachtswoman Ellen MacArthur and other competitors in the Vendée Globe 2000 challenge, a round-the-world race, could never once forget it was a fight against time, virtually at all costs. All the yachts were fine-tuned, out-and-out racing machines. Yet even when speed and efficiency are paramount, robustness still matters. In her autobiography, Ellen MacArthur says of the Vendée Globe 2000 challenge: 'This race shall be won by the most reliable boat . . . that which can push enough, for long enough but keep things together'. And so it was.

What a contrast, though, to *Sara-Ann* and her ancestors, which were built for an entirely different purpose: oyster dredging. An inescapable fact is that there will always have to be a compromise between, on the one hand, making a yacht fast, lively, responsive and manoeuvrable – yet still able to keep going whatever; and, on the other, designing one that is less 'highly strung': to steer by itself (unaided, and with the helm lashed), to have a kind motion at sea, and so on.

That, essentially, is what it can boil down to: the stark contrast between the new, examplified by contenders for the Vendée Globe,

Cowes Regatta or the America Cup; and the old, or replicas of the old – like *Sara Ann* and other packhorses of a bygone era. Despite Frederick Taylor's assertions to the contrary, there is seldom the 'one best way'; it is horses for courses, compromise and trade-offs all the way. This is the case for boats, and the same is true in just about everything else. One thing for sure, though, is that with insufficient robustness, efficiency is an elusive dream.

Cutting things fine, in the quest to be best, can be hazardous in less obvious ways. Consider, as an illustration, what in fact nearly happened to Ellen MacArthur in another pursuit of speed and the 'cerebral climax'. In February 2005 MacArthur and seventy-five feet of carbon fibre (plus high-tech trimmings) – weighing only eight tons – arrived in Falmouth, smashing the solo record around the planet, in seventy-one days. So critical was weight, though, that even freshwater was excess baggage. But relying on desalination nearly lost her the coveted prize. Despite the yacht's tremendous robustness, all of a sudden the 'B&Q system' began to look fragile; simply because of one weak link in the chain (though not the yacht itself) which MacArthur, unaided, managed to fix.

It was not just personal pride and reputation that was on the line, either. MacArthur's achievement, and her book which described it, *Race Against Time*, was possible only through substantial sponsorship and backing. Seen through corporate eyes the venture was one huge business gamble, although, of course, they were banking on it being robust; in one sense, the sponsors were under the same international spotlight as the superstar herself. Had the desalination machines (or anything else) completely conked out and had Ellen MacArthur, consequently, not broken the record, their kudos – if nothing else – might have taken a severe dunking.

When it comes to breaking records, it is not just modern and high-tech achievements we should marvel at. The speed of clipper ships like the *Cutty Sark*, used to transport cargoes of tea and wool in the late 1800s, was legendary. In 1966, English aviator and yachtsman Francis Chichester had a crack at beating the 'fast' outward clipper-ship passages of 100 days. With a sailing time of 107 days to Sydney, and returning to Plymouth in 119 days, he certainly came close to it. As it happened, the record was beaten – but not for another decade – by *With Integrity*. Formerly *Great Britain II*, this yacht was winner of the around-the-world 1975/6 Financial Times Clipper Race. With an overall sailing time of 134 days, it was the first to beat the clipper record originally set by *Patriarch*: a staggering sixty-nine days out and sixty-nine days back.

To his credit, Chichester made the first one-stop, round-the-world voyage, single-handed, and broke several other records, too. Besides, his yacht was far smaller than the *Cutty Sark*, as was *With Integrity* and, to be fair, length is a big driver of speed in sailing vessels.

Judging from Chichester's remarks later, though, you'd never have guessed that his close conquest involved cutting-edge technology of the day. As the following passage from a piece Chichester wrote in *Life* magazine explains, *Gypsy Moth IV* seemed as much as, or more of, a handful than the old clippers, and at times they were certainly no easy ride:

> Now that I have finished, I don't know what will become of *Gipsy Moth IV*. I only own the stern while my cousin owns two thirds. My part, I would sell any day. It would be better if about a third were sawn off. The boat was too big for me. *Gipsy Moth IV* has no sentimental value for me at all. She is cantankerous and difficult and needs a crew of three – a man to navigate, an elephant to move the tiller and a 3'6" [1.1 m] chimpanzee with arms 8' [2.4m] long to get about below and work some of the gear.

Of course not all modern yachts are quite so fickle and badly behaved, though I'm not sure my father would agree. In fact, so wild was *Gipsy Moth IV* at sea that Chichester had an extra piece added to the keel in Sydney. It helped stop her yawing and going off-course, especially in a following sea; but the addition did little when it came to improving stability in terms of reducing the yacht's tendency to capsize.

That is not the only irony of this particular tale. In the case of the

Cutty Sark, in her day, she must have pulled through one ferocious storm after another; what conditions were like is, in fact, well chronicled. Yet, in keeping with robust-yet-fragile principles, from cutting-edge science, the most unlikely event is what can easily cripple any system; and that is how the *Cutty Sark* very nearly met her heavenly maker, too: not in Davy Jones's locker, as it happened, quite literally, up in the sky. While undergoing major restoration in Greenwich near London (ironically in dry dock), a fire very nearly blazed her to the ground in 2007. In fact the ship's teak planking did go up in smoke, and virtually all that remained of her hull was the iron framing. So her shape still remained.

The *Cutty Sark* and *Patriarch* were by no means the only robust ocean speedsters produced in Victorian Britain, though. Consider, as a very different example, the much smaller (8.5-metre) *Curlew*. For many years she found sanctuary down in South Georgia, though nowadays she is resident at Falmouth's Maritime Museum, on England's south coast. Although not a seabird, she is almost as graceful.

Broadly similar to a Falmouth working boat, *Curlew* is a Falmouth quay punt – designed to be part of a bygone service industry, to cater for the needs of incoming ships. Built in the 1890s, she is original, not a replica boat like our oyster dredger. Besides her impressive seaworthiness and globe-trotting ventures, *Curlew* is amazingly fast. If speed is one hallmark of efficiency, and robustness another, then *Curlew* is truly a high flier. As testament, Pauline and Tim Carr, her former owners, periodically sailed her to England, Antigua and other distant horizons, to participate in local regattas. Curiously, this agile centenarian was both renowned and feared for her remarkable turn of speed. So much so, her owners collected many trophies; the only trouble was that *Curlew* did not have enough room in the cabin to store them all.

Perhaps more astonishing still is that the Carrs' voyages in *Curlew* were made without an engine, let alone the latest electronic gizmos. On most counts, GPS and other support systems are invaluable aids to ocean cruising; *Sara-Ann* certainly carried GPS, and several other electronics besides. (Once, coming out of the Underground station in

London, I even used one, secretly, to find the offices of my publishers, Atlantic Books.) An inescapable fact, though, is that they can and do let you down, so there is wisdom in learning to navigate the old-fashioned way in today's silicon world.

Recall, for example, what happened on the 'Sindbad Voyage'. The slow trip across the Indian Ocean had taken its toll. By the time the expedition reached China, as mentioned in the Prologue, few of the vessel's electronic gadgets were functioning.

Fast-forward twenty years later and equipment failure, similarly, befell *Sara Ann*. Barely one hour after leaving Denmark, on the trip back to Whitby, the electronic autopilot suddenly failed; only this time it was not an electronic problem, but failure of a mechanical pin. Nevertheless, the effect was identical: the yacht's self-steering suddenly stopped working. For a modern yacht, especially a highly-strung racer, the only solution would be for the crew to take turns to steer, 24/7, for the entire North Sea crossing. What we did was simply lash the helm and let *Sara Ann* sail herself, with just an occasional tweak to the helm, all the way back to port.

Greater speed and agility, in our eyes, were worth sacrificing for the boat's ability to get back on track, unaided, when knocked off course. Self-correcting behaviour provides an invaluable 'buffer' and is one signature of a robust system; in jargon-free language, it boils down to things working as they should do, with minimal outside help or intervention. That is one of the most important benefits of robustness to engineered systems, and in natural ecosystems, too; that is if they are not weakened too much in the wake of economic growth, as part of our pursuit of '*efficiency* of development and industry'.

That is another of the book's core messages. In the case of *Sara Ann*, being on 'autopilot', quite literally, also gave the crew time to relax and look forward to hot-buttered toast back home – done, naturally, on the old-fashioned Aga cooker, built with similar levels of robustness to *Sara Ann* and our old Bentley: slow-tech, in some ways, but ahead of the times in others, and worth it all the way.

Shortly after I first drafted the Epilogue, Robin Knox Johnston, winner of the first non-stop yacht race around the world, sent out a message. Back then, in 1969, he was in a heavy wooden boat, *Suhaili*, one that could not have been more slow-tech. In the 2006 race, though, his yacht could not have been more high-tech. This is part of his message, transmitted on 15 November 2006, reported by Robin Knox-Johnstone in *Yachting World*:

Speed 3.4 knots. My average speed since the start is pretty close to *Suhaili*'s – the boat I first sailed round the world in 1969 . . . I am not a natural revolutionary, but I am beginning to find myself supportive of the Luddite movement. I was thinking about some of the differences between this trip and *Suhaili* thirty-eight years ago, and, apart from the obvious developments in the boats, the big difference is the time we now have to devote to communications but also the way we have become dependent upon electronic aids. That's fine so long as they work. This dependence comes with a terrible price, the enormous cost in time trying to get it to work properly.

I wonder whether anyone has looked into the man hours being spent on just trying to get the latest technology to work. We have all been shamed into thinking we must have this stuff, but it's like the Emperor's clothes, we need to turn back on the producers and say enough is enough, let's have some quality please before you sell us your product . . .

SELECT READING

Research for *Slow-Tech* probably began, subconsciously, in the 1960s, while sailing and sitting in the back of our family's racing Bentley. It began more seriously in 2004. Most writing took place during 2006 and 2007, in the office, at home, on aeroplanes, in cafés and even on the roadside; parts of the book were written in Eritrea, Sri Lanka and Bermuda.

In the course of my research, I drew on numerous conversations, articles, books, radio and TV broadcast as well as extensive technical material. Here is a very small selection of works that were particularly helpful and/or which will provide the reader with further information. Searches on the web should give some good hits, too.

Prologue

W.O. Bentley, *My Life and My Cars* (Hutchinson, 1967); Tom Cunliffe, *Hand, Reef and Steer: Traditional Sailing Skills for Classic Boats* (Adlard Coles, 2004); Clare Hay, *Bentley Speed Six* (Number One Press, 2008); Tim Severin, *The Sindbad Voyage* (Hutchinson, 1982).

Introduction

Malcolm Gladwell, *The Tipping Point* (Little, Brown, 2000); James Gleick, *Faster: The Acceleration of Just About Everything* (Little, Brown, 1999); Carl Honoré, *In Praise of Slow* (Orion, 2004); Erica Jen (ed.), *Robust Design: A Repertoire of Biological, Ecological, and Engineering Case Studies* (Oxford University Press, 2005); Andrew Price, Matt Keeling and Ian Stewart, 'A robustness metric integrating spatial and temporal information: application to coral reefs exposed to local and regional disturbances', *Marine Ecology Progress Series*, Vol. 331 (2007), p. 101; Andreas Wagner, *Robustness and Evolvability in Living Systems* (Princeton University Press, 2005).

Chapter 1

Ian Bremmer, *The J Curve: A New Way to Understand Why Nations Rise and Fall* (Simon & Schuster, 2006); Jared Diamond, *Collapse: How Societies Choose to Fail or Succeed* (Viking/Penguin, 2004); H.R.P. Dixon, *The Arab of the Desert* (George Allen & Unwin, 1972); Thomas Homer-Dixon, *The Upside of Down: Catastrophe, Creativity and the Renewal of Civilization* (Island Press/Shearwater Books, 2006); G. Tyler Miller Jr, *Living in the Environment: Principles, Connections, and Solutions* (Brooks/Cole, 2005); John Reader, *Cities* (Vintage, 2005); Brian Walker and David Salt, *Resilience Thinking: Sustaining Ecosystems and People in a Changing World* (Island Press, 2006).

Chapter 2

James Buchan, *Frozen Desire: The Meaning of Money* (Picador, 1997); John Gray, *False Dawn* (Granta Books, 1998); Robert Costanza *et al.*, 'The value of the world's ecosystem services and natural capital', (*Nature*, Vol. 387, (1997), p. 259: Carl Honoré, *In Praise of Slow* (Orion, 2004); Nicolette Jones, *The Plimsoll Sensation: The Great Campaign to Save Lives at Sea* (Abacus, 2007); Will Hutton, *The State We're In* (Vintage, 1996) and *The World We're In* (Little, Brown, 2002); Robert Kanigel, *The One Best Way: Frederick Winslow Taylor and the Enigma of Efficiency* (Little, Brown, 1997), the subject matter for which is F.W. Taylor's influential work, *The Principles of Scientific Management* (Harper and Brothers, 1911); Richard Koch, *The 80/20 Principle: The Secret of Achieving More With Less* (Nicholas Brealey, 2004); Jeffrey McNeely, 'As the world gets smaller, the chances of invasion grow', *Euphytica*, Vol. 148 (2006), p.5; Jane Owen and Diarmuid Gavin, *Gardens Through Time* (BBC Books, 2004).

Chapter 3

R. Bisgrove and P. Hadley, 'Gardening in the Global Greenhouse: The Impacts of Climate Change on Gardens in the UK' (Technical Report, UKCIP, Oxford, 2002); James Lovelock, *Gaia: The Practical Science of Planetary Medicine* (Gaia, 1991); Clive Ponting, *A Green History of the World* (Penguin, 1991); Jules Pretty, *Agri-Culture: Reconnecting People, Land and Nature* (Earthscan, 2002); Jules Pretty *et al.*, 'Resource-conserving agriculture increases yields in developing countries', *Environmental Science and Technology*, Vol. 40 (2006), p. 1114; Colin Tudge, *So Shall We Reap* (Penguin, 2003); John Zarb, 'The root of the problem', *Organic Farming* (Winter 2004/5).

Chapter 4

D.R. Bellwood *et al.*, 'Confronting the coral reef crisis', *Nature*, Vol. 429 (2004), p. 827; David Dobbs, *Reef Madness: Charles Darwin, Alexander Agassiz, and the Meaning of Coral* (Pantheon, 2005); T.A. Gardener *et al.*, 'Long-term region-wide declines in Caribbean corals', *Science*, Vol. 301 (2003), p. 958; Poul Harremoës *et al.*, *Late lessons from early warnings: the precautionary principle 1896–2000* (European Environment Agency, Environmental issue report No. 22, 2001); Terrence Hughes et al., (2005), 'New paradigms for supporting the resilience of marine ecosystems', *Trends in Ecology and Evolution*, Vol. 20 (2005), p. 380; Michael Pearson and Ahmed Shehata, 'Protectorates management for conservation and development in the Arab Republic of Egypt', *Parks*, Vol. 18 (1998), p. 29; Charles Sheppard (ed.), *Seas at the Millennium: An environmental evaluation* (Elsevier Science, 2000).

Chapter 5

John Beddington and Geoff Kirkwood (eds.), 'Fisheries: A Future?', *Philosophical Transactions of the Royal Society B*, Vol. 360 (2005), No. 1413; FAO, *The State of World Fisheries and Aquaculture* (SOFIA, Food and Agricultural Organization of the UN, Rome, Italy, 2002); Charles Glover, *The End of the Line: How Over-fishing Is Changing the World and What We Eat* (Ebury Press, 2005); Callum Roberts and Julie Hawkins, *Fully-Protected Marine Reserves: A Guide* (WWF, US, 2000); Callum Roberts, *The Unnatural History of the Sea* (Island Press, 2007).

Chapter 6

H. Khordagui, 'Power and desalination plants', in N. Khan *et al.* (eds), *The Gulf Ecosystem: Health and Sustainability* (Backhuys 2002), p.173; Fred Pearce, 'High and dry in Aswan', *New Scientist*, No. 1924, 7 May 1994 p.28; F.Y. Al-Yamani and N.Y. Khan, 'Changes in riverine input and loss of wetlands', in N. Khan *et al.* (eds), *The Gulf Ecosystem: Health and Sustainability* (Backhuys, 2002), p.235.

Chapter 7

Bernabé Cobo, 'Inca Religion and Customs' (University of Texas Press, 1990); Lewis Page, *Waste and Blundering in the Armed Forces: Lions, Donkeys and Dinosaurs* (William Heinemann, 2006); Henry Petroski, *Small Things Considered: Why There Is No Perfect Design* (Alfred A. Knopf, 2003); Edward Tenner, *Why Things Bite Back: Technology and the Revenge of Unintended Consequences* (Vintage, 1997).

SELECT READING

Epilogue

Alex Beilby, *To Beat the Clippers: The Financial Times Clipper Race* 1975–6 (London, Allen Lane, 1976); Alun Davies, *The History of the Falmouth Working Boats* (Troutbeck Press, 1995); Ellen Macarthur, *Race Against Time* (Penguin/Michael Joseph, 2005).

INDEX

INDEX

INDEX

INDEX

INDEX